KEEPING THE FEAST

Society of Biblical Literature

Early Christianity and Its Literature

David G. Horrell, Editor

Warren Carter
Amy-Jill Levine
Judith M. Lieu
Margaret Y. MacDonald
Dale B. Martin

Number 16

KEEPING THE FEAST

METAPHORS OF SACRIFICE IN
1 CORINTHIANS AND PHILIPPIANS

by

Jane Lancaster Patterson

SBL Press
Atlanta

Copyright © 2015 by SBL Press

Library of Congress Cataloging-in-Publication Data

Patterson, Jane Lancaster.
    Keeping the feast : metaphors of sacrifice in 1 Corinthians and Philippians / by Jane Lancaster Patterson.
        p. cm. — (Society of Biblical Literature. Early Christianity and its literature ; Number 16)
    Includes bibliographical references and index.
    ISBN 978-0-88414-065-8 (pbk. : alk. paper) — ISBN 978-0-88414-066-5 (ebook) — ISBN 978-0-88414-067-2 (hardcover : alk. paper)
    1. Sacrifice—Biblical teaching. 2. Metaphor in the Bible. 3. Bible.Corinthians, 1st—Criticism, interpretation, etc. 4. Bible. Philippians—Criticism, interpretation, etc. I. Title.
    BS2655.S23.P38 2015
    227'.206—dc23   2015022161

Printed on acid-free paper.

CONTENTS

Acknowledgments

It is ironically fitting that the subject of this study is sacrificial metaphors, as the project has asked so much of those around me who have helped to bring it to completion. Principally, my doctoral advisor, Victor Paul Furnish, stayed the course over a long period of time, offering the guidance, clarity, and encouragement I needed at each point along the way. He modeled in all of his dealings with me the ethical patterns that are the subject of this dissertation, a life that is lived for the well-being of others. From him, I learned not only how to speak of these things, but what it means to live them. Words fail me in thanking him sufficiently.

The readers of the original dissertation—Jouette Bassler, Roy Heller, and Melissa Dowling—also remained patient and supportive far beyond what one could expect. They embody for me the Pauline virtue of encouragement. I am deeply grateful to the editorial committee in the Christianity and Its Literature series at the Society of Biblical Literature, especially Gail O'Day. Their responses were invaluable in the process of moving from a dissertation to a book.

John Lewis, my colleague and coworker in the Gospel at St. Benedict's Workshop, carried the major burden of our work for two years, as I focused on the original dissertation. Every page bears the imprint of our common work and the many conversations we have had over the years. Since then, my students and colleagues on the faculty at Seminary of the Southwest have willingly engaged in conversations on sacrifice as I thought this project through out loud. In particular, Cynthia Briggs Kittredge, Dean and President, and Scott Bader-Saye, Academic Dean, have provided a context where scholarship is fostered in a lively community of support and discussion.

In my teaching I have sometimes spoken on the role of benefactors in the New Testament, those people who incarnated their values through their use of money (Luke 8: 1–3; Rom 16:1–2, etc.). Likewise, this project would never have been completed without the generous assistance of the Episcopal Church Foundation, the Schubert Ogden Fellowship, the Graduate Study Fellowships of Southern Methodist University, and the community of supporters of St. Benedict's Workshop, San Antonio, Texas.

Finally, my family sacrificed much, over many years, to support me in this work, and it is to them that I dedicate it: Emily, Jacob, and Dow.

Austin, Texas
January 2015

ABBREVIATIONS

PRIMARY SOURCES

2 En.	2 Enoch
Ant.	Josephus, *Jewish Antiquities*
Ben.	Seneca, *De beneficiis*
Il.	Homer, *Iliad*
J.W.	Josephus, *Jewish War*
Let. Arist.	Letter of Aristeas
m. Pesah.	Mishnah Pesahim
Od.	Homer, *Odyssey*
Oed. Tyr.	Sophocles, *Oedipus tyrannus*
Phaedr.	Plato, *Phaedrus*
Piet.	Philodemus of Gadara, *De pietate*
Poet.	Aristotle, *Poetics*
Prom.	Aeschylus, *Prometheus vinctus*
Resp.	Plato, *Respublica*
Rhet.	Aristotle, *Rhetoric*
Rom.	Ignatius, *To the Romans*
Spec. Laws	Philo, *On the Special Laws*

SECONDARY SOURCES

ABD	Anchor Bible Dictionary. Edited by David Noel Freedman. 6 vols. New York: Doubleday, 1992.
AcBib	Academia Biblica
AnBib	Analecta Biblica
ANRW	Aufstieg und Niedergang der römischen Welt: Geschichte und Kultur Roms im Spiegel der neueren Forschung. Part 2, Prin-

	cipat. Edited by Hildegard Temporini and Wolfgang Haase. Berlin: de Gruyter, 1972–.
ANTC	Abingdon New Testament Commentaries
AThR	*Anglican Theological Review*
Bib	*Biblica*
BibInt	Biblical Interpretation Series
BJS	Brown Judaic Studies
BRev	*Bible Review*
BTS	Biblical Tools and Studies
CBQ	*Catholic Biblical Quarterly*
CRINT	Compendia Rerum Iudaicarum ad Novum Testamentum
EgT	*Eglise et théologie*
EncJud	*Encyclopedia Judaica*. Edited by Fred Skolnik and Michael Berenbaum. 2nd ed. 22 vols. Detroit: Macmillan Reference USA, 2007.
GBS	Guides to Biblical Scholarship
GNS	*Good News Studies*
GOTR	*Greek Orthodox Theological Review*
HNTC	Harper's New Testament Commentaries
HTR	*Harvard Theological Review*
HTS	Harvard Theological Studies
Int	*Interpretation*
JAAR	*Journal of the American Academy of Religion*
JBL	*Journal of Biblical Literature*
JRitSt	*Journal of Ritual Studies*
JSNT	*Journal for the Study of the New Testament*
JSNTSup	Journal for the Study of the New Testament Supplement Series
JSOT	*Journal for the Study of the Old Testament*
JSOTSup	Journal for the Study of the Old Testament Supplement Series
JSS	*Journal of Semitic Studies*
JTS	*Journal of Theological Studies*
LAI	Library of Ancient Israel
LCL	Loeb Classical Library
LEC	Library of Early Christianity
LHBOTS	Library of Hebrew Bible/Old Testament Studies
LQ	*Lutheran Quarterly*
NICNT	New International Commentary on the New Testament

NovT	*Novum Testamentum*
NTS	*New Testament Studies*
PRSt	*Perspectives in Religious Studies*
RB	*Revue biblique*
RBL	*Review of Biblical Literature*
RBS	Resources for Biblical Study
RelSRev	*Religious Studies Review*
ResQ	*Restoration Quarterly*
RSPT	*Revue des sciences philosophiques et théologiques*
RSR	*Recherches de science religieuse*
SBLDS	Society of Biblical Literature Dissertation Series
SBS	Stuttgarter Bibelstudien
SJLA	Studies in Judaism in Late Antiquity
SNTSMS	Society for New Testament Studies Monograph Series
TDNT	*Theological Dictionary of the New Testament.* Edited by Gerhard Kittel and Gerhard Friedrich. Translated by Geoffrey W. Bromley. 10 vols. Grand Rapids: Eerdmans, 1964–1976.
Them	*Themelios*
TS	*Theological Studies*
TynBul	*Tyndale Bulletin*
USQR	*Union Seminary Quarterly Review*
VT	*Vetus Testamentum*
VTSup	Supplements to Vetus Testamentum
WBC	World Biblical Commentary
WMANT	Wissenschaftliche Monographien zum Alten und Neuen Testament
WUNT	Wissenschaftliche Untersuchungen zum Neuen Testament
WW	*Word and World*
ZAW	*Zeitschrift für die alttestamentliche Wissenschaft*
ZTK	*Zeitschrift für Theologie und Kirche*

1

INTRODUCTION

Metaphors and sacrifices have in common that they both turn one thing into something else. But what does it mean when all this alchemical power is combined in *metaphors* of *sacrifice*? Paul's metaphors have the power to turn bodies into temples, communities into fields. Sacrifices turn farm animals into smoke that reaches God in heaven, a pleasing odor for the divine. Metaphors drawn from the sacrificial system turn crucifixion into glory, shame into honor, death into life. This study of sacrificial metaphors in Philippians and 1 Corinthians is a revised version of my dissertation, presented at Southern Methodist University in 2009. But my engagement with the subject matter began as a dutiful question to William J. A. Power, Professor of Old Testament at Southern Methodist University, during my years of coursework in the doctoral program there. "What do you wish students of the New Testament knew more about, in the area of Hebrew Bible?" I asked, naively. His answer came quickly: "Sacrifice. They know *nothing* about sacrifice." In the next breath, I regretted asking the question. I was reluctant to spend what appeared to me to be a very long semester studying sacrifice. That imagined long semester has turned into more than a decade of study, but a decade that was more rewarding intellectually than I had even hoped for. In addition, many other scholars also joined the conversation about both metaphors and biblical sacrifice during that period of time, and kept me returning again and again to examine both the practice and its rhetorical use in the New Testament.

There are gulfs of difference that must somehow be crossed, if one is to attempt even to approach an understanding of sacrifice in the ancient world. A practice that now needs a heavy freight of explanation was so inevitably a part of the culture of ancient Israel that it needed no explanation or justification or rationale whatsoever when it is introduced in Gen 4:3–7: "In the course of time, Cain brought to the Lord an offering"

Likewise, Leviticus, the biblical "Priests' Manual," begins the directions on the offering of sacrifice without any justification for the practice: "When any of you bring an offering" (1:2). This very inevitability of the practice in ancient times is a stumbling block for modern readers of the New Testament, who tend to approach metaphors of sacrifice as something rare and exotic, heavy with theological significance, and not the simple warp and woof of everyday religious experience that they were for their original audience. The comparison of the crucifixion of Jesus of Nazareth to a sacrifice has become reified as church doctrine, rather than an active vehicle of explanation to people who have a common experience of sacrifice.

From early on, I began to see that the whole mood of sacrifice as it was practiced was potentially quite different than I had imagined it. From the outside, sacrifice appears to be about death, about the ritual killing of a portion of those animals whose lives are most closely bound up with the well being of the human community. But in one of the few interpretative passages of Leviticus, the blood of the animal, poured out or dashed upon the altar, is described as the animal's *life* (*nephesh*) made manifest, not its death (Lev 17:11, 14; see also Gen 9:4, Deut 12:23).[1] Within the rhetoric of Yom Kippur, at least, the Hebrew sacrifices affirm the power of the blood of the offered animals to set humans in right relationship with God and their neighbor to banish whatever would threaten fullness of life. Another unexpected dimension of the practice of sacrifice is its centrality to celebrations in the ancient world. In both the Jewish and Greco-Roman cultures, sacrifices were often intrinsic to celebration, as the sacrificial rituals consecrated the meat for a feast. As someone said to me early on, "Jane, think of a barbecue, not a church service."

Perhaps most important, the system of Hebrew sacrifices was as varied as any grammar of relationship. Sacrifices were offered to God for a variety of occasions, some prescribed by the religious calendar, but others offered spontaneously in thanksgiving or as a vow or in expiation. Lack of acquaintance with the practice has caused many readers of the New Testament to collapse the entire sacrificial system into atonement, as though Yom Kippur were the only day on the calendar and sin the only reason to offer sacrifice.

None of what I have discovered about sacrifice in the Hebrew tradition is terribly new, but it has surprised me to find how little this knowledge

---

1. See the discussion of the blood as life in William K. Gilders, "The Identification of Blood with 'Life,'" in his *Blood Ritual in the Hebrew Bible: Meaning and Power* (Baltimore: Johns Hopkins University Press, 2004), 12–32.

has been applied in the study of New Testament sacrificial metaphors. For example, even a very careful and influential Christian scholar may tend to read the sacrifices of Leviticus through the lens of Romans, rather than the reverse.[2] Further it is common among scholars to muddle the categories of martyrdom and sacrifice, even though one of the terms (sacrifice) is a metaphor and the other (martyrdom) is simply an interpretation of a literal death.[3] Moreover, virtually no attention has been paid to the relationship between the rhetorical purposes of individual Pauline letters and the types of sacrifice that predominate in a given letter. For example, what role do metaphors of sacrifice play in the encouragement Paul offers to the Philippians? How do the metaphors of Passover and covenant in 1 Corinthians fit into Paul's strategy of counteracting the community's factionalism? Further, why are the metaphors of atonement so pointedly drawn in Rom 3:23–26 that they have become lodged in the Christian imagination as the fundamental understanding of the meaning of Jesus' crucifixion? This final question is not an explicit topic of this book, but it is my hope that this project encourages some readers to look more critically at the sacrificial metaphors in Romans.

The alchemy that sacrificial metaphors appear to effect for the earliest Christians is one primarily of a radical shift in agency. The execution of Jesus of Nazareth at the hands of Roman soldiers becomes, through the use of a sacrificial metaphor, an act of God intended to bring human beings into right relationship with God and one another (Phil 2:5–11; Rom 3:23–26). Agency is shifted from the Romans to God, and the outcome is shifted from destruction to vindication and new creation.

Sacrifice: From Practice to Metaphor

Of course, one of the principal differences between the discussion of sacrifice in the Hebrew Scriptures and that of the New Testament is that, in the latter, discussion of sacrifice has slipped almost entirely into the realm

---

2. In this case James G. Dunn, "Paul's Understanding of the Death of Jesus," in *Sacrifice and Redemption: Durham Essays in Theology*, ed. S.W. Sykes (Cambridge: Cambridge University Press, 1991), and Dunn, *The Theology of Paul the Apostle* (Grand Rapids: Eerdmans, 1998), 212–27.

3. For a recent book-length example, see Jarvis J. Williams, *Maccabean Martyr Traditions in Paul's Theology of Atonement: Did Martyr Theology Shape Paul's Conception of Jesus's Death?* (Eugene, OR: Wipf & Stock, 2010).

of metaphor, leaving unresolved the question of the relationship between early followers of Jesus and the Jewish cult before the razing of the Temple at Jerusalem in 70 CE.[4] This is not to say that sacrifice was always spoken of in strictly literal terms in the Hebrew Scriptures. The prophetic discussion of behavior incongruent with sacrifice (e.g., Mic 6:6–8; Ps 50) became the foundation for metaphorical reinterpretation of sacrifice in the Hellenistic period by various Jewish writers who did not see themselves as mitigating the importance of the cult. In parallel fashion, the metaphorizing of sacrifice by early followers of Jesus need not mean that they no longer perceived the Jewish cult as valid. Rather, the use of metaphors of sacrifice may have been the way for Jews in the Diaspora to maintain a sense of daily contact with the Temple cult far away in Jerusalem.[5] The writings of Philo, as well as Jewish apocryphal and pseudepigraphal texts,[6] equate obedience to Torah with the offerings in the Temple:

> The one who keeps the law makes many offerings; one who heeds the commandments makes an offering of well-being. The one who returns a kindness offers choice flour, and one who gives alms sacrifices a thank offering. (Sir 35:1–4)[7]

The sense of such interpretations is not to denigrate the offerings in the Temple, but to raise up the effectiveness of obedience to Torah. For those who are able to participate in the Temple cult, their offerings in God's presence call them to a life of daily holiness, to live by an ethic congruent with the cult;[8] for Jews in the diaspora, such interpretations provide a way to

---

4. In order to keep the referent clear, I am capitalizing "Temple" when referring to the Jewish Temple in Jerusalem. When I refer to temples more generally, I use the lowercase, "temple." This is a purely arbitrary convention, but it is helpful for clarity in this particular project.

5. See the discussion of the relationship between the synagogue and the Temple in Donald Binder, *Into the Temple Courts: The Place of the Synagogues in the Second Temple Period*, eds. Michael V. Fox and Mark Allan Powell, SBLDS 169, (Atlanta: Society of Biblical Literature, 1999).

6. Those quoted here, Sirach, the Letter of Aristeas, and the Prayer of Azariah, are all most likely from the second century BCE.

7. See also Sir 34:21–24; Tob 4:10.

8. In this way, these texts reiterate the force of much of the prophetic literature on sacrifice (see more discussion on this subject in the critique of Finlan's schema of spiritualization of sacrifice).

live faithfully, to make offerings of daily life, as it were, far from Jerusalem. This excerpt from the Letter of Aristeas makes a similar point:

> [The king] praised him generously, and asked the tenth guest, "What is the highest form of glory?" The reply was, "Honoring God. This is not done with gifts or sacrifices, but with purity of heart and of devout disposition, as everything is ordained by God and ordered according to his will." (Let. Arist. 234 [Shutt])[9]

The Prayer of Azariah, though most likely written in the second century BCE, is imaginatively set during the period of the Babylonian exile. Lacking a way to offer sacrifice, an attitude of the heart—contrition—becomes the substitute for the cult:

> In our day we have no ruler, or prophet, or leader, no burnt offering, or sacrifice, or oblation, or incense, no place to make an offering before you and to find mercy. Yet with a contrite heart and a humble spirit may we be accepted, as though it were with burnt offerings of rams and bulls, or with tens of thousands of fat lambs; such may our sacrifice be in your sight today, and may we unreservedly follow you, for no shame will come to those who trust in you. (Dan 3:38–40 LXX)

The passages above certainly resonate in Rom 12:1: "I encourage you, brothers [and sisters], by the mercies of God, to offer your bodies as a sacrifice, living, holy and acceptable to God, which is your rational [*logikēn*] worship." All of these passages emphasize the essential congruence between the practice of sacrifice and devotion expressed in moral attitudes and actions.

Two Sets of Tools: Social Science and Literary Criticism

Bruce Malina has written that "biblical interpretation, as the investigation of linguistic communications from the past, requires at least two sets

---

9. See also 2 En. 45, in the J rescension, in which the activities of the cult are seen as merely a test for purity of heart: "Does the Lord God demand bread or lamps or sheep or oxen or any kind of sacrifices at all? That is nothing, but he demands pure hearts, and by means of all those things he tests people's hearts" (Andersen). Also Judith: "For every sacrifice as a fragrant offering is a small thing, and the fat of all whole burnt offerings to you is a very little thing; but whoever fears the Lord is great forever" (Jdt 16:16); and Josephus's paraphrase of 1 Sam 15:22 in *Ant.* 6.147–150.

of tools: one set of a linguistic sort that can deal with texts as texts, and not as words or sentences or supersentences, and another set of an historical sort that can deal with the past in some cross-cultural way."[10] In her article on the intersection of social scientific study and the study of the New Testament,[11] Susan Garrett remarked that "there are a variety of methodological problems calling for both sustained theoretical reflection and test-case analyses: for example, the relationship between social reality and various metaphors used by early Christians (e.g., familial or household language used to describe the church, or slave-terminology used to describe discipleship)."[12] Sacrifice is a part of the social reality of first-century Christians that has come into their ethical and theological reflection principally by means of metaphor.

This study combines historical and sociological attention to ancient practices of sacrifice with a consideration of how metaphors function cognitively and rhetorically, in order to clarify the use of sacrificial metaphors in two of Paul's letters. Both of these areas of inquiry are needed, in order to grasp the rhetorical power of metaphors drawn from contemporary cultic practices. Hence, chapter 2 offers an overview of metaphor theory; chapter 3 discusses ancient sacrificial practices and reflection, in both Greco-Roman and Jewish contexts, and chapter 4 reviews the history of scholarly interpretations of the meaning of sacrifice. The present study is directed toward fruitful exegetical outcomes, toward increasing comprehension of the counsels of 1 Corinthians and Philippians, by the use of both literary and social scientific methods.

Three fairly recent studies of cultic metaphors in the Pauline literature bear mentioning. The earliest is Michael Newton's *The Concept of Purity at Qumran and in the Letters of Paul* (1985). In Newton's view, Paul conceives of his Christian churches in a way analogous to that of the Qumran community, as a substitute for the Jerusalem Temple. He uses E. P. Sanders's structure of entrance into and maintenance of membership in a religious community to examine the function of the language of purity at Qumran and in Paul's letters. In Newton's rendering, Paul's

---

10. Bruce J. Malina, "The Social Sciences and Biblical Interpretation," *Int* 36 (1982): 229.

11. Susan Garrett, "Sociology of Early Christianity," *ABD* 1:89–99.

12. Here Garrett references Dale Martin, *Slavery as Salvation: The Metaphor of Slavery in Pauline Christianity* (Yale University, 1990); Garrett, "Sociology of Early Christianity," 98.

cultic language is more real than metaphorical. For Paul, the Christian community *is* the (new) Temple, and his counsels follow from that foundational supersessionist assumption. If, however, one does not assume from the outset that churches have replaced the Temple as the locus of faithful devotion to God, then Paul's language of purity may be analyzed as metaphorical constructions. To do so enables a more subtle understanding of the creative and persuasive power of this body of language in his letters.

Two more recent studies of cult and metaphors are Stephen Finlan's *The Background and Content of Cultic Atonement Metaphors* (2004) and Albert Hogeterp's *Paul and God's Temple* (2006). These two works are witnesses to an upsurge in interest by biblical scholars in the Jewish cult over the last ten years, as is signaled by the institution of the "Sacrifice, Cult, and Atonement" consultation of the Society of Biblical Literature, inaugurated at the 2007 Annual Meeting. Recent scholarly interest in the topic of sacrifice generally is also attested by the publication of *Ancient Mediterranean Sacrifice* (edited by Jennifer Knust and Zsuzsanna Varhelyi, 2011) and *Ritual and Metaphor* (edited by Christian Eberhart, 2011). Finlan's and Hogeterp's studies concern themselves with Paul's cultic language and thus overlap somewhat with the subject matter of this work but are not identical with it, and neither occupies itself with attention to the rhetorical function of metaphor as such.

Finlan's work concerns itself with the study of metaphors of atonement in Romans. The most important aspect of his work that is also heeded in this study is his description of Paul's metaphors as sometimes mixed but not confused. Finlan is especially concerned that modern readers be clear about exactly which sacrifice or other cultic ritual is the referent of a given metaphor. For example, modern readers have become habituated to confusing the sacrifice of atonement on Yom Kippur with the scapegoat ritual that occurs on the same day. Though the two actions are connected, they have very distinct meanings and roles in the process of atonement. Their confusion leads to a failure to understand clearly what Paul is saying about the death of Christ in such passages as 2 Cor 5:21, Gal 3:13, and Rom 8:3 and dulls the reader's sense for the creativity of Rom 3:21–26. Clarity about the sacrificial system is important in the present work also, because it is equally important here not to confuse what Paul calls the Passover sacrifice (1 Cor 5:7) with a sacrifice of atonement, or any other element of the sacrificial system. To do so is to misunderstand the specific rhetorical strategy behind metaphors of the Passover.

Albert Hogeterp's study of the metaphors of Temple and cult in 1 and 2 Corinthians amplifies some of what will be attended to in the present work, as we are focusing on at least one letter in common. Hogeterp discusses primarily the role of metaphors of the Temple in Paul's rhetorical strategy to counter factionalism at Corinth with images of a holy building. As will be shown, the metaphor of the Passover contributes its own overtones to this rhetoric of building up community.

Hogeterp studies the metaphors of the Temple primarily in their sequence in the letters, without examining how they relate to the structure of the letters as a whole. By contrast, I have chosen to examine the metaphors of sacrifice in 1 Corinthians and Philippians in part because of a formal quality that they share, the placement of a very poignant narrative from the life of Christ, described in sacrificial terms or patterns, roughly at their centers (Phil 2 and 1 Cor 11). It was the way in which that placement recalled for me the centrality of sacrifice in Jewish practice that made me want to attend to how these narratives function in the arrangement of the two letters. Together with other sacrificial metaphors, the Christ Hymn of Phil 2:5–11 and the narrative of 1 Cor 11:23–26 establish a pattern for Christian life that is intuitively grasped through the structure of each letter.

Finlan and Hogeterp disagree on the question of whether Paul's use of metaphors of sacrifice is indicative of a conviction that the Jewish sacrificial system has been superseded by belief in Jesus Christ. It will be seen that I have come to agree with Hogeterp, that Paul's metaphors of sacrifice (or Temple) do not indicate such a replacement of the cult. This issue may indicate the importance of maintaining clarity with regard to the rhetorical purpose of each instance of cultic metaphor, rather than trying to develop a supposed Pauline "theology of sacrifice." Once one has decided that Paul has such a thing as a theology of sacrifice as a whole, and that such a theology of sacrifice would be a specific element in Christian belief, one has given primacy to a working metaphor that may not be supported by the texts, when taken individually. In what follows, sacrifice is examined as a *tool* of Paul's thought rather than an *object* of his thought.

Like the subject of sacrifice, metaphor has recently increased as a focus of study for biblical scholars. Neither Hogeterp nor Finlan gives more than scant attention to the issue of how metaphors function, assuming a fairly simple Aristotelian understanding of metaphors as a figure of speech. Likewise, in a study of Paul's metaphors more generally, David Williams depends upon Aristotle's brief definition ("the application of an alien name by transfer"), which he references only in a footnote in *Paul's Metaphors:*

Their Content and Character (1999).[13] Williams's project is based upon the assumption that what is needed in the interpretation of an ancient metaphor is more information about its reference. For example, to understand Paul's counsel, "Do you not know that your bodies are a temple of the Holy Spirit?" (1 Cor 6:19) what is most needed is more information on the Jerusalem Temple. Williams is not incorrect about the need for a more accurate historical imagination, but without attention to how metaphors function, one cannot really grasp the point of the comparison. By contrast, this study presents some historical foundations for understanding references to sacrifice in their ancient context, but also explores the complex rhetorical function and creativity of sacrificial metaphors.

As in the case of the studies mentioned, Dale Martin's important study of the metaphor of slavery in 1 Cor 9:16–18 is more concerned with elucidating the social context of slavery and the rhetorical move to speak of slavery to Christ as soteriological than with the linguistic function of metaphors per se.[14] On the other hand, Bonnie Howe's work on 1 Peter, *Because You Bear This Name: Conceptual Metaphor and the Moral Meaning of 1 Peter* (2006), offers an extensive overview of theories of metaphor, from Aristotle to cognitive linguistic theory, to aid in the understanding of the moral teaching of 1 Peter, with a view toward its applicability today. Thus, there remains a need for giving the same kind of sustained attention to Paul's use of metaphors of different types, and particularly to the cultic metaphors that have had a profound effect upon Christian theology and practice, while being so little understood in their literal reference.

Chapter 2 of this study highlights the literary methods that are employed to study Paul's use of sacrificial metaphors. I stand among others who find it very fruitful to use cognitive theories of metaphor in the study of metaphors in the New Testament.[15] Categories developed in the work of Lakoff and Johnson serve here in the process of analyzing how metaphors "work" in human thought, and how cultic metaphors in particular function rhetorically in two of Paul's letters.[16] Such metaphors help to make a

13. David J. Williams, *Paul's Metaphors: Their Content and Character* (Peabody, MA: Hendrickson, 1999), 4.

14. Martin, *Slavery as Salvation*.

15. In addition to Bonnie Howe, see Reidar Aasgaard, "Family and Siblingship as Metaphors: A Metaphor-Theoretical Approach," in his *'My Beloved Brothers and Sisters!' Christian Siblingship in Paul* (London: T&T Clark, 2004).

16. George Lakoff and Mark Johnson, *Metaphors We Live By* (Chicago: University

leap of thought from the known to the unknown, and their "entailments" (the various related moods, images, and meanings that cling to them) color the literary work in which they stand. Metaphors of sacrifice in the Pauline corpus are evidence of a relatively early phase of Christian thinking about how to make some meaning out of the death of Christ and about what constitutes a faithful response by the believer. Thus, part of what may be gained from this work is a lively appropriation of metaphors of sacrifice from a time before they became so accepted that they have become moribund as true metaphors and become deceptively straightforward-seeming Christian doctrine. The intention here is to observe metaphors "at work," so to speak, rather than metaphors that have become part of an accepted system of thought.

Tools of rhetorical criticism then extend the study of discrete metaphors to elucidate how the constellation of metaphors of sacrifice used by Paul in a given letter contribute to his persuasive strategy for addressing the distinct issues of that congregation. I examine in particular how cultic metaphors figure in the structure of 1 Corinthians and Philippians as a whole, and how the entailments of metaphors of Passover (1 Corinthians) and thank offerings (Philippians) resonate throughout those letters.

PHILIPPIANS AND 1 CORINTHIANS AS TEST CASES

Chapters 5 and 6 are exegetical studies of the use of sacrificial metaphors in Philippians and 1 Corinthians as an element in Paul's overall persuasive strategy in each of those letters. In each case, it appears that a particular sacrifice (in Philippians, the *shelamim* (sacrifices of thanksgiving); in 1 Corinthians, the Passover) has been developed in such a way that members of the community would be able, in the future, to return to their understanding of the sacrifice and its entailments for further moral guidance.

Attention to the metaphors of sacrifice makes sense of elements of these letters that have otherwise appeared baffling, such as the combination of suffering and joy in Philippians, or Paul's warning that failure to "discern the body" in the Lord's Supper (1 Cor 11:29) is an invitation to chaos and destruction upon the community. But more than that, attention to the entailments of the sacrificial metaphors connects them to most of

---

of Chicago Press, 1980). Lakoff and Johnson subscribe to what is known as the cognitive linguistic understanding of metaphor.

the principal counsels of the letters. These metaphors are used to make an imaginative point not in one passage only, but to link arguments in different sections of the letters.

Having examined Philippians and 1 Corinthians, then, in the final chapter one is in a position to examine the sacrificial metaphors in Romans in at least a cursory way. It will be seen that, though Romans contains some very vivid instances of sacrificial metaphors (especially 3:21–26 and 12:1–2), there is not the same sustained use of a particular sacrificial complex as an imaginative guide for the community's ongoing ethical reflection. The final chapter continues the use of cognitive metaphor theory, together with attention to the actual sacrificial practices that constitute the metaphorical references, to link the cultic metaphors to Paul's persuasive program in Romans.

Listening for these metaphors and their entailments has changed my own approach to Paul's letters. While the letters' interpretation requires all the expected literary tools for dealing with a text, I have come to experience them less as texts, and more as music; as a kind of complicated fugue, a performance to process aurally over the time it takes to hear it. Certain metaphors resound long after the passage in which they occur, and their entailments weave in and out of the surrounding arguments. Attention to sacrificial metaphors as an element in the overall thematic arrangement of a letter can serve to elucidate how the letters function persuasively by lodging in the imagination, long after the last note is heard.

SACRIFICE AS METAPHOR IN PAULINE RHETORIC

METAPHOR AND SYMBOL

Clearly, before any early Christian began to use metaphors of sacrifice in teaching or argumentation, there was the actual practice of sacrifice in Jewish and Greco-Roman worship. That statement may seem so obvious that it hardly bears mentioning, but the fact often becomes lost in Christian theologizing, in which the move from sacrificial practice to sacrificial metaphor has become obscured by what appears to be the givenness of the metaphor of sacrifice. While in the first century CE sacrifice was a *familiar* category that could be employed to explain the *not-yet-understood* implications of Jesus's life and death for the Christian moral life, the reverse is now the case: almost no one in the developed world has any familiarity at all with cultic practices of sacrifice, yet they use the term frequently and casually in its metaphorical sense. These metaphorical understandings are then clumsily played back upon the original practice.

Still, there is a kind of metaphorical dimension even to the practice of sacrifice itself.[1] Using the categories of Clifford Geertz, it might be appropriate to say that the practice of sacrifice is a "[sacred] symbol complex"[2] in Hellenistic Jewish and Greco-Roman religions; but it is a *metaphor* in earliest Christian theologizing. Sacred symbols or symbol complexes

---

1. Lakoff and Johnson say of religious rituals in general that they "are typically metaphorical kinds of activities, which usually involve metonymies—real-world objects standing in for entities in the world as defined by the conceptual system of the religion. The coherent structure of the ritual is commonly taken as paralleling some aspect of reality as it is seen through the religion" (*Metaphors We Live By*, 234).

2. Clifford Geertz, *The Interpretation of Cultures: Selected Essays by Clifford Geertz* (New York: Basic Books, 1973), 132.

dramatized in rituals or related in myths, are felt somehow to sum up, for those for whom they are resonant, what is known about the way the world is, the quality of the emotional life it supports, and the way one ought to behave while in it. Sacred symbols thus relate an ontology and a cosmology to an aesthetics and a morality: their peculiar power comes from their presumed ability to identify fact with value at the most fundamental level, to give to what is otherwise merely actual, a comprehensive normative import.[3]

By repetition, symbolic rituals gradually come to be taken as expressing the truth about some state of affairs that would be incomprehensible without the ritual. In this way, rituals function like conventional metaphors. But what Paul was developing were *new* metaphors to speak of *new* states of affairs and a new ordering of life, as he saw it.

Newly created metaphors in particular have something of the provisional about them. They do not necessarily describe the world as it is and ever shall be. Rather, they always retain what is peculiar to metaphors: the ability to say that something is both like and not-like something else. Paul Ricoeur speaks of the "is and is not" quality of metaphor as "tensional" or paradoxical: "The paradox consists in the fact that there is no other way to do justice to the notion of metaphorical truth than to include the critical incision of the (literal) 'is not' within the ontological vehemence of the (metaphorical) 'is.' In doing so, the thesis merely draws the most extreme consequence of the theory of tension."[4] When Paul uses the metaphor of sacrifice to speak of the death of Christ, or Christian living in general, or his own apostolic call in particular, he is saying that each of these is both like and unlike the practice of sacrifice. The metaphor of sacrifice is one way among others (e.g., ransom, or buying and selling) to unpack the implications of the cross of Christ. Whether the metaphor of sacrifice *becomes* a sacred symbol for Christians over time is another matter.

The obvious lack of logic in the choice to see the execution of Jesus of Nazareth as a holy sacrifice points to the power of the metaphor. By means of the metaphor of sacrifice, the early Christian community claimed agency, purpose, and divine intention at precisely the point in their story

---

3. Ibid., 127.

4. Paul Ricoeur, *The Rule of Metaphor: Multi-Disciplinary Studies of the Creation of Meaning in Language,* trans. Robert Czerny et al. (Toronto: University of Toronto Press, 1977), 255.

when it would seem that they (and their God) were least effective, least powerful. For Jesus's first followers, his crucifixion was surely one of those occurrences that Geertz describes as threatening the human ability to find order in the world:

> There are at least three points where chaos—a tumult of events which lack not just interpretations but *interpretability*—threatens to break in upon man: at the limits of his analytic capacities, at the limits of his powers of endurance, and at the limits of his moral insight.[5]

The death of Jesus may have threatened the ability of his disciples to make sense of the world in all three of these areas: at the limits of their analytic capabilities, at the limits of their power of endurance, and at the limits of their moral insight.[6] The use of the metaphor of sacrifice was one way in which they sought to reclaim interpretability.[7] The writings of Paul, because they are the earliest Christian writings we have, are the best source for a glimpse of this imaginative leap in its early stages. The task, then, is to bracket out what one might know of later Christian theologizing on sacrifice, in order to focus as clearly as possible on each Pauline text and the train of thought made manifest there. This study is not so much concerned with any schema

---

5. Geertz, *Interpretation of Cultures*, 100.

6. See Neil Elliott's discussion of the relationship between the historical realities of the Roman practice of crucifixion and Paul's interpretation of the cross in "The Anti-imperial Message of the Cross," in *Paul and Empire: Religion and Power in Roman Imperial Society*, ed. Richard A. Horsely (Harrisburg, PA: Trinity Press International, 1997), 167–83.

7. In this effort the author of 2 Maccabees, especially in chapter 7, of course, precedes them. A key difference between the vindicating resurrection proposed in 2 Maccabees and that of the early Christians is the Christian claim that the risen Christ somehow remains present in and among the community of believers. One might say that we are choosing to stay with the concept of sacrifice as metaphor, before it becomes ramified as a theological model in early Christian thought. Sallie McFague draws a simple, but useful contrast between a metaphor and a model: "The simplest way to define a model is as a dominant metaphor, a metaphor with staying power. Metaphors are usually the work of an individual, a flash of insight which is often passing. But some metaphors gain wide appeal and become major ways of structuring and ordering experience" (*Metaphorical Theology: Models of God in Religious Language* [Philadelphia: Fortress, 1982], 23). But see also Janet Martin Soskice's warning against the "conflation of the categories of 'model' and 'metaphor,' reducing their distinction to "a matter of degree," though she agrees that they are in many ways comparable (*Metaphor and Religious Language* [Oxford: Clarendon, 1985], 101).

of "development" of a Pauline "theology of sacrifice" as it is with the use of the metaphor as a rhetorical tool in particular arguments made with particular communities in mind, in this case in 1 Corinthians and Philippians.

Because I am concerned to study the metaphor at a relatively early stage in its use, I have made some very basic judgments about the chronology of the Pauline letters,[8] although I am expressly *not* concerned to trace any sort of supposed chronological development in Paul's use of the metaphor of sacrifice. For example, while I think it bears mentioning that the letter to the Romans is later than 1 Corinthians, it would be misleading to attribute the differences in the use of cultic metaphors in the two letters *primarily* to a supposed maturation of Paul's thoughts on sacrifice as they relate to Christian living. The differences in the use of cultic metaphors in the two letters are due more to the distinct purposes of the letters, and to the issues and circumstances of their recipients, than to their place in an assumed development of Paul's theology. The object here is to catch Paul in the act of working out the complex of meanings that are born when one begins to use sacrifice as a metaphor in Christian thinking, and to allow the specific concerns of 1 Corinthians and Philippians to surface through a study of their particular range of uses of sacrificial metaphors. It is also important to remember that Paul is not necessarily the sole creator of these metaphors, however freshly and provisionally he may appear to be using them. His is one voice preserved from a multi-vocal conversation among early Christians whose frame of reference was both Greco-Roman and Jewish religious practice.

ANCIENT THEORIES OF METAPHOR

The point of this section and the two following is not to give a comprehensive account of discussion on metaphor throughout the ages, but to bring to light some reflection on metaphor in three broad categories: first, a glimpse into Aristotle's and Plato's discussion and use of metaphor, as a window into ancient thought on metaphor; secondly, a broad overview of some of the twentieth-century discussion of metaphor organized by a consideration of some of the key terms currently in use; and thirdly, a

---

8. I am assuming that 1 Thessalonians dates from the early 50s; 1 Corinthians from the mid-50s, together with Philippians and Philemon; that the separate pieces of 2 Corinthians are later than 1 Corinthians; and that Romans is Paul's latest letter. Galatians would be most difficult to date with any precision.

discussion of the cognitive theory of metaphor. The concentration is upon those theories that shed the most light on Paul's use of cultic metaphors in 1 Corinthians and Philippians.

Aristotle's concise definition of metaphor is the customary starting-place for considerations of metaphor: "A metaphor is the application of a word that belongs to another thing" (*Poet.* 14 [Halliwell]). Most writers on metaphor stress the fact that Aristotle limited the scope of metaphors to a matter of individual words. But, while he viewed metaphors as having mainly to do with nouns (rather than a larger frame of meaning), he saw their role in creating new ways of understanding: "Metaphors must not be far-fetched, but we must give names to things that have none by deriving the metaphor from what is akin and of the same kind, so that, as soon as it is uttered, it is clearly seen to be akin" (*Rhet.* 3.2.12 [1405a] [Freese]). The ability to create such a connection Aristotle saw as a matter of genius: "Much the greatest asset is a capacity for metaphor. This alone cannot be acquired from another, and is a sign of natural gifts: because to use metaphor well is to discern similarities" (*Poet.* 22.5–6 [1459a] [Halliwell]; see also *Rhet.* 3.10.1–4 [1410b]).

This basic move—to see the similarity between things that are, on the face of it, dissimilar—is exactly what must be attended to in Philippians and 1 Corinthians. In Philippians, Paul draws a similarity between the ritual pattern of a thank offering and the death of Jesus, then further draws the similarity to include the moral patterns of himself, Timothy, and Epaphroditus, and finally urges the Philippians to adopt the same pattern of moral discernment in self-offering. In 1 Corinthians, Paul makes a comparison between the moral life of the Corinthians and patterns in Passover observance, such as rigorously cleaning out the "yeast," attending to the community's holiness, and properly celebrating the covenant meal. In drawing out these similarities, he develops a way for members of the two communities to carry out their own ongoing moral discernment, for which there are no precedents in their immediate context. His genius (as Aristotle might have called it) was to forge these similarities, working from the known (sacrifice) to the unknown (Christ-appropriate faithfulness) and to use these similarities to guide the communities' ways of life.

While Plato has the reputation of being critical of metaphors in general,[9] an examination of his own *use* of metaphors reveals them as very

---

9. This critique rests upon Plato's distinction between the true forms of things

sharp instruments for thought. In *Phaedrus*, Socrates introduces his imagery for the soul as a "figure," or "likeness" (ἔοιϰεν): "To tell what [the soul]
really is would be a matter for utterly superhuman and long discourse, but
it is within human power to describe it briefly in a figure [ἔοιϰεν]; let us
therefore speak in that way. We will liken the soul to the composite nature
of a pair of winged horses and a charioteer" (*Phaedr.* 246a [Fowler]). He
goes on extensively to describe the difficult interaction between the charioteer and the two winged horses, as a way to speak of internal realities that
cannot be seen. He expects his hearer (Phaedrus) to be attracted to the
heavenly images he describes, and to adjust his orientation accordingly,
toward the "fitting pasturage" that is found only in heaven (*Phaedr.* 248b
[Fowler]). Plato's use of such an extended metaphor is very much akin to
Paul's use of the Christ Hymn in Philippians, which opens up the community's view into heavenly realities; or it might be compared to the narrative
of the Lord's Supper in 1 Corinthians, which likewise reveals the transcendent significance of that community's practice. In all of these cases, the
extended metaphor helps the speaker to describe a very complex reality
in a relatively short space, and to suggest a set of thoughts and actions
congruent with the image.

Terms for the Study of Metaphor

Several twentieth-century philosophers have contributed to a vocabulary
for the study of metaphor. Since I will continue to use some of these terms,
I offer here a brief description of some of the most widely employed terms.

In the 1930s, I. A. Richards adopted the names "tenor" and "vehicle" to
refer to the word being discussed and the word (or concept, place, person,
event) to which it is being compared, respectively.[10] In the sentence "Life is
a journey," *life* is the tenor, and *journey* is the vehicle. The terms "ground"
and "figure" or "target" and "source" are equivalents to tenor and vehicle.
Below, I discuss the terms target and source in relation to semantic fields.

Ricoeur elaborated upon I. A. Richards's description of metaphors as
"tensive," and brought to light the way in which metaphors put peculiar

---

(their ideal), their existence in the world as objects subject to decay, and their representation in works of art and poetry. This third category is thus a mere imitation of an
imitation (see *Resp.* 10).

10. I. A. Richards *The Philosophy of Rhetoric*, 2nd ed. (Oxford: Oxford University
Press, 1976).

pressure on the verb "to be," causing it to mean both "is" and "is not." This insight into the incongruity of metaphorical speech is especially significant for the study of the early production of sacrificial metaphors in relation to the death of Jesus and the shape of Christian moral life. While this body of metaphors has become conventional to the point of being taken as more or less literal by many, it is important for the study of mid-first-century Christian texts to maintain a keen sense of their novelty and surprise.

Ricoeur also examined and clarified the proper frame for understanding a metaphor's purpose and meaning. In *The Rule of Metaphor*, Ricoeur first considers Aristotle's discussion of metaphors as being essentially a matter of *semiotics*.[11] In such a case, the individual words that compose the metaphor itself are considered to be their proper frame of reference. Without negating Aristotle's understanding, Ricoeur later poses an additional semantic frame of meaning for a given metaphor, a move which expands the frame to include the sentence or paragraph,[12] or finally the entire work ("poem") that contains the metaphor. While Ricoeur develops this thought within a larger consideration of the truth of metaphors,[13] his position that a metaphor's proper frame might be a work as a whole is key to this particular study.

While the Christian Gospels are composed of many discrete units of tradition, edited and shaped into a whole, the 1 Corinthians and Philippians are more or less unitary in their conception and execution, and thus rhetorically coherent.[14] The particular point of this study is that the proper frame of understanding for the cultic metaphors in Philippians and 1 Corinthians is the entire letter in which they appear. The metaphors based upon the *shelamim* sacrifices in Philippians and the metaphors drawn

---

11. Ricoeur, *Rule of Metaphor*, 1977.

12. Others, such as Eva Kittay (*Metaphor: Its Cognitive Force and Linguistic Structure* [Oxford: Clarendon Press, 1987]), also understand the sentence to be the appropriate frame of a metaphor.

13. I.e., whether or not a metaphor, with its is/is not quality, can properly refer to reality (see Ricoeur, *Rule of Metaphor*, 221–28). For the purposes of this study, we are not concerned as much with the truth-value of Paul's cultic metaphors as with their aptness for his particular rhetorical purposes.

14. I say "for the most part" in order to acknowledge the insertions and patchwork character of some of the epistles. Both 1 Corinthians and Philippians have been subject to scholarly debate concerning their unity (Philippians) and possible non-Pauline additions (1 Cor 14:33b–36). But for the most part, they remain coherent documents, especially when compared to the compositional history of the Gospels.

from the Passover in 1 Corinthians occur multiple times in each letter, shaping and coloring the reader's interpretation even in passages in which they do not specifically occur.

Another, related, way in which metaphor theory has expanded from simple consideration of the two terms involved in the metaphor is manifested in the work of Eva Kittay, who built upon Ferdinand de Saussure's understanding of semantic fields to develop a semantic field theory of metaphor. According to Kittay, what is transferred from one term to the other in a metaphor is not a simple one-to-one nominal reference, but an entire semantic field of related elements and concepts.[15] Using Aristotle's understanding of metaphor as constituting a "transfer of meaning," she says that this transfer "can be seen as a process in which the structure of one semantic field induces a structure on another content domain."[16] This expanded sense of what exactly is transferred by the use of a metaphor—and especially in the use of extended or repeated metaphors in a single work, as in the case of the cultic metaphors of Philippians and 1 Corinthians— supports the thesis that the sacrificial metaphors in Philippians and 1 Corinthians bring with them a host of entailments, evaluations, emotions, implied moral behavior, and so on.

Additionally, Kittay agrees with others who have contributed to the cognitive theory of metaphor in holding that metaphors do not simply remark upon a similarity between two things (or two semantic fields); they *create* a similarity between two things. By studying the early Christian use of sacrificial metaphors in the letters of Paul, one has a chance to observe the *creation* of similarities among the Jewish and Greco-Roman sacrificial systems, the crucifixion of Jesus, and the moral formation of early Christian believers.

COGNITIVE THEORY OF METAPHOR

The understanding of metaphor that is the main guide in this study is the cognitive theory of metaphor described by George Lakoff and Mark Johnson in their coauthored work, *Metaphors We Live By*.[17] Lakoff and Johnson

---

15. Eva Feder Kittay, *Metaphor: Its Cognitive Force and Linguistic Structure* (Oxford: Clarendon, 1987), 258–300.

16. Ibid., 258.

17. A good overview of the history of the interpretation of metaphors since the time of Aristotle, including an overview of the cognitive linguistic approach to the

understand metaphor to be far more than a feature of language. Rather, the making of metaphors is integral to human understanding, to living in and making sense of the world: "It is as though the ability to comprehend experience through metaphor were a sense, like seeing or touching or hearing, with metaphors providing the only ways to perceive and experience much of the world."[18] Thus, metaphors are not merely tools of expression, but tools of thought itself,[19] as the process of human cognition "is fundamentally metaphorical in nature."[20] The foundational metaphors of a culture structure both people's thoughts and their actions, as they seek to understand the basic structures of the world and to live in proper relationship to those structures. What follows is a series of points made by Lakoff and Johnson that will serve to open up and elucidate the sacrificial metaphors in Philippians and 1 Corinthians.

According to Lakoff and Johnson, metaphors have an experiential basis related to human physicality. This characteristic of metaphor is sub-

---

study of metaphor outlined in Lakoff and Johnson is in the first half of Bonnie Howe's *Because You Bear This Name: Conceptual Metaphor and the Moral Meaning of 1 Peter*, BibInt 81 (Leiden: Brill, 2006), 11–160.

18. Lakoff and Johnson, *Metaphors We Live By*, 239. See also Lakoff's homage to Reddy in "The Contemporary Theory of Metaphor": "The contemporary theory that metaphor is primarily conceptual, conventional, and part of the ordinary system of thought and language can be traced to Michael Reddy's ... now classic essay, 'The Conduit Metaphor,' which first appeared in the first edition of this collection. Reddy did far more in that essay than he modestly suggested. With a single, thoroughly analyzed example, he allowed us to see, albeit in a restricted domain, that everyday English is largely metaphorical, dispelling once and for all the traditional view that metaphor is primarily in the realm of poetic or 'figurative' language. Reddy showed, for a single, very significant case, that the locus of metaphor is thought, not language, that metaphor is a major and indispensable part of our ordinary, conventional way of conceptualizing the world, and that our everyday behavior reflects our metaphorical understanding of experience. Reddy was the first to demonstrate them by rigorous linguistic analysis, stating generalizations over voluminous examples" (in *Metaphor and Thought*, ed. Andrew Ortony [Cambridge: Cambridge University Press, 1993] 203–4).

19. As Sallie McFague writes in *Metaphorical Theology*, "metaphorical thinking constitutes the basis of human thought and language" (15). Further, "The principal tasks of conceptual thought—analysis, classification and synthesis—all depend on [the] process of 'drawing out' similarities within dissimilars" (34). See also I. A. Richards's chapter on metaphor in *The Philosophy of Rhetoric*: "*Thought* is metaphoric, and proceeds by comparison, and the metaphors of language derive therefrom" (94, emphasis original).

20. Lakoff and Johnson, *Metaphors We Live By*, 3.

sequently reflected in cultural systems of orientation and valuation, such as *up is happy* and *down is sad*. There is an overall "cultural coherence" to these physical relationships that Lakoff and Johnson track in Western society in this way: happy is up, sad is down; conscious is up, unconscious is down; health and life are up, sickness and death are down; having control or force is up, being subject to control or force is down; more is up, less is down; high status is up, low status is down; good is up, bad is down; virtue is up, depravity is down; rational is up, emotional is down.[21] There is some variation in valuation across cultures, such that some cultures value balance over an up vs. down prioritization, and some value passivity over activity. But in spite of these differences, basic human physicality nonetheless creates a large degree of consistency across cultures.

Subcultures may deviate from some of the generally held values of a society, but they do so at risk of opposition from outsiders and incoherence for insiders. An example of such deviation would be people who believe that *less is more* in a culture that generally regards *more* as *up* and *up* as *better*. These deviations in value may become a source of intense social conflict.[22] It appears that Paul employs sacrificial metaphors precisely to undermine the system of *up is honorable, down is shameful* values and decision-making in the Greco-Roman context of his churches. Phil 2:6–11 is a clear example of such an inversion of values, as the one who was ἐν μορφῇ θεοῦ descends to take on the form of God's slave, a decision that ironically results in his exaltation. Ultimately, the conviction that *up is good* is maintained, though the Messiah's vindication may be sensible only to the community of faith.

The crucifixion of the Messiah Jesus, followed by the vindicating proclamation of his having been raised, comprise a sequence of events difficult for his followers to justify to others confidently without the use of a powerfully explanatory metaphor. The metaphor of sacrifice, with its *loss is gain, death is life* logic, fits together with an upside-down apocalyptic worldview to make sense of a Christian proclamation that subverts the dominant value system. As Lakoff and Johnson say, there will be significant conflict when a subgroup of a culture deviates from the basic metaphorical construction of values of the culture. This conflict is apparent in all of the documents of the New Testament. As we will see in subsequent

21. Ibid., 14–21.
22. Ibid., 22–24.

chapters, in both Philippians and 1 Corinthians, seeking high status is problematic, seeking low status is prized (1 Cor 8); the risk of sickness and death are valued, while seeking one's personal safety is devalued (Phil 2:20–21, 29–30), et cetera. In a grand moral reversal, those who seek what is down will (ultimately) be raised to the highest point. The combination of both physical experience (up is life, down is death) and cultural valuation make Paul's countercultural message confusing to his churches and in need of constant reiteration and explanation. Metaphors of sacrifice help to connect this shift in fundamental values to something already known (by both Jews and adherents of the Greco-Roman religions), and to justify it.

A second important property of metaphors is their capacity not only to reveal but to hide: "In allowing us to focus on one aspect of a concept," a metaphor "can keep us from focusing on other aspects of the concept that are inconsistent with that metaphor."[23] Likening the execution of Jesus to a sacrifice removes Roman culpability from the picture and recasts God as the principal agent. When sacrificial metaphors are then extended to the Christian moral life, Rome as the governing authority becomes a minor, transitory player, and God becomes the one whose power must be recognized and whose favor must be sought (Phil 2:12–13). Rather than oppose Roman power directly, sacrificial metaphors allow the believing community to disempower and side-step Rome altogether.[24] It is a given author's rhetorical choice to decide what a metaphor will hide or reveal, by choosing which aspects of a comparison to stress, and which to ignore. In Rom 3:25, Paul mentions the blood of Jesus at his crucifixion, not because crucifixion is a bloody way to die, but because blood manipulation is central to the Jewish sacrifice of atonement, to which Paul is comparing Jesus's death.

Who gets to say which metaphors become deeply rooted in a people's understanding of the structure of the world? Certain metaphors have a strong explanatory power that is confirmed over time as they are used and as people act in accordance with them. But there is another social aspect to the use of metaphors: "whether in national politics or in everyday interaction, people in power get to impose their metaphors."[25] Certainly the metaphor of sacrifice seems to have had an immediate explanatory power

---

23. Ibid., 10.

24. This move is consistent with Paul's counterintuitive assertion of the triumph of his proclamation in spite of opposition in Phil 1:12–18.

25. Lakoff and Johnson, *Metaphors We Live By*, 157.

for early Christians, but one must also ask in whose interest it might have been for the metaphor of sacrifice to be singled out as central to Christian theology over the following centuries. Was the metaphor simply so apt that it became inconceivable not to use it, or was it primarily useful for a particular person or social group? Sacrifice can be a high-stakes metaphor in moral instruction, as it asks a person to give up his or her self-interest in support of something said to be of larger value. Who determines the scale of value, and on what grounds? Remembering that metaphors both reveal and hide aspects of reality, one should have a healthy suspicion concerning who benefits from any particular revelations and concealments.

When a metaphor is put into play, it brings with it a set of *entailments*,[26] meanings that cling to the metaphor and which are brought along with it into its new reference.[27] Consequently, there is more than a one-to-one correspondence between a metaphor and its tenor, and this dynamic increases with the complexity of the metaphor involved. For instance, the metaphor of sacrifice entails a web of related ideas involving (among many other things) atonement, priesthood, holiness, oath-making, eating, community, thanksgiving, death, life, cleanliness, men's work and women's work. This complexity in the entailments of cultic meta-

---

26. The concept of the "entailment" is not far removed from what Stökl Ben Ezra calls the "*imaginaire*," a term developed by French philosophers and historians to describe the "ensemble of conceptions of a given collective," including the "unsequenced motifs" and "associations" that cluster about an important concept. As he says, "For example, the 'German *imaginaire* of Christmas' may include such motifs as Christmas tree, snow, Santa Claus, gifts, 'Silent Night,' family, scent of cinnamon cookies, solitude, frostiness, sledge, church, heated house, frosted windows, holidays, coziness, etc." (*The Impact of Yom Kippur on Early Christianity: The Day of Atonement from Second Temple Judaism to the Fifth Century* [Tübingen: Mohr Siebeck, 2003], 8–10). I use the term *entailment* because it refers specifically to associations that cling to metaphors, though the two terms point to a similar phenomenon of the clustering of a wide variety of associations about a significant term.

27. The concept of entailments is related to what Max Black calls the "resonance" of a metaphor, its ability to "support a high degree of implicative elaboration" (see "More about Metaphor," in *Metaphor and Thought*, ed. Andrew Ortony [Cambridge: Cambridge University Press, 1993], 26). A related claim made by Black is that the "secondary subject" in a metaphorical statement is "to be regarded as a system rather than an individual thing. Thus, I think of Wallace Stevens's remark that 'society is a sea' as being not so much about the sea (considered as a thing) as about a system of relationships ... signaled by the presence of the word 'sea' in the sentence in question" ("More about Metaphor," 27).

phors is part of the way in which they may have a tendency to resonate beyond their immediate context. For instance, in 1 Corinthians the Passover metaphor is not confined to its explicit mention in 5:7 but resonates throughout the letter in discussions of yeast, puffing up, holiness, and community order. It is by way of entailments that the proper frame for considering strong sacrificial metaphors becomes an entire epistle rather than a single sentence.

Structural metaphors are those that are more complex than many of the most common and conventional metaphors, such as "ideas are money" or "he has a *wealth* of ideas."[28] While some structural metaphors have become conventional, many are created for particular rhetorical purposes, and employ "one highly structured and clearly delineated concept to structure another."[29] Examples of structural metaphors in the Pauline literature might be "Christian moral life is a thank offering" (Rom 12:1) or "The death of Jesus is a sacrifice of atonement" (Rom 3:25). These two examples alone demonstrate some of the complexity involved in relating two highly developed structures to one another. In each case, the known quantity is assumed to be the sacrificial metaphor, which elucidates the less-known tenor, the Christian moral life or the effects of Jesus's execution on subsequent believers.

In addition to the complexity arising from the use of structural metaphors, Paul also sometimes mixes them, as in 1 Cor 3:9 ("For we are God's servants working together; you are God's field, God's building").[30] Each of these vehicles comes with an attendant cloud of entailments that interact and play off one another as the reader attempts to decipher how they were intended to interact with one another. These overlapping and complex structural metaphors have the power to resonate across an entire letter, coloring other images and trains of thought.

In his work on cultic atonement metaphors, Stephen Finlan clarifies that a mixed metaphor is not necessarily a confused metaphor.[31] The prohibition against mixing metaphors that is learned by American school-

---

28. Lakoff and Johnson, *Metaphors We Live By*, 48.

29. Ibid., 61.

30. A subtle background to this metaphor may be Jer 1:10, but the effect is still to put before the Corinthians two very complicated metaphors for how they might think of their life together.

31. Stephen Finlan, *The Background and Content of Paul's Cultic Atonement Metaphors*, AcBib 19 (Atlanta: Society of Biblical Literature, 2004).

children is not a barrier for Paul's creativity in drawing metaphors from multiple realms of human experience and combining them in a single argument. The desire on the part of scholars to unify Paul's thought may work against a full understanding of his vision of, for example, the different facets of the significance of the death of Jesus. One obvious example of such a quick movement of thought is encountered at 1 Cor 6:19–20, where the cultic metaphor of the Temple gives way suddenly to the image of money exchanged in the redemption of a slave or prisoner. It appears that Paul expects the reader to experience the multiplication of metaphors not as confusion, but as a confirmation of his counsel: "therefore glorify God in your own body" (1 Cor 6:20). The holiness of the body *and* its value are both at stake.

One of the most important characteristics of metaphor is its predictive capacity.[32] A metaphor "uses the similar to move into the unknown."[33] In discussing the use of models in the sciences, Janet Martin Soskice contends that "the task of theory construction itself is customarily the task of constructing models to explain better what we do not yet fully understand, rather than that of building models of states of affairs whose nature is clear to us."[34] In earliest Christianity, the metaphor of sacrifice is proposed in just such a way; it is put forward as an explanation of things not yet completely understood. Once the metaphor is used, it works in the same way that powerful scientific models work: it explains, predicts, and implies rational human responses to the state of affairs it describes. In a sense, a lively metaphor is out in front of one's ability to conceive of a thing, drawing the person after it, unraveling all the ways in which the metaphor appears to make sense of something previously incomprehensible.

Beyond the predictive capacity of the metaphor is the way in which some powerful metaphors do not merely explain, but actually *create* simi-

---

32. Aristotle's description of the generative quality of metaphors is worth noting here: "We all naturally find it agreeable to get hold of new ideas easily: words express ideas, and therefore those words are the most agreeable that enable us to get hold of new ideas. Now strange words simply puzzle us; ordinary words convey only what we know already; it is from metaphor that we can best get hold of something fresh" (*Rhet.* 3.10.1–2 [1410b]). This predictive quality of metaphors is encountered in what Lakoff and Johnson call "imaginative rationality," an experiential mode of thought that goes beyond the binaries of objectivism and subjectivism (Lakoff and Johnson, *Metaphors We Live By*, 185–237).

33. McFague, *Metaphorical Theology*, 36.

34. Soskice, *Metaphor and Religious Language*, 103.

larities between the tenor and the vehicle, such that a culture's perceptions and ongoing experiences of the tenor are profoundly changed. Such is the case with the crucifixion of Jesus in Christian tradition. The power of the sacrificial metaphor in relation to the crucifixion altered the meaning of Jesus's execution to such an extent that its original political reality is now a subject that needs to be taught, explained, and justified.

In the opening of his essay "Thick Description: Toward an Interpretive Theory of Culture," Clifford Geertz quotes from Susanne Langer's[35] description of the power of certain new ideas: "The sudden vogue of such a *grande idée*, crowding out almost everything else for a while, is due, she says, 'to the fact that all sensitive and active minds turn at once to exploiting it. We try it in every connection, for every purpose, experiment with possible stretches of its strict meaning, with generalizations and derivatives.'"[36] Moreover, though Geertz goes on to explain that such *grandes idées* tend to lose their power over time, sacrifice has become so embedded in Christian thought (particularly in relation to the crucifixion of Christ) that it has almost lost its metaphorical sense and become, to a certain extent, literalized, or what some would call a "dead" metaphor. Dead metaphors have lost the tension between "is" and "is not," "like" and "unlike." As McFague says, "The greatest danger [for a powerful metaphor] is assimilation—the shocking, powerful metaphor becomes trite and accepted.... What has occurred, of course, is that similarity has become identity; the *tension* that is so critical in metaphor has been lost."[37]

George Lakoff, however, decries the use of the term "dead metaphor" as too imprecise to be useful, since so-called dead metaphors actually "die" in a variety of ways, with different consequences for the understanding of the terms involved.[38] It could be the case that the source domain has

35. Susanne Langer, *Philosophy in a New Key: A Study in the Symbolism of Reason, Rite and Art*, 4th ed. (Cambridge: Harvard University Press, 1960).

36. Geertz, *Interpretation of Cultures*, 3. Geertz is using Langer's discussion to put the scientific concept of "culture" on the table, to "[cut] the culture concept down to size." Geertz is criticizing a concept used within the field of anthropology, but I find his remarks equally useful here, in examining an occurrence within a culture.

37. McFague, *Metaphorical Theology*, 41. Ashton also writes on this subject, "One difficulty that frequently crops up when reading Paul is that his metaphors have lost their shine: overuse has left them worn and lustreless: they are dead metaphors" (*The Religion of Paul the Apostle* [New Haven: Yale University Press, 2000], 132).

38. George Lakoff, "Metaphorical Issues: The Death of Dead Metaphor," *Metaphor and Symbolic Activity* (1987), 243–47. But see also in Lakoff and Johnson, *Meta-*

become unknown to the people using the metaphor; it could be that the metaphorical meaning has actually replaced the primary meaning of a word; it could be that the metaphor has become conventional in its use. Simply calling all of these cases dead metaphors obscures what has actually happened to the concepts in question.

In the case of metaphors of sacrifice in Christian rhetoric, several different things have happened, opening a sizeable gap in understanding between the original users of the metaphors and their modern interpreters. Most current users and interpreters of sacrificial language have little to no understanding of the original source domain. In particular, very few are aware of the nuances of the different sacrifices in Jewish or Greco-Roman cultic practice, resulting in the domination of interpretations relating to atonement, the only kind of sacrifice with which many people are even superficially familiar. Modern use of the word "sacrifice" to refer to almost any burdensome task or relationship can confuse the matter further. The fact that using sacrificial terms to speak of the death of Jesus has become conventional (or assimilated, as McFague says above) masks the original shock value of equating a travesty of justice with a holy ritual. To extend the shock value, Paul actually used submission to wrongful execution as a moral model (Phil 2).

When sacrificial metaphors undergo all of these different changes over the centuries, they do not die (since they continue to be used as a tool of cognition), but they do not necessarily continue to mean the same things they did to their original users. It is my hope that this study may recover some of the shock and tension of the original use of sacrificial metaphors in Paul's letters.

Because metaphors are not just a way of saying something obliquely that could be said more directly without the metaphor, and because metaphors are often the only way to apprehend or express a reality, their use usually implies a set of actions, a way of living, coherent with the metaphor. Lakoff and Johnson hold that, "In all aspects of life ... we define our reality in terms of metaphors and then proceed to act on the basis of the metaphors. We draw inferences, set goals, make commitments and execute plans, all on the basis of how we in part structure our experience,

---

phors We Live By, the example of "*foot* of the mountain," a metaphor among others that they characterize as "idiosyncratic, unsystematic, and isolated.... If any metaphorical expressions deserve to be called 'dead,' it is these, though they do have a bare spark of life" (55).

consciously and unconsciously, by means of metaphor."[39] For instance, the so-called "war on poverty" established a way of viewing poverty and a way of addressing its problems that inspired certain kinds of actions and precluded others.[40] The more people live, act, and make moral choices on the basis of a particular metaphorical understanding, the more they affirm its validity and begin to see it as a fact of the structure of the world.

New metaphors, or new uses of existing metaphors, not only describe a state of affairs that had not been described before, but they are actually capable of creating new realities by inspiring a new set of behaviors congruent with the metaphor. In the letters of Paul, one encounters the author trying the concept of sacrifice in many connections, for many purposes, and experimenting with possible stretches of its strict meaning, with generalizations, derivatives, and entailments. When Paul enjoins his community to behavior appropriate to people whose actions comprise "a living sacrifice" (Rom 12:1), one assumes that they internalize this metaphor, experience their choices of action in terms of the metaphor, and develop a complex of ideas around the experience. In this way, the metaphor of sacrifice, as it relates to the moral life of the community, begins to take hold, not only as an idea or a tool for understanding, but as a lived reality.

Metaphor and Rhetoric

Because we cannot hear the voices of Paul's conversation partners in Philippi, we cannot know how members of the community received his establishment of sacrificial patterns of living as a moral model (Phil 1:21–26; 2:6–11, 19–24, 25–30). If this pattern is intended to be a corrective to the leadership of Euodia and Syntyche (4:2), we do not know whether or not it was either understood or successful. We do not know whether his rhetorical strategy was met with acquiescence or irritation. We do not know whether the recipients of the letters felt that Paul was contradicting his own moral counsel by "strong-arming" them in commending to

---

39. Lakoff and Johnson, *Metaphors We Live By*, 158.

40. See the related discussion of metaphors and problem setting in social policy in Schön's chapter, "Generative Metaphor: A Perspective on Problem-Setting in Social Policy," in Ortony's *Metaphor and Thought* (137–63), and discussion of the need for more apt metaphors for relating appropriately to environmental degradation in K. L. Cox's "A Clouded View: How Language Shapes Moral Perception," *USQR* 63 (2010): 84–96.

them a sacrificial pattern of life. To what extent was Paul's own self-interest involved in the choice of this high-stakes metaphor? What we can see is that Paul used the sacrificial pattern in Philippians repeatedly and pointedly, shaping it to reveal that self-abnegation in the present leads to exaltation in the end.

In the letters of Paul, sacrificial metaphors are used primarily as high-stakes tools of persuasion. I say "high stakes," because their sphere of reference is so serious and so central to religious life for both Jews and adherents of the various Greco-Roman religions. When the grounding for a particular counsel is "because your body is a temple," or "because Christ is our Passover sacrifice," then the counsel in question is not easily dismissed. The chapters that follow on sacrificial metaphors in Philippians and 1 Corinthians use recent rhetorical studies of those letters, in order to establish a framework for showing how the metaphors relate to the overall structure and themes of each letter.

Margaret Mitchell describes 1 Corinthians rhetorically as "a single letter of unitary composition which contains a deliberative argument persuading the Christian community at Corinth to become reunified."[41] According to Aristotle's τέχνη ῥητορική, deliberative rhetoric is a strategy of persuasion containing admonitions and exhortations concerning the audience's future behavior (*Rhet.* 1.2). Mitchell further amplifies this description by noting that deliberative rhetoric was used mainly in the political sphere.[42] The very name for early Christian communities, the ἐκκλησία, comes likewise from the political sphere, where it referred to a legislative assembly of citizens. Paul's first letter to the Corinthians might be seen then, broadly, as a written substitute for an address to the gathered assembly.[43] In it Paul seeks to persuade the community to certain

41. Margaret Mitchell, *Paul and the Rhetoric of Reconciliation: An Exegetical Investigation of the Language and Composition of 1 Corinthians* (Louisville: Westminster, 1991), 1. Paul's principal proposition in 1 Corinthians, according to Mitchell, is stated at 1:10, παρακαλῶ δὲ ὑμᾶς, ἀδελφοί, διὰ τοῦ ὀνόματος τοῦ κυρίου ἡμῶν Ἰησοῦ Χριστοῦ, ἵνα τὸ αὐτὸ λέγητε πάντες καὶ μὴ ᾖ ἐν ὑμῖν σχίσματα, ἦτε δὲ κατηρτισμένοι ἐν τῷ αὐτῷ νοῒ καὶ ἐν τῇ αὐτῇ γνώμῃ.

42. Mitchell, *Paul and the Rhetoric of Reconciliation*, 65. As can be seen in Aristotle's brief enumeration of the subjects that fall naturally to deliberative rhetoric: ways and means, war and peace, defense of the country, imports and exports, and legislation (*Rhet.* 1.7).

43. Paul, of course, was temporarily not able to be present with the community at Corinth, and so the letter represented him and his thoughts to the ἐκκλησία; but

patterns of behavior in the future. Hogeterp has rightly, I think, characterized the future for which Paul advocates as "proper community building."[44]
Mitchell's basic assumptions and conclusions concerning the rhetoric of 1
Corinthians are employed in chapter 6 to track the metaphors of cult and
sacrifice as they occur within the structure of the letter.

Duane Watson has proposed a rhetorical analysis of Philippians, in
which he categorizes this letter also as an example of deliberative rhetoric,[45]
and he argues for the unity of Philippians, based on his analysis. The exigence of Philippians (the situation that has occasioned the letter), according to Watson, is the "appearance of a rival gospel in Philippi,"[46] provok-
ing Paul's response to the situation, expressed in the proposition: "Only
let your life be worthy of the gospel" (1:27). Thus, he sees the letter as
concerned mainly with the question, "What is a manner of life worthy of

---

it is only through the written word that we now have access to *any* ancient rhetoric. As George Kennedy says, "Rhetoric originates in speech and its primary product
is a speech act, not a text, but the rhetoric of historical periods can only be studied
through texts" (*New Testament Interpretation through Rhetorical Criticism* [Chapel
Hill: University of North Carolina Press, 1984], 5).

44. Albert Hogeterp, *Paul and God's Temple: A Historical Interpretation of Cultic
Imagery in the Corinthian Correspondence*, BTS 2 (Leuven: Peters, 2006), 302–4.
Mitchell characterizes this purpose, using more clearly political or civic terms, as the
cessation of factionalism and the urging of concord and unity (*Paul and the Rhetoric
of Reconciliation*, 65–66). For a counter-argument to this characterization, see R. Dean
Anderson, *Ancient Rhetorical Theory and Paul* (Kampen: Kok Pharos, 1996), 231–38.

45. In contrast to Kennedy, who calls it "largely epideictic" (Kennedy, *New Testament Interpretation*, 77), though he might be of the opinion that the epideictic passages are in the service of purposes more akin to that of deliberative rhetoric. Stowers
acknowledges that, "Most types of letters used in the Greco-Roman world were associated with the *epideictic* division of rhetoric" (*Letter Writing in Greco-Roman Antiquity*,
LEC 5 [Philadelphia: Westminster, 1986], 27), but he also says that rules for types of
speeches could be adapted for letters: "So, for example, a letter of consolation written
by a person with rhetorical training may more or less follow the form of the concilia-
tory speech" (Stowers, *Letter Writing*, 34). The deliberative form seems to fit more
closely Paul's aims in Philippians, as Watson makes clear, with 2:19–30 serving as an
epideictic digression to praise Timothy and Epaphroditus as examples of those who
are "standing firm in the gospel" (1:27). And, as we discussed in relation to 1 Corinthians, there is linguistic evidence to suggest that a political form of rhetoric would be
appropriate for Paul's construal of Christian community (see esp. Phil 3:20).

46. Duane F. Watson, "A Rhetorical Analysis of Philippians and Its Implications
for the Unity Question," *NovT* 30 (1998): 58.

the gospel?"[47] Metaphors drawn from the sacrifices of thanksgiving help to describe the moral pattern of such a life.

One of the most important aspects of rhetoric is the arrangement, or disposition (τάξις) of a speech. Kennedy comments that "a speech is linear and cumulative, and any context in it can only be perceived in contrast to what has gone before, though a very able speaker lays the ground for what he intends to say later and has a total unity in mind when he first begins to speak."[48] In *Phaedrus*, Plato likens the organic arrangement of a discourse to the human body: δεῖν πάντα λόγον ὥσπερ ζῷον συνεστάναι σῶμά τι ἔχοντα αὐτὸν αὑτοῦ, ὥστε μήτε ἀκέφαλον εἶναι μήτε ἄπουν, ἀλλὰ μέσα τε ἔχειν καὶ ἄκρα, πρέπουτ' ἀλλήλοις καὶ τῷ ὅλῳ γεγραμμένα (264c). Furthermore, Wuellner says that there is an "anatomy" or an "architecture" to a speech or a text.[49] One of the interesting features of both Philippians and 1 Corinthians is the placement at the "heart" (to continue the anatomical metaphor) of each letter of a powerful representation of Christ (1 Cor 11:23–26; Phil 2:5–11). Both of these depictions have sacrificial overtones. Chapters 5 and 6 analyze these passages both according to the rhetorical purposes of their immediate contexts as well as the significance of their placement in the arrangement of the whole of the letters in which they stand.

In recent decades, the scholarly construct of Paul as the individual author of his letters addressing various groups of so-called opponents[50] has come under criticism, primarily by feminist scholars, who decry the uncritical assumption of an imagined gulf between the wise apostle and his wayward and infantilized communities: "Imagining the locus of Paul's theology to be in his own mind means that efforts to reconstruct the process are focused individually rather than socially."[51] Initiated by the work of Elisabeth Schüssler Fiorenza on early Christian communities, there is

47. Ibid., 60.

48. Kennedy, *New Testament Interpretation*, 5.

49. William Wuellner, "Where Is Rhetorical Criticism Taking Us?" *CBQ* 49 (1987): 456.

50. Cynthia Briggs Kittredge, *Community and Authority: The Rhetoric of Obedience in the Pauline Tradition*, HTS 45 (Harrisburg, PA: Trinity Press International, 1998), 7.

51. Cynthia Briggs Kittredge, "Rethinking Authorship in the Letters of Paul: Elisabeth Schüssler-Fiorenza's Model of Pauline Theology," *Walk in the Ways of Wisdom: Essays in Honor of Elisabeth Shüssler-Fiorenza*, ed. Shelly Matthews, Cynthia Briggs Kittredge, and Melanie Johnson-DeBaufre (Harrisburg, PA: Trinity Press International, 2003), 322.

an attempt on the part of scholars such as Cynthia Briggs Kittredge and Antoinette Clark Wire[52] to develop an ear for the many voices in Paul's communities that can be heard through and beneath the words of the canonical text, and to validate the thoughts and practices of these other early Christians, even (or perhaps especially) those whom Paul opposes. For example, in her response to a group of papers on "The Politics of the Assembly at Corinth," Wire writes,

> Our task is to shake off what Horsley calls the subjection of Paul to being read as the authoritative expression of Christianity and begin to read his voice alongside that of his opponents as the beginning of our deliberating tradition, with serious arguments and strong rhetoric flying both ways. Only then can we overcome the yet more virulent subjection of our ancestors in Corinth, and since, to being dismissed as people without authority. By this route we might even begin to shake the subjection of God to the imperial world.[53]

Sacrificial metaphors have their real life not in the mind of Paul, but in the community for whom they help to make sense—or fail to make sense—of Christian living. As Kittredge says,

---

52. Antoinette Clark Wire, *Corinthian Women Prophets: A Reconstruction through Paul's Rhetoric* (Minneapolis: Fortress, 1990). See also Luise Schottroff on a Pauline passage that will be crucial to the present study, 1 Cor 11:17–34, "Paul quotes the Last Supper narrative in order to protest against the manner in which one group of Christians in Corinth celebrated the Lord's Supper. This conflict is not between Paul and 'the Corinthians,' but between groups within the Corinthian community (11:18, 19). Paul's letter takes up the cudgels for one side in this dispute. The image of the apostle and his 'opponents' which has left its mark on the history of the exposition of his letters is ecclesiogenetic. It takes for granted a smoothly flowing continuity between a 'correct' Pauline church and today's church on the one hand, and a pattern (then and now) of 'opponents', 'sectarians' and 'splinter-groups' on the other hand. This dualistic antithesis fails to do justice to the plurality of community praxis in early Christianity; besides this, it attributes to Paul an absolute authority which he did not possess at that period, an authority to which he did not even lay claim. He was one teacher and apostle among many women and men who lived the gospel together and engaged in discussion and dispute about the correct interpretation of Torah in their situation" ("Holiness and Justice: Exegetical Comments on 1 Corinthians 11:17–34," *JSNT* 79 [2000]: 52–53).

53. Antoinette Clark Wire, "Response: The Politics of the Assembly in Corinth," in *Paul and Politics: Ekklesia, Israel, Imperium, Interpretation: Essays in Honor of Krister Stendahl*, ed. Richard A. Horsley (Harrisburg, PA: Trinity Press International, 2000), 127–82.

For his rhetoric to be effective, Paul counts on sharing at least some elements of the symbolic universe of his audience. While they probably shared some elements, they may have construed others differently. Paul writes to create and construct that shared knowledge of the symbolic universe.[54]

The metaphors of sacrifice in 1 Corinthians and Philippians are simultaneously explicit evidence of Paul's strategies of communication and persuasion and implicit evidence of the larger community conversation in which Paul is only one participant. The following chapter discusses Greco-Roman and Jewish sacrificial practices that were the basis for both Paul's rhetoric and the responses of his communities.

---

54. Kittredge, *Community and Authority*, 7.

3

SACRIFICE AS A GRECO-ROMAN AND JEWISH PRACTICE

While it makes sense logically that Paul might develop a language of temple and sacrifice that would be as valid for the Greco-Roman cults as for the Jewish cult, in fact part of what will become clear in chapter 6 is how Paul's metaphors of temple and sacrifice in 1 Corinthians seem to have as their principal referent the Jewish cult in particular, and not a more generalized reference to ancient cults of all kinds.[1] It is the Jewish system of texts and practices in which Paul is a learned specialist. His expertise and authority are based in his experience and education in that context. First Corinthians 10 is full of interpretive references to Jewish history and teaching that Paul expects his hearers not only to comprehend but to receive as binding upon themselves and upon their moral choices. The fact that Paul chooses the Passover, one of the central Jewish sacrifices,[2] as paradigmatic for his counsels in 1 Corinthians is evidence of how thoroughly he is grounding his communities in a Jewish matrix of meaning.

The metaphors of sacrifice in Philippians, however, appear to work within both Jewish and Greco-Roman frames of reference, because the ritual pattern of the Jewish *shelamim* (sacrifices of thanksgiving) is not highly distinct from the basic Greco-Roman pattern of sacrifice and festal meal. The following section sketches some of the broad background that Paul's communities might have brought to bear on his language, an interpretive context that he might have presupposed in their reception of his

---

1. I say this, while recognizing, as John Pairman Brown has shown, that the Jewish cult has much in common with the cults of others living around the Mediterranean ("The Sacrificial Cult and Its Critique," *JSS* 24 [1979]: 159–73). Still, Paul appears to make just those qualifications that will link his statements to the Jewish cult in particular, e.g., the ναός θεοῦ of 1 Cor 3:19.

2. Elsewhere he refers to Yom Kippur (Rom 3:25), the other principal sacrifice of the Jewish year.

counsels. Unfortunately, we may never fully understand just how Paul's Gentile communities received his metaphorical references to specific Jewish cult and Jewish lore. From Paul's own point of view, however, the sacrificial metaphors he uses are intended to underscore the invitation to the Gentiles to become part of the people of the Jewish God, YHWH.

GRECO-ROMAN COMMENSAL SACRIFICES

The most common sacrificial practice in the Greco-Roman religions was, to use Hans-Josef Klauck's term, the slaughter-sacrifice,[3] in which some of the meat is offered to the god(s), followed by a communal meal. The sacrificial rituals recounted in Homer's *Iliad* and *Odyssey* (ca. 700 BCE) offer idealized accounts of the pattern of events that remained the more or less the standard sequence for the commensal sacrifices. The ideal gives some insight into the emotional tenor of these sacrifices, which were generally occasions for rejoicing. The mood of joy should not be entirely forgotten as a possibility in a Pauline reference such as Phil 2:17, where Paul speaks of his "being poured out as a libation over the sacrifice and offering of your faith." As he adds, "I am glad and rejoice with all of you." I am not denying the pathos of his statement, but given the celebratory atmosphere of most of the dedicatory sacrifices, rejoicing is a natural accompaniment.

The most detailed account of the ideal pattern occurs in Homer, *Od.* 4.430–535. While this account predates the period we are most concerned with, both the actions described and the mood of the event remain the standard throughout the Hellenistic period, and the events described accord with what one sees depicted on pottery and in sculpture throughout ancient Greece. The sacrifice in the fourth book of the *Odyssey* is offered to Athena by Nestor and his family as they welcome Telemachus. The sequence begins the night before, with prayers to Athena. Then, on the morning of the sacrifice, a person is sent to the fields to choose a heifer as the sacrificial victim. Cows were the most expensive offering, and the one considered normative, while sheep and goats were, in fact, the most common.[4] A goldsmith is sent for, "to sheathe the heifer's horns in gold" (*Od.* 4.475 [Fagles]), and "Athena came as well to attend her sacred rites" (*Od.*

---

3. Hans-Josef Klauck, *The Religious Context of Early Christianity*, trans. Brian McNeil (Minneapolis: Fortress, 2003), 40.

4. Jan N. Bremmer, "Greek Normative Animal Sacrifice," *A Companion to Greek Religion*, ed. Daniel Ogden (Oxford, Blackwell: 2007), 133–34.

4.485 [Fagles]). The sacrifice then proceeds with the heifer's horns being sheathed with gold, to delight the goddess. Men lead the heifer in procession to the place of sacrifice, bringing fresh water in a bowl decorated with flowers, together with barley in a basket. Nestor, leading the ceremony, prays to Athena and flings a tuft of the heifer's hair into the fire. The water and barley are splashed from their containers suddenly upon the animal, to evoke a surprised nodding of the head, interpreted as the animal's assent to the sacrifice. Thrasymedes strides up and very quickly kills the victim with an axe through the neck tendons, after which the animal is bled out into a basin held by Perseus. The blood was then poured out upon the altar. What follows sounds very like a recipe:

> They quartered her quickly, cut the thighbones out
> and all according to custom wrapped them round in fat,
> a double fold sliced clean and topped with strips of flesh.
> And the old king burned these over dried split wood
> and over the fire poured out glistening wine
> while young men at his side held five-pronged forks.
> Once they'd burned the bones and tasted the organs,
> they sliced the rest into pieces, spitted them on skewers
> and raising points to the fire, broiled all the meats. (Homer, *Od.* 4.510–20 [Fagles])

Then the full meal begins:

> They roasted the prime cuts, pulled them off the spits
> and sat down to the feast while ready stewards saw
> to rounds of wine and kept the gold cups flowing. (Homer, *Od.* 4.527–529 [Fagles])

If we step outside the narrative for a moment, to analyze it, the passage from the *Odyssey* clearly illustrates the contention of Marcel Detienne, namely, that Greek sacrifices had mainly to do with cuisine. Indeed, the usual name for the sacrifice was the same as that for a butcher, μάγειρος. But sacrifice was a formal, stylized practice of cuisine that reflected the structures of Greek society. In ordinary sacrificial practice, only elite males were in the inner circle of the sacrifice, where the viscera were roasted and eaten. The god received the inedible portions (bones wrapped in fat), offered up as smoke. Other diners received the rest of the meat, boiled and distributed. As Stowers says of these later Greek sacrifices, "Taking apart the animal in a certain way and distributing the meat … elicited patterns that reinforced the relationships of honor and power in the city."[5] To return to the narrative, while the sacrifice is occurring Telemachus is being cared for, almost as an extension of the sacred ritual:

> During the ritual lovely Polycaste, youngest daughter
> of Nestor, Neleus' son, had bathed Telemachus.
> Rinsing him off now, rubbing him down with oil,
> she drew a shirt and handsome cape around him.
> Out of his bath he stepped, glowing like a god,
> strode in and sat by the old commander Nestor. (Homer, *Od.* 4.521–526 [Fagles])

A key characteristic of sacrifices is evident in this idealistic account from the *Odyssey*: the boundary between human beings and the gods seems to disappear, as Athena attends the sacrifice and Telemachus's appearance is transformed into something godlike.

In the first book of the *Iliad*, a sacrifice is called for, but this offering is set in motion by a need for reconciliation. The sacrifice is necessitated by Agamemnon's refusal to return the daughter of Chryse, a priest of Apollo, who was kidnapped and taken as bounty. When Agamemnon refuses to accept any ransom for the girl, Chryse appeals to Apollo for revenge, and Apollo responds by inflicting a plague upon the Greek soldiers. A prophet announces to Achilles and the other Greeks that they must appease Apollo in order to stop the plague, and so they set out to return the daughter, Chryseis, and to make an acceptable sacrifice to the god. The result of the sacrifice is reconciliation between Apollo (and his priest), and this gathering of Greek soldiers, and also a feast of well-being and overflowing joy. The god is not merely appeased, but, as in the sacrifice above, is assumed to join the human experience of delight over the food, the singing and dancing:

> When their work was done and the meal prepared, they feasted, and no one went without a fair share. Their hunger and thirst satisfied, the young men filled the mixing-bowls to the brim with wine and went round the

5. Stanley Stowers, "Greeks Who Sacrifice and Those Who Do Not: Toward an Anthropology of Greek Religion," *The Social World of the First Christians: Essays in honor of Wayne E. Meeks*, ed. L. Michael White and O. Larry Yarborough (Minneapolis: Fortress, 1995), 329.

whole company, pouring some into each cup for a libation to the god. And for the rest of the day the young Greek warriors sang and danced to appease the god with a beautiful hymn celebrating the Archer Apollo, to which he listened with delight. (Homer, *Il.* 1.467–475 [Jones])

The effect of all that was done that day—the returning of Chryseis to her father, Apollo's priest; the prayers and sacrifice; the feasting and delight—spills over onto the following day, as the Greeks live into the experience of reconciliation with Apollo and with his earthly priest, Chryse:

When the sun set and darkness fell, they lay down to sleep by the hawsers of their ship. But when early-born, rosy-fingered Dawn appeared, they set sail for the broad Greek camp, taking advantage of a favourable breeze the Archer-god had sent them. They put up their mast and spread the white sail. The wind filled its belly, and a dark wave hissed loudly round her keel as the vessel gathered a way and sped through the swell, forging ahead on her course. So they returned to the broad Greek camp, where they dragged the black ship high up on the sandy shore and kept it upright with wooden props. That done, they dispersed to their several huts and ships (Homer, *Il.* 1.475–488 [Jones]).

Klauck writes of sacrifices in the first century, "To ascertain what those involved actually felt, we can retain as the lowest common denominator what Plutarch says[6]: namely, the experience of some kind of presence of the divine, combined with the very tangible joyful feast."[7] These classical excerpts express ideals, but those ideals infused the sense of what the practice, as it was encountered in the ritual calendar of feasts, was about.

Commensal sacrifices were the basic form of sacrifice known to people in the ancient Mediterranean world, and they accompanied most festivals and social celebrations of all kinds.[8] Indeed, as Stowers writes, succinctly: "Except under extraordinary circumstances, Greeks ate only meat that had

---

6. "For that which is delightful in the feasts is not the quantity of wine or the roasted flesh, but the good hope and the belief that the god is present with his help and accepts what is taking place" (*Suav. Viv. Epic.* 21 [1102a], quoted by Klauck, *The Religious Context of Early Christianity*, 39).

7. Klauck, *The Religious Context of Early Christianity*, 41.

8. Peter Lampe offers a succinct outline of a typical Greco-Roman dinner party, whether it was a purely social occasion or a dinner given by an association of some sort, in "The Corinthian Eucharistic Dinner Party: Exegesis of a Cultural Context (1 Cor 11:17–34)," *Affirmation* 4.3 (1991): 1–15.

been sacrificed."[9] He continues, underscoring the centrality of sacrifices in the observance of practically every sort of formal occasion:

> At a birthday party, a city festival, a social club—wherever people ate meals with meat—a sacrifice took place. When the gods were thanked, placated, or beseeched for blessings—beginning a meeting of the city council, setting out for war, after the birth of a child, entering manhood—Greeks sacrificed. All significant political bodies in the Greek city (e.g., *ekklēsia, boulē*, prytany,[10] boards of officials, boards of generals, archons) were male sacrificing bodies that conducted no significant political activity without sacrifice.[11]

It was in such a context that the Corinthians celebrated the Lord's Supper (κυριακὸν δεῖπνον) of 1 Cor 11:17–34 and that they debated how fully to participate in the social life of their city (1 Cor 8, 10). Abstention from civic sacrifices was seen as defiant and deviant in a culture that organized itself around and through this central practice.

What is hidden in the poetical accounts comes to the surface in the work of contemporary scholars, such as Stowers, who bring together a close observation of the practice with an interpretation of the social relationships established by the placement of people within the ritual. Stowers views "sacrifice as a map or ideogram of Greek social relations."[12] While sacrifices changed somewhat over time, and varied from place to place, a constant was that they both shaped and reflected relationships of status and honor in the Greek polis:

> The procession ended when a circle was ceremonially drawn around the participants, the altar, and the animal. At the center of this circle stood those who exercised authority in whatever social unit, whether polis, tribe, or cult association, upon which the sacrifice effected its powers. From the center of the circle outward and by size and quality of the portion distributed, the practice established a hierarchy.[13]

---

9. Stowers, "Greeks Who Sacrifice," 294.

10. In Athens, the presidency, a period of one-tenth of a year, during which the president of each φυλή presided in turn in the βουλή and ἐκκλησία.

11. Stowers, "Greeks Who Sacrifice," 294–95.

12. Ibid., 325.

13. Ibid., 326.

The implication of status and honor in sacrificial choreography may be one of the issues affecting the practice of the Lord's Supper in Corinth (1 Cor 11:17–34). Just how closely knit are the worlds of the Greco-Roman cult and nascent Christianity can be seen in Acts 14:8–18. While in the town of Lystra, Paul and Barnabas heal a man who had not been able to walk since birth. The townspeople proclaim them gods, calling Barnabas "Zeus" and Paul "Hermes." The priest of Zeus, therefore, "brought oxen and garlands to the gates; he and the crowds wanted to offer sacrifice" (Acts 14:13). As in the story from the *Iliad* above, this desire to sacrifice is festive, a desire to make an offering of thanksgiving for an act perceived to be reconciling, gods and human beings brought together in well-being through an act of healing. The Jewish Paul rejects the pagan sacrifice, but the story points up a part of the context in which Christian metaphors of sacrifice were being made. An occasion of thanksgiving is considered a natural occasion for sacrifice.

Covenantal Sacrifice

In her article "Sacrificial Violence in the *Iliad*," Margo Kitts offers an important contrast between commensal sacrifices and covenantal sacrifices, noting that in the former, "what is remarkable … is that the dying of the animal is never mentioned, not during any commensal sacrifice in the *Iliad* (but cf. *Od.* 3:439–63, as quoted above, and 14:418–36),"[14] while the gruesome death of the animal seems almost to be the point of sacrifices made to seal a covenant: "If Homeric commensal sacrifice ignores violence, oath-sacrifice has violence at its very heart."[15] Like Detienne, Kitts sees commensal sacrifices as primarily about "cuisine." Paying close attention to the language used to describe commensal sacrifices in the *Iliad*, she notes that "the focalization is on the activity of the cooks,"[16] while the death of the animal is rushed: "the pace of this verse [*Il.* 24.622][17] is a bit hurried, as if to eclipse the animal's death between those first moments when his

---

14. Margo Kitts, "Sacrificial Violence in the *Iliad*," *JRItSt* 16 (2002): 29.
15. Ibid., 31.
16. Ibid., 29.
17. "At that, swift Achilles sprang up and slew a white-fleeced sheep, and his comrades flayed it and made it ready well and in good order, and sliced it skillfully and spitted the morsels, and roasted them carefully and drew everything off the spits" (Homer, *Il.* 24.622 [Jones]).

head is held up and his throat cut, and the next, when he is flayed."[18] Kitts
ascribes the reason for the lack of attention paid to the victim's death in
a commensal sacrifice to the demands of its literary genre, the epic poem
about war: "Set against war's carnage, the sacrificial feasting scenes would
seem to express a conviviality far removed from the travails of war, and
one might hazard that what they offer the audience is precisely a respite
from the wartime tensions which occupy the rest of the poem."[19]

On the other hand, in the covenantal sacrifices in the same poem,
"the deadly ramifications of violating the cosmic principles behind oaths
and kindred commitments permeate the [text] and are amplified by the
somber tone and stiff formality."[20] For example, the verse that describes
the killing of the lambs for the oath-sacrifice in book 3 reads:

> He spoke, and cut the lambs' throats with the pitiless bronze; and laid
> them down on the ground gasping and failing of breath, for the bronze
> had robbed them of their strength. (Homer, *Il.* 3.292 [Jones])

And the punishment for breaking the oath is described thus:

> Zeus, most glorious, most great, and you other immortal gods, which-
> ever army of the two will be first to work harm in defiance of the oaths,
> may their brains be poured out on the ground just as this wine is, theirs
> and their children's; and may their wives be made to serve other men.
> (Homer, *Il.* 3.298 [Jones])

The consequences of a broken oath are shame and violent death for the
perpetrator, and these consequences radiate out from him to all his family.
Kitts says, "Clearly, oath-sacrificing rituals are serious events and feature
killing as the high point of the ritual. As insinuated in the Homeric curse-
prayers which accompany the oath, the killing of the victim and the rituals
surrounding its death are meant to be analogic to the anticipated punishment of the perjurer who violates the oath."[21]

What Kitts's work offers the reader of Paul is a possible context for the
otherwise strange conclusions Paul draws from the Corinthians' failure to
"discern the body" in the Lord's Supper: "For this reason, many of you are

---

18. Kitts, "Sacrificial Violence in the *Iliad*," 29.
19. Ibid., 31.
20. Ibid., 31.
21. Ibid., 32.

weak and ill, and some of you have died" (διὰ τοῦτο ἐν ὑμῖν πολλοὶ ἀσθενεῖς καὶ ἄρρωστοι καὶ κοιμῶνται ἱκανοί, 1 Cor 11:30). Having already made very prominent the death of "the Lord Jesus" (11:26), and having established participation in the meal as acceptance of a "new covenant" (11:25), Paul draws out the clear consequences of violating that covenant (11:27). More will be said on this subject below when the passage is addressed more fully, but two important things to note at this stage are, first, how a conclusion drawn by Paul that seems mystifying to a modern reader may have made perfect sense in its original setting, and secondly, the significance of identifying the particular sacrifice at issue in any use of metaphors of sacrifice, in this case a covenantal sacrifice.

CRITIQUE OF SACRIFICE

There was a substantial philosophical critique of traditional religion and sacrifice among the Greek philosophers, but a similar critique has been mistakenly assumed to be the case in interpretation of Paul's metaphors of sacrifice. While this body of critical literature has been compared to writings of the New Testament, under the assumption that early Christians were similarly critical of the Jewish cult and had replaced it with metaphors of sacrifice and a commitment to ethical living by faith in Jesus Christ, there is no basis for hearing such a critique in Paul's use of metaphors of sacrifice. The important background for making Paul's cultic metaphors more intelligible is, I would argue, a more ample sense for the meaning of ordinary sacrificial language as it was understood primarily by first-century Jews, and secondarily by first-century participants in the Greco-Roman cults. Paul's use of cultic metaphors relies upon the power of the practice, not upon its denigration. A statement such as, "For our paschal lamb Christ has been sacrificed" (1 Cor 5: 7) depends upon the validity of the Passover, not a critique of Passover. Likewise, a question like, "Do you not know that your body is a temple of the Holy Spirit?" (1 Cor 6:19) depends upon the assumption of holiness for its persuasive power.

In the main, what stands out in the ancient literature is the unthinkableness of refusing to offer sacrifices. In his treatise *De pietate*, Philodemus quotes Epicurus as saying,

> Let us sacrifice to the gods ... devoutly and fittingly on the proper days, and let us fittingly perform all the acts of worship in accordance with the laws, in no way disturbing ourselves with opinions in matters concern-

ing the most excellent and august of beings. Moreover, let us sacrifice justly, on the view that I was giving. For in this way it is possible for mortal nature, by Zeus, to live like Zeus, as it seems. (Philodemus, *Piet.* 880–890 [Obbink])

According to Epicurus, it was important to conform to the sacrificial practices of his day, for by them one might even be drawn to a godly pattern of life. The Epicureans were criticized by Plutarch for "putting on a show" out of fear of others' opinions (*Contra Epic. beat.* 1102b),[22] but even so, Epicurus's support for sacrificial practice underscores the centrality of the practice for civic and social life.

Ovid's entertaining description of the festivals of the Roman calendar in poetic form, the *Fasti*, satirizes the relational quality of ancient sacrifices, the very human ways in which gods and humans were seen to relate to one another through the medium of sacrifice. For example, he has Flora say, with more than a hint of mockery,

We [gods], too, are touched by honor; we delight in festivals and altars; we heavenly beings are a greedy gang. Often when by sinning a man has disposed the gods against him, a sacrificial victim has been a sop for crimes. Often have I seen Jupiter, when he was just about to launch his thunderbolts, hold his hand on the receipt of incense. But if we are neglected, we avenge the wrong by heavy penalties, and our wrath exceeds just bounds. (Ovid, *Fast.* 5.297–302 [Frazer])

Price cautions the modern reader from taking such accounts as indicative of a thoroughgoing attitude of *do ut des* in Greco-Roman sacrifices, as though every sacrifice were a gift offered cynically, only to receive something in return. "Such criticism misses the point," he says. "Like other systems of gifts and counter-gifts, the Greek ritual system assumed choice on both sides. Gifts to the gods were not a way of buying the gods, but of creating goodwill from which humans might hope to benefit in the future."[23] Like any human practice, generous gift-giving to gods or to humans is subject to corruption. Just because gift-giving *might* become coercive, this fact does not delegitimize *all* gift-giving.

---

22. Quoted by Obbink, 436.

23. Simon Price, *Religions of the Ancient Greeks*, vol. 9 of *Key Themes in Ancient History*, ed. P. A. Cartledge and P. D. A Garnsey (Cambridge: Cambridge University Press, 1999), 38–39.

THE JEWISH SACRIFICIAL SYSTEM

While the book of Leviticus describes the procedures for the offering of Jewish sacrifices, it nowhere offers an interpretation of the meaning of sacrifice, and this reticence is consistent with other cultures in the ancient Mediterranean.[24] The sacrifices described in Leviticus fall into two major categories, propitiatory sacrifices (relating to atonement and purification) and dedicatory sacrifices (gift-giving sacrifices, sacrifices of well-being or thanksgiving). For the purposes of this study, it is not necessary to describe the sacrificial system of Leviticus in great detail, nor to rehearse the many scholarly disagreements over the authorship or dating of the text. The role of Leviticus for this study is in the development of a broad overview of the Jewish system of sacrifices for distinct purposes. Paul's use of metaphors of sacrifice is attentive to these distinctions. There are, however, some issues relating to Leviticus that have surfaced in the literature recently that do have a bearing on our topic.

Jacob Milgrom's groundbreaking work on Leviticus has more or less defined the issues of interpretation for other commentators on Leviticus. In particular, his assertion that the *hattat* sacrifice (sacrifice for sin, Lev 4) has as its object the purification of the sanctuary (and not the offerer) has been both influential and controversial. Milgrom contends that the person who brings the *hattat* is cleansed by means of his or her remorse, before even entering the sanctuary. The blood of the victim (its "life," Lev 17:1) has the effect of a "ritual detergent" in cleansing the sanctuary of the "spiritual miasma" of the offerer's sin.

James Watts has presented an interesting critique of Milgrom and others, as he questions all theories that presuppose that the sacrificial system described in Leviticus is "realistic," that it necessarily corresponds to the actual system of practice in the Jewish Temple.[25] Watts connects such a realistic approach to the theory of functionalism, that religious systems (such as sacrifice) support the basic social structures of a group of people. In the functionalist construal, religious texts are interpreted as sources of data for understanding the wider social context which they

---

24. See James W. Watts, *Ritual and Rhetoric in Leviticus: From Sacrifice to Scripture* (Cambridge: Cambridge University Press, 2007), 180–81. Watts notes that the few such explanations in Greek culture were provoked by a need to defend the practice in the face of criticism or to justify a change in practice.

25. Ibid., 5.

straightforwardly reflect and support. As Watts says of Milgrom and some of his followers,

> Gane[26] presupposed, with his teacher Milgrom, that ancient ritual texts provide modern interpreters direct access to the rituals whose dynamic structure and cognitive tasks he can interpret. His method found an internal logic in rituals rather than exposing their social function, but he did not address the problem that texts may reflect interests and meanings different from the rituals they describe.[27]

Watts's contribution is to unmask the rhetorical strategies of Leviticus, to show that the book is not a mere bank of raw data on the Jewish sacrificial system, but an extended argument for particular concerns of the priestly writers. As he says succinctly, "*texts are not rituals, and rituals are not texts.*"[28]

Two related aspects of the rhetorical strategy of Leviticus are important to consider. The first has to do with the divine authority claimed by the authors of Leviticus. Watts calls attention to the narrative framework of the book, that "casts Leviticus 1–7 as divine prescriptions delivered through Israel's paradigmatic lawgiver, Moses."[29]

Second, Watts questions the priority of the whole burnt offering (*olah*)[30] as reflective of the actual pattern of Jewish sacrifices:

> The *olah*, "burnt offering," is the paradigmatic offering in the Hebrew Bible. Of all the many technical terms from Israel's cultic worship, the *olah* is most frequently mentioned, and, when multiple offerings are listed, it is almost always listed first. The *olah*'s prominence cannot be credited to its actual dominance in ritual: the *shelamim*, "peace or communion offerings," that were eaten by worshippers and priests must have outnumbered the offerings burnt whole on the altar. The offerings would otherwise have impoverished both priests and lay people. That expectation is confirmed by the passages that list the numbers of both kinds of offerings: *olot* account for only one out of six animals offered by the elders of Israel according to Numbers 7, and slightly more than one

---

26. Roy E. Gane, *Ritual Dynamic Structure* (Piscataway, NJ: Gorgias, 2004).

27. Watts, *Ritual and Rhetoric,* 12.

28. Ibid., 29, emphasis original.

29. Ibid., 46.

30. *Olah* means literally "that which goes up." It is a reference to the smoke of the whole burnt offering ascending to God.

out of ten at Hezekiah's temple rededication according to 2 Chronicles 29. Nevertheless, except when reveling in the sheer number of offerings, the stories and ritual instructions of the Bible grant the *olah* pride of place.[31]

Watts attributes the priority of the *olah* as the paradigmatic sacrifice to an interpretive move by the priests. This move corresponds to the emphasis given in descriptions of other sacrifices in the Torah, such as the near-sacrifice of Isaac (Gen 22:1–19), where the stress of the passage is on the total self-dedication and obedience of the offerer: "The implication of its rhetorical prominence then is that the *olah* represents the purest form of divine service."[32] Secondarily, according to Watts, the emphasis on the *olah* served to mask the financial importance of the *minhah* and *shelamim* sacrifices to the priestly establishment.

The significance of Watts's interpretation for understanding Paul's metaphors of sacrifice is his affirmation that the *shelamim* were the customary form of sacrifice in actual practice, the offering most frequently experienced by Jews. The *shelamim* also have the most in common with the Greco-Roman practice of sacrifice generally. When Paul refers to sacrifice in Philippians, without any qualifier, it is my contention that his repeated language of rejoicing suggests that he has the *shelamim* in mind. At the same time, it would appear that he also assumes the interpretive framework established by the priestly writers in giving the *olah* pride of place, as a sign of total, unreserved commitment on the part of the offerer. The *shelamim* are set within an understanding of sacrifice as a sign of complete self-offering, even when their principal emotional content may be joy and thanksgiving.

A second critique of Milgrom that touches upon this work is that offered by Klawans, who says that "running through [Milgrom's] commentary is the presumption that linguistic usage develops in one direction, from the literal to the metaphorical."[33] Klawans criticizes Milgrom's whole approach to the sacrifices (as opposed to the ethical and holiness regulations of Leviticus) as "evolutionist," saying that

---

31. Watts, *Ritual and Rhetoric*, 63.

32. Ibid., 71.

33. Jonathan Klawans, "Ritual Purity, Moral Purity, and Sacrifice in Jacob Milgrom's *Leviticus*," *RelSrev* 29 (2003): 25.

Milgrom's denigration of sacrifice goes hand in hand with his assumption that metaphor is a relatively late development in human thought.
As I have tried to argue elsewhere,[34] a full contextual understanding
of sacrifice in ancient Israel requires that we remove both sacrifice and
metaphor from evolutionist schemes like Milgrom's which place literal
understandings of sacrifice in a primitive stage of human development,
and metaphor in a relatively late stage.[35]

Klawans's critique is important for the support it gives to the understanding that Paul was using metaphors of sacrifice at the same time that he
participated in the cult itself. Neither metaphor nor actual practice took
precedence over the other. Rather, the metaphors drew meaning, legitima-
tion, and power from the ongoing cult.[36]

Paul's Relationship to the Temple and the Jewish Cult

Leander Keck's exploration of the question of Paul's continuity or discon-
tinuity with his life as a Pharisee[37] recounts the recent history of scholarly
consideration of Paul's relationship to Judaism after the revelation of Jesus

---

34. Jonathan Klawans, "Pure Violence: Sacrifice and Defilement in Ancient
Israel," *HTR* 94 (2001).

35. Klawans, "Ritual Purity, Moral Purity, and Sacrifice," 25.

36. Christfried Böttrich summarizes the long history of Christian interpretation
that would have seen Paul's metaphorizing of the cult as a signal of the separation of
Christians from Jews, in "Ihr seid der Tempel Gottes." Böttrich goes on to counter
this traditional view: "A widely held thesis that has governed exegesis for centuries
now goes as follows: according to early Christian understanding, the displacement
of the Jerusalem Temple cult was a natural outcome of the revelation of God in Jesus
Christ. The cult was therefore all but nullified, replaced later by the ethic of Jesus. All
cultic terminology in use by Christian communities was, then, seen as expressive of
spiritual realities only. According to this way of thinking, Pauline Temple metaphors
were understood as evidence of a turning away from previous convictions about the
sanctuary. This point of view has taken shape principally on the basis of a supposed
contrast between the Jewish cult and Christian spirituality, and emphasizes from the
outset a split between Judaism and nascent Christianity" (Christfried Böttrich, "'Ihr
Seid der Tempel Gottes': Tempelmetaphorik und Gemeinde bei Paulus," in *Gemeinde
Ohne Tempel, Community Without Temple: Zur Substituierung und Transformation
des Jerusalemer Tempels und seines Kults im Alten Testament, antiken Judentum und
frühen Christentum*, ed. Beate Ego, Armin Lange, and Peter Pilhofer [Tübingen: Mohr
Siebeck, 1999], 412), my translation.

37. Leander Keck, "The Quest for Paul's Pharisaism: Some Reflections," in *Justice*

Christ "in him" (Gal 1:16). What stands out from the point of view of one studying the Jewish sacrificial system is the overwhelming emphasis of scholars, including Keck, on Paul's *ideas* rather than his *actions*, or cultic practices, about which they are silent. Of course, through the letters of Paul, one gains access to his thought and not his actions, but it is interesting that there is not more curiosity expressed about his relationship with the practice of the cult. It is the nature of Paul's thought (his use of Scripture, his attitude toward the Law, his understanding of the role of Abraham as compared to Moses) that Keck and others are studying, rather than evidence of his practical relationship with the Temple. In his summary, Keck does note Paul's continuity with the "Pharisaic concern for ritual purity,[38] pointing out that there remains "a major area for fruitful investigation" in "Paul's understanding of the sanctification of the ordinary and its roots in his former Pharisaism."[39] But how did Paul regard the Jewish Temple and its sacrificial system after his revelation, and how likely is it that, as reported in Acts, Paul continued to participate in the Temple sacrifices as a believer in Jesus?

Friedrich Horn explores aspects of this question in a paper given at Aberdeen in 2006, in which he sees no textual evidence in the Pauline letters for Paul's having substituted faith in Christ for the entire Temple cult.[40] He also notes the lack of criticism of the Temple cult in Paul's use of metaphors referring to it: "The thematic confluence of Temple, Spirit, and holiness is put forward without any corresponding criticism of the Herodian temple."[41] Horn traces the use of cultic metaphors in Jewish literature, and then comments on the boldness of Paul's vision, in which he draws his Gentile believers precisely into the sphere of holiness and Temple, through their life in the Christian community.[42] Horn takes up the question of whether Paul's audacity with regard to metaphorical inclusion of

---

and the Holy: Essays in Honor of Walter Harrelson, ed. Douglas A. Knight and Peter J. Paris (Atlanta: Scholars Press, 1989).

38. Ibid., 175.

39. Ibid..

40. Friedrich Willhem Horn, "Paulus und der Herodianische Tempel," *NTS* 53 (2007): 190.

41. Ibid., 190.

42. Ibid., 191: "Während die Tempelmetaphorik in judenchristlicher Theologie gleichfalls eine Bewältigung der Trennung vom Heiligtum intendiert und—parallel zu Qumran—grundsätzlich am tempeltheologischen Denken festhält, weitet Paulus in der Korintherkorrespondenz dieses tempeltheologische Denken auf Heidenchristen

Gentiles in the Temple extended to inviting Gentiles into the Jewish-only areas of the actual Temple, as he is accused of doing in Acts (21:28). While one cannot decide this question conclusively, he points to Paul's description of the "offering of the Gentiles" in Rom 15:16 and the importance of the Temple imaginatively for Paul's Gentile Christians, through his use of Temple-related metaphors:

> Clearly, beginning with the use of Temple metaphors in the Corinthian correspondence, and continuing through the depiction of the Gentiles as an offering for God in Rom 15:16, there is a gradual reorientation of Gentile believers in respect to the Temple. At the same time that the Temple remains a Jewish boundary marker against the Gentiles, it is also becoming an identity marker not only for Jews, but for Jewish and Gentile Christians.[43]

While explicit information concerning Paul's activities in the Temple, such as is found in Acts, is lacking in Paul's own letters, it appears that he continued to regard the Temple as God's dwelling place, and used metaphors of the Temple cult (such as the mercy seat, ἱλαστήριον, of Rom 3:25–26) as a positive extension of an activity in the Temple to an analogous occurrence in the Christian narrative.[44] Ultimately, we cannot answer the question of how much Paul continued to participate in the Temple cult on his few visits to Jerusalem. For any Jew living in the Diaspora, the Temple had power largely in the imagination. But the work of Horn establishes an important grounding for a separation of Paul's metaphorical use of images of the Temple cult from the idea of a necessary criticism of the cult, and leaves open the distinct possibility of his ongoing participation in Jewish sacrificial practice.

ENTAILMENTS OF METAPHORS OF THE SHELAMIM

We have seen above how the *shelamim* were interpreted, in part, by their setting within the sacrificial system that prescribed the *olah* as the paradig-

---

aus. Dies markiert nicht eine Substitution, sondern öffnet jüdische Tempeltheologie im Blick auf Heidenchristen und bezieht sie ein."

43. Ibid., 203, my translation.

44. Ibid., 200: "Paul extends the existing intra-Jewish use of Temple metaphors in a positive way to Gentile Christians, and within the framework of his piety affirms the possibilities for Christian believers' orientation to the Temple" (my translation).

matic sacrifice. Thus, the *shelamim* were also seen, within that system, as representing the whole-hearted dedication of the offerer. Despite the priority of the *olah*, the *shelamim* were probably the most frequently offered of all the sacrifices, as they were the most common means for people to eat meat. Milgrom says of these "offerings of well-being":

> The *šĕlāmîm* falls into three categories of motivation: *nĕdābâ* 'freewill'; neder 'vow'; and toda 'thanksgiving' (7:11–16). The common denominator of these motivations is rejoicing: "You shall sacrifice the *šĕlāmîm* and eat them, rejoicing before the Lord your God" (Deut 27:7). The freewill offering (*nĕdābâ*) is, on logical ground, the most frequently sacrificed, for it is the spontaneous by-product of one's happiness, whatever its cause. *nĕdābâ* can even be found as a surrogate for *šĕlāmîm* (Num 15:3, 8).[45]

One of the distinctive characteristics of Paul's letter to the Philippians is its blending of obedient suffering on account of one's wholehearted dedication with equally wholehearted rejoicing. For example, Paul rejoices that Christ is proclaimed, even if the proclamation is from false motives that cause him personal suffering (1:18). He enjoins the Philippians to exercise patient and unified endurance of suffering (1:27–2:4), ushering in Paul's joy (2:2). The exaltation of Jesus Christ at the end of the Christ Hymn is tied to his willingness to suffer a complete emptying-out of his glory in the first half of the hymn (2:5–11).[46] Epaphroditus is set before the community as a model of complete dedication, nearly dying in the offering of his service (2:25–27), but his recovery brings about the joy of the Philippians (2:28). The popular English usage of the term *sacrifice* to refer to something irksome or painful, together with the twentieth-century scholarly link of sacrifice and violence impede appropriate interpretation of first-century sacrificial references. Dedicatory sacrifices were marked principally by festive joy and celebration.[47] Paul could rely upon this remembered mood

---

45. Jacob Milgrom, *Leviticus 1–16: A New Translation with Introduction and Commentary*, AB 3 (New York: Doubleday, 1991), 218–19.

46. This is the force of the word διό at the beginning of 2:9.

47. Christian Eberhart, "Sacrifice? Holy Smokes! Reflections on Cult Terminology for Understanding Sacrifice in the Hebrew Bible," in *Ritual and Metaphor: Sacrifice in the Bible*, ed. Christian A. Eberhart, RBS 68 (Atlanta: Society of Biblical Literature, 2011), 21–22, and 24: "Specifically the burnt offering, the cereal offering, and the sacrifice of well-being are often associated with a cheerful, merry, and celebratory atmosphere."

when he blended costly self-offering with invitations to rejoice, conveyed through the use of sacrificial metaphors.

Such a blend of suffering (due to one's unwavering commitment to God) and rejoicing is not uncommon in apocalyptic literature generally, as it seeks to make sense of current suffering of the faithful in light of their eventual vindication by God.[48] In the case of the letter to the Philippians, sacrificial metaphors carry some of the weight of helping to make sense of what is otherwise almost an emotional impossibility: to see within the very experience of suffering or loss a possibility for rejoicing. All sacrifices require the trusting relinquishment of something of value into the hands of God, as may be seen both in the simple offerings of Cain and Abel (Gen 4:3–5) and in the more heartrending and emotionally complex offering of Isaac (Gen 22:1–14). But it is the *shelamim* in particular that call for rejoicing and conviviality as part and parcel of an act of significant relinquishment.[49]

Within the Jewish system of sacrifices, the *shelamim* are the corollary of the basic commensal form of sacrifice found all over the ancient Mediterranean. They are, in the main, a spontaneously motivated offering of thanksgiving and feasting.[50] The potentially universal quality of the *shelamim* is in contrast to the specifically Jewish character of the Passover and its role in commemorating a pivotal event in Jewish history. Interestingly, while Paul is concerned to clarify boundaries for the Corinthians between their table fellowship and that of their idol-worshiping neighbors (10:1–33), he brings up no such issue in Philippi. Perhaps Paul's choice to use metaphors of a specifically Jewish sacrifice in addressing the Corinthians (the Passover) and metaphors of a more general type of sacrifice in addressing the Philippians is more strategic than is generally recognized. As a corollary to this fact, one might note that, in Philippians, Paul also

---

48. For example, one might think immediately of the "suffering Messiah" of the Gospel of Mark (8:27–37).

49. Jan Bremmer speaks of the economic cost of sacrifices in "Greek Normative Animal Sacrifices," 133.

50. Milgrom says of the *shelamim*, "The well-being offering never serves as expiation (but cf. Lev 17). Its function is simply to permit the consumption of meat. The motivation was usually spontaneous and occasioned by a sense of elation" (from "Leviticus," in *The Harper Collins Study Bible NRSV*, ed. Wayne A. Meeks et al. [New York: HarperCollins, 1993], 160).

makes use of a typical "Greco-Roman virtue list"[51] (Phil 4:8) rather than some more identifiably Jewish or Christian list of virtues. Perhaps Paul is purposely avoiding confusion concerning idol-worship in Corinth by using metaphors clearly drawn from the Jewish cult (Passover, the Jewish Temple, the Jewish regulations of purity) rather than metaphors that might just as easily apply to the Greco-Roman cults. Perhaps such discrimination was not necessary for the Philippians. In addition, the particular trials of the Philippians vis à vis their surrounding society (Phil 1:27–30) seem to invite comparison with the self–offering that is characteristic not only of the Jewish *shelamim*, but of the Greco-Roman sacrifices as well. The sacrifices of thanksgiving communicate metaphorically across a wide spectrum of ancient cultic experience.

Another aspect of the *shelamim* that Paul alludes to (Phil 2:17) is the libation that accompanied them. The Greco-Roman practice of libation in the *Odyssey* has been described above. The additional directions for the *shelamim* in Lev 7:11–12, call for oil poured over the cakes brought with the animal offering. And, of course, all of the sacrifices described in Leviticus are, as Paul says of the gifts sent to him by the Philippians through Epaphroditus, "a fragrant offering, a sacrifice acceptable and pleasing to God" (ὀσμὴν εὐωδίας, θυσίαν δεκτήν, εὐάρεστον τῷ θεῷ, Phil 4:18, cf. Lev 3:16, and esp. the refrain of Lev 1:9, 13, 17).

The entailments of the *shelamim*—complete dedication, joy, thanksgiving, fragrance, intimate relationship with God and with one's community—reverberate across the verses of Philippians. The Christ Hymn in the center of Philippians sets the pattern for selfless dedication which leads, along however painful a route, to profound joy. The sacrificial metaphors of Philippians (1:10, 2:17–18, 4:18) are images principally of the *shelamim* sacrifices and put forward an analogous moral pattern in the lives of Paul, of his coworkers, and of the Philippians. Philippians is a short letter and the *shelamim* a relatively uncomplicated form of sacrifice. What follows is an overview of a more complicated sacrifice, the Passover, and its metaphorical use in a more complex letter, 1 Corinthians.

51. Bonnie B. Thurston and Judith M. Ryan, *Philippians and Philemon*, Sacra Pagina 10 (Collegeville, MN: Liturgical Press, 2005), 146.

The Passover and Its Entailments

While it is generally agreed that the Passover and the Festival of Unleavened
Bread were originally separate holidays in ancient Israel, by the time of the
compilation of Exodus the two festivities had become completely linked
with one another (Exod 12:14–15).[52] One witness to the inseparability of
the two by Paul's time is 1 Cor 5:6–8, as Paul moves from the metaphorical
counsel "Clean out the old leaven" (ἐκκαθάρατε τὴν παλαιὰν ζύμην) to the
underlying metaphorical assertion that "Christ our Passover has been sacrificed" (τὸ πάσχα ἡμῶν ἐτύθη Χριστός).[53] Passover is not included among
the sacrifices of Lev 1–7. Eberhart speculates that this omission may be

---

52. See Tamara Prosic's treatment of the origins and history of Passover in *The
Development and Symbolism of Passover until 70 CE*, JSOTSup 414 (London: T&T
Clark, 2004). Her study takes into account recent work on the ancient history of Pal-
estine that sheds doubt upon the biblical, literary concept of Israel as a people distinct
from those of Canaan. She writes, "In contrast to the old historical model whose view
on the ethnic and cultural origins of the Israelites reflected in studies of Passover as
a search for distinctiveness and separate functional entities in its ritual structure, the
new trends provide a basis for an assumption that the festival comes from a single
cultural background and that it is, despite our inability to understand the governing
idea behind it, a coherent unit, both ritually and functionally" (8). On the dating of the
origins of the Passover, she writes, "What we can firmly establish … is not the earliest
period, *terminus a quo*, but the *terminus ad quem* of [the redefinition of its function,
the connection of the agricultural and pastoral festivals with the story of the people's
liberation].… Even dating of that *terminus ad quem* is relative since it depends on
the period when the biblical texts were finally written. If we accept the latest studies
regarding this question, that may be as late as Hellenistic times. So what we could
possibly establish in historical terms is that Passover's ideological and corresponding
functional translation is evident in Hellenistic times, but how far back into the past
from the fourth or fifth century that process started it is not possible to say" (14).

53. Θύω is the appropriate Greek verb to designate sacrificial slaughter. Eberhart
notes that in the LXX the "noun θυσία occurs not only 138 times as translation of the
term זבח, but also 134 times as the equivalent of the term מנחה in both its meaning
for the 'cereal offering' (Lev 2:1, 2, 3, 4, 5, 6, 7, 8, 9, 10, 11, 13, 14,15; 9:4, 17, 18; Num
15:4) and as a general term for 'sacrifice' (e.g., Gen 4:3, 5). Consisting of vegetal sub-
stances, the cereal offering naturally features no act of slaughter. Instead the only ritual
step to be carried out at the sanctuary is the burning rite on the central altar.… There
are, however, other instances where θύω or θυσία is equivalent to the verb or noun
derived from the root זבח and implies the participation in a sacrificial meal (Exod
18:12; 24:5; Deut 17:7; 1 Sam 1:3–4; 2:13–16; 1 Kgs 8:62–66; 19:21; Hos 8:13; 1 Chr
29:21–22)" (Eberhart, "Sacrifice? Holy Smokes," 27–28).

due to the fact that it originated as an apotropaic ritual in the home and not as a Temple sacrifice. He notes, however, the references to Passover as a "sacrifice [פסח זבח] to YHWH" in Exod 12:27 and as an "offering" [קרבן] to YHWH" in Num 9:7, 13.[54] Eberhart draws attention to the fact that the verb used to designate the killing of the Passover lamb (זבח) is not the same as the verb used in the cultic regulations of Lev 1–7 (שחט). The זבח "encompasses a festive meal during which the offerer, together with family and friends, had the privilege of eating sacrificial meat (Gen 31:54; Exod 18:12; 24:5; Deut 27:7; 1 Sam 1:3–4; 2:3–16; 9:12–13; 1 Kgs 8:62–66; 19:21; Hos 8:13; 1 Chr 29:21–22)."[55]

Exodus 12–13 completely intertwines the historical account of the exodus from Egypt with directions for the future commemoration of the event. The original story and its future observance become completely interdependent over the centuries of the commemorative practice, as can be seen in the rabbinical commentary of m. Pesahim:

> In every generation a person is duty-bound to regard himself as if he personally has gone forth from Egypt, since it is said, "And you shall tell your son in that day saying, It is because of that which the Lord did for me when I came forth out of Egypt" (Ex 13:8). Therefore we are duty-bound to thank, praise, glorify, honor, exalt, extol, and bless him who did for our forefathers and for us all these miracles. (10:5 [Neusner])[56]

Similarly, Paul links the story of Jesus "on the night in which he was handed over" (ἐν τῇ νυκτὶ ᾗ παρεδίδετο) to the present practice of the Corinthians: "whenever you eat this bread or drink the wine, you proclaim the death of the Lord until he comes" (ὁσάκις γὰρ ἐὰν ἐσθίητε τὸν ἄρτον τοῦτον καὶ τὸ ποτήριον πίνητε, τὸν θάνατον τοῦ κυρίου καταγγέλλετε ἄχρις οὗ ἔλθῃ, 1 Cor 11:23, 26). Part of the power of Paul's brief recitation of Jesus's statements at the blessing of the bread and wine lies in a similar overlay of the historical onto the present, as though Paul had called Jesus in personally to witness to what was happening in Corinth. Poignantly, Jesus "on the night in

---

54. Ibid.

55. Ibid., 26.

56. I do not intend to suggest by my quoting from the Mishnah that it is an infallible guide to the practice of Judaism before 70 CE, but it is at least an indicator of some of the possible entailments of the Passover in Paul's time, and a guide to *some* of the accepted practices surrounding the observance of the Passover before the destruction of the Temple.

which he was handed over" becomes present again as host, witness, and judge of every future Lord's supper (κυριακὸν δεῖπνον).

In the story of the Passover, the original event of liberation included the painting of the lintels of the Israelites' homes with the blood of the Passover lamb, an apotropaic rite to identify them as the people faithful to YHWH, so that they would not suffer the deaths of their firstborn, as the Egyptians did, when God passed over their houses (Ex 3:23). While it has already been shown that the covenant sacrifices in the Greco-Roman tradition emphasize the death of the animal as a way of reinforcing the sense of danger attendant to breaking the covenant, this apotropaic rite likewise serves to emphasize the fact that God has the terrifying power both to give and to take life.[57] Being in covenant relationship with God, or being the community where God is as fully present as God is in the Temple, is potentially either dangerous or life-giving. Paul's use of metaphors of Passover and covenant have attendant to them this urgency of life and death, of the need to make moral choices that are radically faithful, or else accept the consequences.

Exodus 12:43–50 outlines who may eat the Passover, with a concern that all males who eat of it be circumcised (12:48–49), the preeminent sign of the integrity of the community in its devotion to the one God. The people who gather to eat the Passover are the people who are in covenant with YHWH. When the events of the Passover are recited in the future (Deut 26:1–19), the scope of the event includes covenant with the God of Israel as an implication of the Passover (Deut 26:17–18).[58] This solidarity

---

57. John Dunnill has recognized the connections between the narrative of the Passover and covenant ceremonies, in *Covenant and Sacrifice in the Letter to the Hebrews*: "this joyful communion [the Passover meal] is a covenant-feast: first, the blood-rite separates those inside, enjoying God's favour, from his enemies; second, no one may take part in the Passover except Israelites; third, it is in text and tradition inseparable from the salvation story of Exodus. The ambivalence of God is here dramatized in blood: he is not only the Destroyer whom blood is smeared on doorposts and lintel to drive away, but the Covenant Lord for whom it is a sign of homage and dedication. The aversive form of the blood-rite (sprinkling, 2 Chron. 35:11) was subsequently altered to conform to the throwing action of the covenant-sacrifice in Exodus 24. Within the space marked out by blood, Israel feasts in God's presence" (SNTSMS 75 [Cambridge, Cambridge University Press, 1992], 107–8).

58. Deuteronomy 26 concerns the reciting of the basic story of the Passover when making an offering of the firstfruits. In the Mishnah Pesahim, the recitation is also required as part of the Passover celebration: "He [the father] begins [answering the

of the covenant people could be seen in the first century CE, as people ate by "associations" (kinship or affiliated groups) (m. Pesah. 7:13a), who provided and ate their lamb, herbs, and bread together. What is important to hear in all of this is the thread that links Passover to covenant and to the image of the people of Israel as a unified whole, the "whole assembly of the congregation of Israel" (m. Pesah. 5:5b). The vast pilgrimages to Jerusalem in the first century CE at the time of the Passover, would have given the participants a sense of this gathered nation.[59] Philo also highlights the unifying aspect of pilgrimage to the Jewish temple: "the sacrifices and libations are the occasion of reciprocity of feeling and constitute

---

questions] with disgrace and concludes with glory, and explains [the Scriptures from], *A wandering Aramaean was my father* ... until he completes the entire section" (10:4.J).

59. Josephus depicts several occurrences of the pilgrimage to Jerusalem, all of which heighten the sense of the unity and number of the people. I have italicized elements that reiterate what I see as important entailments of metaphors of Passover. He describes the first celebration of the Passover in the Second Temple thus: "As the Feast of Unleavened Bread was at hand, it being the first month, which the Macedonians call Xanthicus but we call Nisan, *all the people streamed out of the villages* to the city to celebrate the festival *in a state of purity* with their wives and their children, according to the law of the fathers. They offered the sacrifice which was called the Passover, on the fourteenth day of the same month, and then feasted seven days. They spared no expense, but offered whole burnt offerings to God and performed sacrifices of thanksgiving, because God had led them again to the land of their fathers and to its laws, and had disposed the mind of the king of Persia favorably toward them. So for these reasons the men offered the largest sacrifices and used great magnificence in the worship of God (Josephus, *Ant.* 11.4.8.109–112 [Marcus]). In his discussion of the protest against Archelaus at the time of the Passover (4 BCE), Josephus writes, "*An innumerable multitude of people come out of the country, and from abroad also*, in order to worship God" (*Ant.* 17.9.3.213 [Marcus]). Josephus's estimation of the number of people who gathered for the Passover in 70 is, no doubt, exaggerated (see E. P. Sanders, *Judaism: Practice and Belief 63 BCE–66 CE* [Philadelphia: Trinity Press International, 1992], 126), but his point was to indicate how many people were killed when the Romans destroyed Jerusalem: "Cestius, desiring to inform Nero, who was inclined to condemn the nation, of the power of the city, requested the high priests to take a count, if possible, of the entire population. So these high priests did so upon the arrival of their feast which is called the Passover. On this day they slay their sacrifices from the ninth hour until the eleventh, *with a company of not less than ten belonging to every sacrifice—for it is not lawful for them to have the feast singly by themselves*—and many of us are twenty in a company. These priests found the number of the sacrifices was two hundred and fifty–six thousand five hundred; which, if we assume no more than ten feasted together, amounts to two million seven hundred thousand and two hundred persons." (Josephus, *J.W.* 6.9.3.422–427 [Thackeray])

the surest pledge that all are of one mind" (*Spec. Laws* 1.70 [Colson]). Unification and covenant are some of the themes that Paul is similarly drawing together in 1 Corinthians.[60]

While the earliest commemorations of the Passover may indeed have taken place in and around people's homes, and would not therefore technically be part of the sacrificial system, by the late Second Temple period the Passover resembled the other sacrifices, by taking place in the Temple courts, with the blood gathered in bowls by the priests and dashed upon the altar, not upon the people's lintels (m. Pesah. 5). It should be remembered that the Temple was as much a symbol of the *nation* of Israel (as a political entity) as it was a religious center, and in this way Mitchell's description of 1 Corinthians as an example of deliberative rhetoric (from the political sphere) may be more related to the imagery of the community as Temple than has previously been acknowledged. In any case, Paul's description of Jesus as the *sacrificed* (ἐτύθη) paschal lamb underscores just how thoroughly the Passover had become connected with the sacrificial system of the Temple. So, while the Lord's Supper in Corinth is presumably taking place in a home, the gathered community might logically be conceived as God's Temple (1 Cor 3:16–17; 6:19; 2 Cor 6:16).

This image of the community as Temple also plays the role of intensifying the question of the people's ritual purity, which was a requirement for the celebrating of Passover in Jewish tradition (Num 9:6–12; m. Pesah. 7). Further, as regards the language of purity, the combining of the Passover with the Feast of Unleavened Bread adds another layer of literary entailments connected with purity that enhances those of the Passover

---

60. Federico Colautti makes the same point concerning the descriptions of the Passover by Flavius Josephus in "The Celebration of Passover in Josephus: A Means of Strengthening Jewish Identity?" (*Society of Biblical Literature Seminar Papers 2002*, SBLSPS 41 [Atlanta: Society of Biblical Literature, 2002]). He writes, "First of all it seems quite clear that Passover was already a literary *topos*, capable of serving as a background for one of the most important concepts that [Josephus] desires to convey, namely, that those who attempted to gain political independence, in reality brought destruction to the people. A consequence of this presentation is that the correct or incorrect interpretation of Passover outlines the boundary between the true and false members of the Jewish people.... Bearing in mind that [Josephus] insists on the significance of purity and of the *politeia/politeuma* in relating these arguments to Passover, it could be proposed that [Josephus] considered Passover as one of the fundamental practices which were necessary to preserve and strengthen the Jewish identity" (305).

sacrifice itself.[61] The scrupulosity that surrounded the cleaning out of all leaven takes up the better part of two chapters of the m. Pesahim (1–2). Paul picks up this language of purity to describe the community at Corinth (1:2, 8). I disagree with Jeffrey Siker who hears echoes of Yom Kippur (or other propitiatory sacrifices) in the connection of purity with Passover in 1 Cor 5:7. Right preparation was traditionally part of the Passover experience, with the cleaning out of leaven an important part of the ritual that came to express both inner and outward purity.[62] What Siker calls the "Yom Kippuring of Passover" is, to my ear, a post-Pauline phenomenon, made possible mainly after the destruction of the Temple and the loss of the clearly distinct sacrifices of the Jewish system. I thoroughly agree with Siker when he comments on: "the ease with which Paul works this ritual language into his discussion. This is all the more remarkable given that Paul uses these Jewish sacrificial images while addressing a Christian community that appears to be primarily Gentile in makeup."[63] But when he goes on to say that Paul's use of the Passover metaphor expresses the community's view of Jesus as the "*true* paschal lamb,"[64] I part ways with him. This is precisely the move that confuses Paul's use of metaphors in relation to Jewish ritual practice. To say that Jesus functions as the paschal lamb of the Gentiles is not to delegitimize the traditional Jewish paschal lamb, but to establish an equation between the two, in terms of their efficacy in

---

61. Robin Routledge explains that, "In ancient times, the leaven that caused bread to rise was prepared by leaving dough lightened by grape and other juices in a warm place to ferment. Because this process took several days, and because it was seen as something of a mystery, old leaven was preserved and added to successive batches of dough. The leaven thus provided a link with the past; and the absence of leaven symbolized a break from the past and the desire for a new beginning. This was particularly appropriate in the context of the Passover celebration" ("Passover and Last Supper," *TynBul* 53:2 [2002]: 207).

62. Siker says, "Paul appears at least obliquely to import the notion of doing away with sin, an idea inherent to the meaning of Yom Kippur, into a Passover reading of Jesus as the sacrificial Lamb. Thus in 1 Cor 5:6–8 we may be seeing a kind of recombinant ritualizing in the process of formation already at this eearly stage of Christian theologizing, the "Yom Kippuring" of Passover" (Jeffrey S. Siker, "Yom Kippuring Passover: Recombinant Sacrifice in Early Christianity" in Eberhart, *Ritual and Metaphor*, 68–69).

63. Ibid., 69.

64. Ibid., 69, emphasis added.

bringing a people out of slavery into the freedom of right relationship with
God and their neighbor.

Paula Fredriksen refers to the Passover as "the archetypical festival
of liberation,"[65] and that is certainly its narrative setting in the various
places where it is recounted in the Hebrew Bible. In Joshua, the liberat-
ing event extends all the way into the "land flowing with milk and honey,"
where the generation born during the exodus was circumcised and the
entire liberated community celebrated the Passover again together (Josh
5:2–12). It is only when the entire exodus is over, and people have crossed
the Jordan, that God says, "Today I have rolled away from you the disgrace
of Egypt" (Josh 5:9). Liberation and covenant are deeply related to one
another through the yearly commemoration of the Passover. The directions concerning the Passover in the Mishnah Pesahim stress the theme
of liberation: He brought us forth from slavery to freedom, anguish to joy,
mourning to festival, darkness to great light, subjugation to redemption....
(10:5). Indeed it was customary to eat the meal reclining, as free people,
not sitting, as was the custom for servants.[66] This theme of freedom from
slavery is characteristic of Paul's thinking concerning what has happened
to those who are in Christ, as can be seen most clearly in Gal 2:4, 5:1, and
5:13. But the language of freedom also shows up in 2 Cor 3:17, and entailments of the Passover drama from slavery to freedom may inform 1 Cor
7:21–24.[67]

Passover is also the preeminent sacrifice for marking Israel's return to
faithfulness at various points in history. Hezekiah's reforms and rededication of the Temple are celebrated first by sacrifices at the Temple itself,
but they become a feature of life for all of Israel only when "all Israel and
all Judah" are invited to come to Jerusalem to celebrate the Passover as a
nation (2 Chr 30:1–9). The festival is an occasion for the people to "return
to YHWH [שובו אל יהוה], the God of Abraham, Isaac, and Israel, so that

---

65. Paula Fredriksen, "Did Jesus Oppose the Purity Laws?" *BRev* 11.3 (1995):
19–25, 42–46.

66. Mishnah Pesah. 10:1, "even the poorest Israelite should not eat until he
reclines at table." See Louis Jacobs, "Passover," *EncJud* 15:679; Routledge, "Passover
and Last Supper," 209; Mark 14:18; John 13:22, 28.

67. Imagine the shock value of the language of freedom in Gal 5:1, giving way to
Paul's heated criticism of circumcision in 5:2, when one takes into consideration the
entailments of the Passover. Such a passage may clarify one of the reasons why Paul
does not use cultic metaphors in the letter to the Galatians.

he may turn again [וישב] to the remnant of you who have escaped from the hands of the kings of Assyria" (2 Chr 30:6). When the people gather, they remove from Jerusalem all the altars besides the central sanctuary (2 Chr 30:14) before they sacrifice the Passover lamb. We read that "the priests and the Levites were ashamed," presumably because of their previous inattentiveness to the demands of the Torah. Perhaps what is most interesting for comparison to Paul's extension of Passover to the community of Gentiles in Corinth, is the description of the northern tribes' unpreparedness (or unwillingness?) to conform at 2 Chr 30:17–20:

> For there were many in the assembly who had not sanctified themselves; therefore the Levites had to slaughter the Passover lamb for everyone who was not clean, to make it holy to the LORD. For a multitude of the people, many of them from Ephraim, Manasseh, Issachar, and Zebulun, had not cleansed themselves, yet they ate the Passover otherwise than as prescribed. But Hezekiah prayed for them, saying, "the good LORD pardon all who set their hearts to seek God, the LORD the God of their ancestors, even though not in accordance with the sanctuary's rules of uncleanness. The LORD heard Hezekiah, and healed the people. (NRSV)

In spite of their lack of appropriate purification, the northern tribes are made ready for the festival by the prayer of Hezekiah. Then the nation keeps the festival for seven days "with great gladness" (2 Chr 30:21), and then agrees to celebrate it for seven *more* days "with gladness" (2 Chr 30:23). Following the festival, the people continue to exercise their fervor by destroying all the ancient sanctuaries in competition with the Jerusalem Temple (2 Chr 31:1). The question here is not what the passage means about the history of Israel, but how it affected *Paul's* sense of the Passover, and his sense of God's demands and God's mercy. In this passage, the observance of the Passover is a sign of the nation's repentance and unity. Paul carries forward these meanings of the Passover into his correspondence with the ἐκκλησία in Corinth.

A celebration of the Passover also marks the rebuilding of the Temple after the return of the Babylonian exiles, following the decree of Cyrus. The Temple is dedicated with sacrifices, and then the first observance after the dedication is the Passover (Ezra 6:19). Here, the emphasis is on the purity of the priests and Levites[68] who offer the sacrifice and the separa-

---

68. Purity is a particular concern of Ezra.

tion from "the pollutions of the nations of the land" by all who participate in the festival. The mood of the celebration is one of gladness and relief: "With joy they celebrated the Festival of Unleavened Bread seven days; for the LORD had made them joyful, and had turned the heart of the king of Assyria[69] to them, so that he aided them in the work of the house of God, the God of Israel" (Ezra 6:22, NRSV).[70] Again, we see the importance of the Passover in narratives marking important turning points in the life of Israel, from slavery, oppression, or faithlessness, to renewed faithfulness to YHWH. These narratives give depth to the meaning of "Christ our Passover" in 1 Corinthians, where they signal a turning point in the life of the community, willingness to give up familiar patterns for whatever God requires, dedication to purity, unity as a nation in right relationship with God—and celebratory joy.

The principal entailments of references to the Passover, as I have outlined them above, include deliverance, covenant, the integrity of the nation of Israel before God, the joyful eating of a communal meal, purity (described as leaven and lack of leaven), apotropaism (danger and life), Temple, preparedness to live in the land God has given, and a collapse of historical distance in the recounting of the narrative of God's liberation of Israel. These are some of the concepts that recur in the discussion of 1 Corinthians. While the Passover was an important celebration for marking the people's return to YHWH after a time of laxity with regard to the Torah, it is not a propitiatory sacrifice, but a commensal sacrifice of celebration. In 1 Corinthians, Paul uses references to aspects of the Passover to ground his counsels concerning the importance of moral purity, separation from idols, and covenant faithfulness to God. References to the Passover may indicate how Paul regards the inclusion of the Gentiles in history: as a people made holy, called to live in the ways of God, appropriately celebratory as they gather for the Lord's Supper in a new land.

---

69. This is an anachronistic reference. The exiles returned under the decree of Cyrus of Persia and then rebuilt the Temple under the reign of Darius.

70. The political interests of the Persians in currying the favor of the returned exiles would most likely not have been a concern of Paul in the development of his understanding of the Passover.

4

SACRIFICE AS AN OBJECT OF STUDY

Sacrifice has been a widely practiced human act, various in its details, variously understood by those who have sought to explain it, and now almost unknown as an actual practice in developed countries. Most of those who have written on the subject would agree that sacrifice "means something" or "accomplishes something" beyond what is strictly observed, though most primary texts on sacrifice focus on what is *done*, not on what it *means*. J. H. M. Beattie wrote in 1980, "sacrificial ritual, like other rites, is a form of art, a drama, which is believed by its performers ... to work. Also as, in a sense, a language—a way of saying something as well as of doing something—it requires its own specific kind of understanding."[1] Since the nineteenth century, there has been extensive research and writing attempting to get at some presumed initiating spark that lies behind the history of the human practice of sacrifice. The popularity of Darwin's theory of evolution added to this conception the assumption that the practices of sacrifice are subject to evolution over time, becoming ever more "spiritual" and/or "moral." What follows is a brief overview of the many-faceted scholarly discussion of sacrifice since the nineteenth century. The purpose of the overview is to bring to the surface some of the main threads in scholarly interpretation of sacrifice, not to choose one among them as the correct interpretation, but to increase the modern interpreter's ability to hear some of the possible nuances of meaning carried by sacrificial metaphors.

---

1. J. H. M. Beattie, "On Understanding Sacrifice," in *Sacrifice*, ed. M.F.C. Bourdillon and Meyer Fortes (London: Academic Press for the Royal Anthropological Institute of Great Britain and Ireland, 1980), 33.

THE "LOGIC" OF SACRIFICE

Foundational anthropological studies of sacrifice include the works of
Edward Burnett Tylor and W. Robertson Smith.[2] In Tylor's rendering, sacrifice is, at its simplest level, a ritual of gift-giving; in Robertson Smith's,
it is a sacred meal. Influenced by the new theories of Darwin, Tylor held
to the idea that religion was subject to rules of evolution, or maturation.
The more closely particular rites were given an ethical interpretation by
their practitioners, the more sophistication Tylor ascribed to the practices;
while, conversely, the more sacrificial rites were spoken of in terms analogous to human relationships, the more childlike and crude he found them.
It was his understanding that a path of development in the rites of sacrifice
could be traced, from simple gift-giving in hopes of pleasing the deity (and
with some hope of reciprocation), to the more abstract idea of homage, in
which the gift is offered to honor the deity (without any sense that such
gifts are of practical use to the deity and without hope of reciprocity), to
what he called the "self-abnegation theory," in which the value of the gift
lies purely in the giver's self-deprivation. For Tylor, each of these interpretations of sacrifice represents a developmental leap over the previous one,
and he was inclined to link the Jewish practice of sacrifice, as described in
the Torah, with the more sophisticated level of development: "Here sacrifice appears not in the lower conception of a gift acceptable and even ben-
eficial to the deity, but with the higher significance of devout homage or
expiation for sin."[3] In making this judgment, Tylor has chosen to privilege
the prophetic (moral) and Levitical (expiatory) discussions of sacrifice
over the many biblical narratives in which sacrifice occurs as a simple act
of gift-giving to God as to a human (Gen 4:3; 8:20; 28:18).[4]

---

2. Edward Burnett Tylor, *Primitive Culture: Researches into the Development of
Mythology, Philosophy, Religion, Language, Art, and Custom,* (New York: Gordon
Press, 1977); W. Robertson Smith, *The Religion of the Semites: The Fundamental Insti-
tutions* (New York: Meridian, 1956).

3. Tylor, *Primitive Culture,* 472.

4. Even in Leviticus, directions are given for the combining of different types
of sacrifices. For example, the ordination of the high priest calls for a sin offering, a
whole burnt offering, and a sacrifice of well-being (Lev 9). None of these sacrifices is
described as more significant or more highly developed than another, but rather each
has its specific purposes, and in the combined sacrifices each part contributes to the
efficacy and to the emotional climate of the whole.

With the publication of his work, *The Religion of the Semites*, in 1889, Robertson Smith countered Tylor's gift-theory by saying that "the leading idea in the animal sacrifices of the Semites … was not that of a gift made over to the god, but of an act of communion, in which the god and his worshippers unite by partaking together of the flesh and blood of a sacred victim."[5] Central to Robertson Smith's construction of ancient sacrifices was the concept of totemism, in which the totem animal of a clan was assumed to be the father of the clan's patriarch, and thus consanguineous with the entire clan. As E. Evans-Pritchard writes[6] of Robertson Smith's theory, "Sociologically speaking, the god was the clan itself, idealized and divinized … and the clan periodically expressed the unity of its members and of them with their god, and revitalized itself, by slaying the totemic creature and eating its raw flesh in a sacred feast, a communion 'in which the god and his worshippers unite by partaking together of the flesh and blood of a sacred victim.'"

In Robertson Smith's imaginative reconstruction, the sacrificial meal breaks down social boundaries between one participant and another, and serves to unite a diverse group of people into a single clan. However, unlike Tylor, his understanding of the development of the expiatory sacrifices is less sanguine, as Israel "grew up" and substituted "a painful and scrupulous anxiety in all approach to the gods" for their earlier "joyous confidence."[7] For Robertson Smith, expiatory sacrifices, such as the whole burnt offering, or *ōlah*, are a later development from the earlier and more fundamental communion sacrifices, but the communion sacrifice is always at least vestigially present, "under" any expiatory sacrifice.

Following closely upon the work of Tylor and Robertson Smith, Henri Hubert and Marcel Mauss worked to establish a fundamental understanding of the logic of sacrifice, using Vedic texts as their principal source.[8] They put forth the theory that the "grammar"[9] of sacrifice is concerned

5. Robertson Smith, *Religion of the Semites*, 226–27.

6. In *Theories of Primitive Religion* (Oxford: Clarendon, 1965).

7. Robertson Smith, *Religion of the Semites*, 257.

8. Henri Hubert and Marcel Mauss, *Sacrifice: Its Nature and Function*, trans. W. D. Halls (Chicago: University of Chicago Press, 1964); originally published as "Essai sur la Nature et la Fonction du Sacrifice," *L'Année sociologique* 2 (1899): 29–138. The work of Hubert and Mauss remains central to discussions of sacrifice, even while they are widely criticized for relying upon a single literary source to delineate a universal theory of the schema of sacrifice.

9. "Grammar" is the term used by E. Evans-Pritchard to describe Hubert and

mainly with the approach and withdrawal of the divine, and with the necessity for human beings to enter into a relationship with the divine, however dangerous such proximity might be.[10] The death of the sacrificial victim is a proxy for the death that would otherwise be the outcome of the offerer's approach to the divine.

Hubert and Mauss were looking for "the unity of the sacrificial system," the most widely seen "procedures of sacrifice" and the "least rich in particular form."[11] They find their unity in the processes of "sacralisation" and "desacralisation," mediated by a sacrificial victim. Thus they distinguish the following discrete elements in the scheme of sacrifice: the entry; the sacrifier;[12] the place, the time, the instruments; the victim; the exit. After the withdrawal of the divine (the exit), the one who has offered sacrifice is morally changed by the death of the victim:

> In sacrifice ... the consecration extends beyond the thing consecrated; among other objects, it touches the moral person who bears the expenses of the ceremony. The devotee who provides the victim which is the object of the consecration is not, at the completion of the operation, the same as he was at the beginning.[13]

Mauss's discernment of the structure of sacrifice, in his foreword (viii) to the 1964 edition of Hubert and Mauss'ss *Sacrifice*.

10. "There is no need to explain at length why the profane thus enters into a relationship with the divine: it is because it sees in it the very source of life. It therefore has every interest in drawing closer to it, since it is there that the very conditions for its existence are to be found. How does it come about that the profane only communicates with the sacred through an intermediary? The destructive consequences of the rite partly explain this strange procedure. If the religious forces are the very principle of the forces of life, they are in themselves of such a nature that contact with them is a fearful thing for the ordinary man. If he involved himself in the rite to the very end, he would find death, not life. The victim takes his place.... *The victim redeems him*" (Hubert and Mauss, *Sacrifice*, 98, emphasis original).

11. Ibid., 95.

12. The term *sacrifier* was coined by Hubert and Mauss and has been picked up by others to denote the person for whose benefit the sacrifice is offered, as distinct from the "sacrificer," the person who actually does the sacrificing, who might be a priest or another person chosen to accomplish the act. Sacrifier and sacrificer may also be one and the same.

13. Hubert and Mauss, *Sacrifice*, 9.

In essence, what Hubert and Mauss describe is a rite of passage for the sacrifier who, via the victim, undergoes a moral change effected by contact with the divine.

Almost a century after the work of Hubert and Mauss, Luc de Heusch[14] roundly criticized them for applying what are basically Roman connotations of the words "sacred" and "profane" to non-Roman cultures; for applying the structure of a rite of passage onto the act of sacrifice without adequate evidence that the two are, in fact, analogous; and for presuming that one text can open up the schema of all sacrifices in all cultures. Still, de Heusch acknowledges that he has not developed a new theory to supplant that of Hubert and Mauss; rather, he substitutes the notions of "the conjunction and the disjunction of spaces, human and nonhuman" for Hubert and Mauss'ss sacralization and desacralization of the sacrifier.

Sacrifice and Purity

In her provocative and influential work, *Purity and Danger: An Analysis of Concepts of Pollution and Taboo* (1966), Mary Douglas (influenced by the structuralist work of E. E. Evans-Pritchard) analyzed the Levitical system of sacrifices as a sophisticated way of ordering an essentially untidy world. She argued that order and classification set boundaries in such a way as to mark out for people what would be considered life-giving and what would be regarded as dangerous and destructive. Her work, which expressed the elegance and ingenuity of the Levitical sacrificial system, offered a significant challenge to the evolutionary view of sacrifice.[15] As she says in the beginning of *Purity and Danger*:

> In this book I have tried to show that rituals of purity and impurity create unity in experience. So far from being aberrations from the central project of religion, they are positive contributions to atonement. By their means, symbolic patterns are worked out and publicly displayed. Within

---

14. Luc de Heusch, *Sacrifice in Africa* (Bloomington: Indiana University Press, 1985).

15. Jonathan Klawans offers a succinct view of Douglas's impact on subsequent interpreters of Leviticus, especially Milgrom, in "Ritual Purity." Klawans expresses concern for ways in which such an understanding of the purity regulations as a coherent system may lead scholars to "fill in gaps" in the supposed system in ways that are not necessarily valid (20).

these patterns disparate elements are related and disparate experience is given meaning.[16]

Part of what Douglas accomplishes is to link what might otherwise be seen as disparate subjects in Leviticus: the instructions on the offering of sacrifices, ethical issues in daily life, and regulations on pollution.

Building to some extent on Douglas's discussion of purity, together with a grounding in E.P Sanders's *Paul and Palestinian Judaism* (1977), Michael Newton published a study comparing the concept of purity at Qumran and in the letters of Paul (1985), focusing especially on the subject of the Temple.[17] Newton attempted to straddle the gulf between acknowledgment of the importance of the Jewish cult for early Christians and a conviction that Paul was arguing "that the Jewish cult was no longer a means of salvation," all while continuing to use cultic terminology as a way of "understanding the Christ event."[18] The simple choice to make a comparison between the rhetoric found in the Qumran scrolls and in the letters of Paul betrays an assumption that the two will share in a critique of the Temple and in the conviction that its leadership was illegitimate. A key point of comparison for Newton is the Qumran community's self-conscious equivalence of Torah study and cultic observance (1QS 6:2–8) and his interpretation of Temple metaphors in Paul as indicating that Paul regarded the *ekklēsia* as a replacement for the Temple. As he writes:

> In the Jewish tradition, out of which Paul came, the Temple in Jerusalem was regarded as the special dwelling place of God, and his continued presence was secured by the expiatory sacrifices that were offered there. These sacrifices were required to maintain the purity of the sanctuary, which was threatened by the defiling force of the sins of the people. *In Paul's mind the Christ event had changed all this. The community of believers now constituted the Temple and in the eschatological times was assured of God's Spirit and his presence among those who were "in Christ."*[19]

---

16. Mary Douglas, *Purity and Danger: An Analysis of Concepts of Pollution and Taboo* (Washington: Praeger, 1966), 2–3.

17. Michael Newton, *The Concept of Purity at Qumran and in the Letters of Paul* (Cambridge: Cambridge University Press, 1985).

18. Ibid., 8.

19. Ibid., emphasis added.

Newton's study can sensitize a reader to the language of purity that links Paul's letters to the traditional Jewish cultic concerns for purity as well as the purity regulations in the Qumran community. But his assumption that Paul saw his communities as a replacement for the Jerusalem Temple is not well-founded and relies upon reading passages about the Temple out of their context in the letters as a whole and without a sense for the state of Paul's thinking and acting, twenty years before the destruction of the Second Temple.

I disagree with Newton on the *function* of the language of purity in Paul's letters. Purity is not the goal for Paul, but is instrumental and dynamic. The churches are a means for God's holiness (of which purity is a part) to escape the walls of the Temple and even the bounds of Israel, to sanctify the nations: the unbelieving spouse (1 Cor 7:12–16), the neighbor (10:23–33), the world (Phil 2:14). In the Jewish cultic system, rites of purification were related to pure-hearted commitment to all the qualities of God's holiness, such as justice and ethical dealing of all kinds. The purity commended by Paul (1 Cor 1:2, 8) does not *replace* cultic purity, but is its everyday manifestation in moral life. What remains so difficult for Paul to describe is how to live in but not of the world, how to live with purity in such a way that it is not guarded (1 Cor 5:9–10), but rather escapes with its full potency into the world.

When Newton brings to bear all the instances of Paul's use of the language of purity on the interpretation of a single use, there is a distortion of the use of the metaphor in each specific context. The idea of the community as replacement for the Jewish Temple becomes a concept that overshadows the use of the metaphor as a rhetorical tool to rally the community to particular moral commitments. The metaphor of the believing community as Temple, reified, becomes the point and not a means in a moral argument that is about something other than calling the community to identify itself as a replacement for the Temple.

PSYCHOLOGICAL INTERPRETATIONS OF SACRIFICE

From the mid-twentieth century, the study of sacrifice began to focus more and more on psychological motivations for sacrifice, and these studies still bear the impress of the early assumption that there must be some universal basis to the practice. Probably no one's work has been more provocative or influential in this vein than that of René Girard, the author of *La violence et le sacré* (1972) and *Des choses cachées depuis la fondation du monde* (1978). It is hardly possible, since Girard, to speak of sacrifice without speaking of violence, while few would agree with the large-scale claim that the "hermeneutic" of sacred violence "stands at the origin of all culture."[20] In Girard's construction, the sacrificial act, basic to all human societies, begins in what he calls "mimetic desire." One subject's desire for a particular object is sparked by a model's possession of that object. A mimetic rivalry ensues between the subject and the model. The more heated the conflict for the desired object, the closer the subject and the model become to one another in their mutual desire for the object. The conflict is ultimately resolved when the escalating violence between subject and model is deflected onto a third party, the scapegoat. The practice of sacrifice is ritualized scapegoating, which protects society at large from the violence of perpetual mimetic rivalry.

In his book *Sacred Violence: Paul's Hermeneutic of the Cross* (1992), Robert Hamerton-Kelly uses Girard's theory to elucidate Pauline sacrificial metaphors pertaining to the death of Jesus. In support of his grand scheme to interpret specific texts, he distinguishes between "the level of theory and the level of analysis: Theories are tested differently than are hypotheses, not by the reliability of correlations but by their power and elegance."[21] In Hamerton-Kelly's view, the theory of sacred violence (the double movement of mimetic desire and scapegoating) has the power and elegance to explicate the human, cultural significance of Paul's sacrificial metaphors that might otherwise go unseen:[22]

> I intend to begin a rethinking of Christianity from the point of view of the divine determinative negation in the Cross of Christ. The Cross is not a sacrificial mechanism but the deconstruction of sacrifice.... It is a dialectical overcoming of sacrifice, which supersedes it while leaving it intact.[23]

In Hamerton-Kelly's rendering, the cross is, for Paul, "a metonymy" of the entire gospel, containing within itself both the history of Christ's life and the pattern for the moral life of his followers:

---

20. Robert G. Hamerton-Kelly, *Sacred Violence: Paul's Hermeneutic of the Cross* (Minneapolis: Fortress, 1992), 28. Stowers says, succinctly, that he considers "the work of René Girard a sacrificial ideology based on Christian and Freudian thought rather than a theory of sacrifice" ("Greeks Who Sacrifice," 295–96 n. 9).

21. Hamerton-Kelly, *Sacred Violence*, 2.

22. "My purpose is to show the generative presence of sacred violence behind the themes of the Pauline text" (ibid., 59).

23. Ibid., 60.

Philippians 2:8 is especially noteworthy because it interprets the Cross
as the symbol of the nonacquisitiveness of Christ, his willingness to give
up even the divine equality rather than to grasp it possessively. Paul
recommends this nonacquisitiveness as the moral pattern for life in the
community (cf. 2 Cor 13:4; Gal 5:24).[24]

For Hamerton-Kelly, Paul's move from traditional Judaism to life as an
apostle of Jesus Christ "and him crucified" (1 Cor 2:2) is the move from
the "Mosaic Law in its role as an instrument of the primitive Sacred"[25] to
a rejection of the whole system of mimetic rivalry and scapegoating, this
rejection represented by the cross. Here the evolutionary view of sacrifice
appears in a new guise.

But two issues are even more problematic for acceptance of the
Girardian explanation of the foundations of sacrifice. The first is that the
scapegoat ritual of Yom Kippur is far from being the paradigmatic Jewish
sacrifice. In fact, it is a kind of anti-sacrifice. Rather than a pure animal
offered to God within a holy space, the Yom Kippur scapegoat is an animal
upon whom the sins of the people are placed, and the animal banished to
the wilderness. The scapegoat sacrifice in the Jewish system is an anoma-
ly.[26] Secondly, the accounts of both Greco-Roman sacrifices and Jewish
sacrifices are almost devoid of language concerning death and violence. As
will be shown in the following chapter, only the covenantal sacrifices speak
of violence, as a threat against the breaking of the covenant. The blood
mentioned in Leviticus and Genesis is the animal's life, not its death. The
intensity of life poured out is *dangerously* alive and needs to be handled
only by priests specially chosen and prepared to do so. This feature of the
ancient interpretation of sacrifices—they are about life and not death—is
one of the elements that so set it apart from modern views of sacrifice that
portray the practice as a bloody, violent, primitive act best left behind.

In her 1981 dissertation, "Throughout Your Generations Forever: A
Sociology of Blood Sacrifice," Nancy Jay argues that there is no use in
searching for a universal "cause" for blood sacrifice, because these sacrifices are not, in fact, universal. They are bound up with the need to establish and strengthen patriarchal and patrilineal kinship systems in certain

24. Ibid., 65.
25. Ibid., 63.
26. Likewise, among the Greek sacrifices the *pharmakos* would not be considered
the most fundamental sacrificial form.

societies. Matrilineal descent is, of course, naturally certain, but Jay contends that, "what is needed to provide clear evidence of jural paternity is an act as definite and available to the senses as is birth."[27] Ritual blood sacrifice provides the needed guarantee of membership in the kinship group.[28]

William Beers built upon on some of the insights of Jay, while developing much further the psychoanalytical origins of sacrifice, using primarily the work of Heinz Kohut in self-psychology and object relations to build his argument.[29] Accepting Jay's principle, that sacrifice has everything to do with male identity formation, Beers focused primarily on the precognitive development of the male child in relation to the mother. As he says in the introduction to his work, "I shall be arguing that sacrifice embodies and conceals the psychological structure of a male anxiety associated with differentiation, separation, and other related transitions. An understanding of narcissistic anxiety is the key to understanding the psychological structure of sacrifice."[30] He outlined four ways in which sacrifice may be examined in relation to a male self-psychological understanding: sacrifice as merger with an idealized self-object, sacrifice as separation from the self-object, sacrifice as a conduit for male rage and violence, and sacrifice as a transfer of assumed omnipotence from the maternal self-object to male peers.

---

27. Nancy Jay, "Throughout Your Generations Forever: A Sociology of Blood Sacrifice" (Brandeis University, 1981), 132.

28. As she explains, "The twofold movement of sacrifice, integration and differentiation, communion and expiation, is beautifully adapted for creating patrilineal descent. Sacrifice can both expiate descent from women (along with other dangers) and integrate the pure and eternal patrilineage. Sacrificially constituted descent, incorporating women's mortal children into an 'eternal' (enduring through generations) kin group, in which membership is recognized by sacrificial ritual, not merely by birth, enables a patrilineal descent group to transcend mortality in the same process in which it transcends birth. Sacrifice is a remedy for having been born of woman because it is a uniquely powerful technique for creating an ideology for the control of the social relations of reproduction in which patrilineal descent groups appropriate as their own the offspring of women's reproductive powers" (Jay, "Throughout Your Generations Forever," 141).

29. William Beers, *Women and Sacrifice: Male Narcissism and the Psychology of Religion* (Detroit: Wayne State University Press, 1992).

30. Ibid., 16.

Sacrifice and Meals, Revisited

Another stream of interpretation of sacrifice in the mid-to-late twentieth century has been a return to Robertson Smith's theory as sacrifice as essentially a meal, without the encumbrance of his commitment to the idea of totemism. Marcel Detienne's influential essay, "Culinary Practices and the Spirit of Sacrifice," made several important points in regard to the Ancient Greek practice of sacrifice that were later adopted by Bruce Chilton in regard to Jewish sacrifices and the New Testament language of sacrifice.[31]

First, Detienne notes "the absolute coincidence of meat-eating and sacrificial practice"[32] in ancient Greece. "All consumable meat comes from ritually slaughtered animals, and the butcher who sheds the animal's blood bears the same functional name as the sacrificer posted next to the bloody altar." Secondly, he notes the implication of sacrificial practice with political power and all levels of political relationships: "Political power cannot be exercised without sacrificial practice." Abstaining from meat, then, was a form of political protest, a way of standing apart from the social order, not a stand taken in support of animals as such. To fail to see this is to underestimate "the [social and political] rupture implied by a deliberate avoidance of meat."

Bruce Chilton stated clearly that there is no global explanation for the whole phenomenon of sacrifice. In fact, he says, "The grand design of explaining sacrifice is itself a product of modern mystification."[33] Instead, like Detienne, he proposes that the interpreter stay close to what may be simply observed in the practice of sacrifice, and in the rules and prohibitions that surround it. Chilton notes, however, that what sacrifice looks like, most obviously, is the preparation and consumption of a meal:

> To the overwhelming majority of modern interpreters who have considered the issue of sacrifice, the most evident part of the activity is the death or destruction of the victim.... But in sacrifice, consumption is probably a better metaphor to describe what is happening than death;

---

31. Marcel Detienne and Jean-Pierre Vernant, *The Cuisine of Sacrifice among the Greeks*, trans. Paula Wissing (Chicago: University of Chicago Press, 1986), 1–20.

32. Ibid., 3.

33. Bruce Chilton, "The Hungry Knife," in *The Bible in Human Society: Essays in Honour of John Rogerson*, ed. M. Daniel Caroll, David J.A. Clines, and Philip R. Davies, JSOTSup 200 (Sheffield: Sheffield Academic, 1995), 137.

the passing of the victim rarely arouses interest, while its preparation and disposal, to the advantage of people or the gods, is specified. What happens most nearly approximates a meal, and sacrificial practice—in the type of food and its consumers—is often associated with culinary practice. Meals, as well as sacrifices, are pragmatic and affective, and may occasion ideological transactions, although the gods are not normally involved. If we wished generally to characterize the typology of sacrifice we have been discussing, then we could say that sacrifice is a feast with the gods, in which life as it should be—chosen and prepared correctly—is taken in order to produce life as it ought to be.[34]

RHETORIC: PRACTICE VERSUS INTERPRETATION

More recently, there has been a shift toward distinguishing between the practice of sacrifice as it was carried out by ordinary people all around the ancient Mediterranean, and the practice as reflected upon, discussed, and interpreted by literate cultic specialists and entrepreneurs, of whom the apostle Paul was one. Recent work by Stanley Stowers and Daniel Ullucci is illustrative of this important shift.[35] Their work calls into question the primary use of literary source material (Greek drama, poetry, philosophy, biblical texts) to interpret sacrificial practice accurately as it was experienced by most (illiterate) people.

While Stowers focuses his attention on Greek sacrificial practice, he holds that most of his main points characterize religiosity across the globe. What he finds fundamental to sacrificial practice is the simple interrelationship of human beings with gods and other "nonobvious" beings in "mundane social exchange."[36] Social exchange could involve any aspect of the whole range of human social behaviors:

Who in the ancient Mediterranean did not know how to give gifts, prepare food for others, share in celebratory meals, clean up a place for others, ask for help, get someone powerful to help you, appease the

---

34. Ibid.

35. Stanley Stowers, "The Religion of Plant and Animal Offerings versus the Religion of Meanings, Essences, and Textual Mysteries," in *Ancient Mediterranean Sacrifice*, ed. J. Knust and Z. Várhelyi (Oxford: Oxford University Press, 2011), 35–56; and Daniel Ullucci, "Contesting the Meaning of Animal Sacrifice," in Knust and Várhelyi, *Ancient Mediterranean Sacrifice*, 57–74.

36. Stowers, "The Religion of Plant Offerings," 37.

hostile, make promises, honor and praise, sing for someone, seek information about another's disposition, whether kindly or hostile, and seek expert or insider advice?[37]

Central to this exchange with the gods was the human social value of reciprocity, extended to a relationship among radical nonequals. The knowledge required for sacrifice was the same simple, practical knowledge and experience of day-to-day social interaction with which anyone would be familiar.

Beliefs attendant to these practices were not the province of specialists only—ordinary people also developed their own understandings of the meanings of their practices. But across a community these understandings might be as various as the number of people who held them. What was essential was the doing of the thing; ideas about what was done were secondary.[38] Those professionals who reflected upon and interpreted sacrificial practices constituted what Stowers calls a "second mode" of religion, the province of "the literate cultural producer," along with religious "entrepreneurs" who adapted and reformed the productions of the specialists.[39] It is the writings of these specialists that have steered the academic study of sacrifice, and perhaps steered it off course. What arises as most significant in the *popular* practice of sacrifice across the board is reciprocity; what arises as most significant in *literary* artifacts on sacrifice is a host of other things, taken to be the "deeper meaning" of sacrifice, such as atonement or obedience or morality, depending upon the point of view of the writer.

Literate religious specialists tended to be oriented to one of two poles, either toward the conservation of traditions by codifying, explaining, and interpreting them, or toward innovation, reinterpreting traditional practices by a new set of standards. Christianity had its beginnings in an intellectual reexamination and reinterpretation within Judaism, as an outcome of criticism of the collusion of first-century Jewish leadership with Rome. The letters of Paul are an artifact of this "entrepreneurial" intellectual reassessment of the 'true' meaning of such things as circumcision (Rom 2:28–9;

---

37. Ibid., 38.

38. Ibid., 37: "Rather than imagining people carrying around highly organized and complete systems of belief that then generate actions, we should imagine that religious inferences and beliefs were evoked as aspects of their practical skills for living life day to day and were dispersed in their practices."

39. Ibid., 41.

1 Cor 7:19; Gal 5:6; Phil 3:3), holiness (1 Cor 1:2, 7:14, etc.), Passover (1 Cor 5:7), and Temple (1 Cor 6:19). Paul's reinterpretations should, then, properly be heard within the framework of centuries of Jewish *scribal* reflection upon religious practices. Additionally, because Paul's letters form a part of an ongoing dialogue with nonliterate participants in the early house churches, one should be attuned to the differences between Paul's point of view and that of his audience, as he seeks to persuade them to adopt his interpretations.

A related approach to the discussion of meaning and sacrifice is that taken by Daniel Ullucci, who questions the appropriateness of the phrase "critique of sacrifice," a term frequently used in the scholarly literature on sacrifice.[40] Like Stowers, Ullucci contrasts the *practice of sacrifice* from the practice of *writing about sacrifice*. People offering a sacrifice need only practical directions on how to carry out the task.

They do not need discursive practices, even though they may attach (multiple) meanings to their actions.[41] Discursive practices characterize literate religious professionals in competition with one another for influence: "Debate over the meaning of sacrifice must be understood as part of this ongoing competition between cultural producers, not as critiques of some essential or universal meaning or purpose of animal sacrifice."[42]

The phenomenon described as "critique" is the wide number of writings in which "the same authors who claim that the gods do not need sacrifice also argue for continued participation in sacrifice."[43] An example of such double vision would be Ps 51:15–19, or on a larger scale Isa 1:1–12 within the context of Isaiah as a whole.[44] Statements directed to God, such as, "you have no delight in sacrifice" are offset by the expressed hope that when Israel is living faithfully, "then you will delight in right sacrifice" (Ps 51:15, 19). According to Ullucci, two aspects of the critique model are fundamentally flawed: it tends to collapse various interpretations of sacrifice into a single category of "critique," and it inscribes

---

40. Ullucci, "Contesting the Meaning of Animal Sacrifice."

41. In fact, the *practice* is so primary that Christians, who became nonsacrificing only with the destruction of the Jerusalem Temple, do not have an explanatory discourse concerning why they do not offer sacrifices until after the composition of the synoptic Gospels, decades after the fall of the Second Temple (ibid., 68).

42. Ibid., 61.

43. Ibid., 57.

44. Ibid., 66.

a modern, Christian supersessionist view of sacrifice upon an ancient interpretive conversation.

As does Stowers, Ullucci grounds sacrifice in basic human practices of reciprocity, where emphasis in the exchange falls upon the ongoing relationship between the two persons involved in the exchange, not on the supposed equality of the things exchanged between them. By the "logic of reciprocity," gods do not have to *need* sacrifices (meat, grain, oil, wine) in any way for these gifts to be nonetheless a crucial means of fostering relationship between gods and humans. Thus, "ancient authors who discuss sacrifice are not critiquing some universal essential meaning of the act. Rather, they are themselves attempting to argue for one particular interpretation."

Ullucci's work is extremely important for weighing the literature on the supposed "critique" or "spiritualization" of sacrifice in biblical Jewish writings. A relatively recent example of this literature is Stephen Finlan's *The Background and Content of Paul's Cultic Atonement Metaphors* (2004).[45] Finlan develops a model for six "levels of spiritualization" that he finds in the Hebrew biblical witness and says that "each level causes or registers a change in sacrificial practice or ideology."[46] Because ideas of spiritualization and critique have been so prominent in the Christian scholarship on sacrifice, it is worth sketching Finlan's schema here, as he brings together in a coherent system the thoughts of many. Finlan's six levels of spiritualization are as follows: (1) The "substitution of one sacrificial offering for another,"[47] such as a historical shift from human to animal sacrifice or the substitution of an animal for a human sacrifice in a particular account.[48] (2) The language describing the import of sacrifice is "increasingly symbolic and moralizing."[49] An example of level two may be found in Philo, *Spec. leg.* 1.277. (3) The "internalization of religious values," claiming that what matters to God is the right attitude. (4) The writer (or speaker) applies

---

45. See also his chapter that contains the scheme of spiritualization, "Spiritualization of Sacrifice in Paul and Hebrews," in *Ritual and Metaphor: Sacrifice in the Bible*, ed. Christian A. Eberhart, RBS 68 (Atlanta: Society of Biblical Literature, 2011), 83–97.

46. Stephen Finlan, *The Background and Content of Paul's Cultic Atonement Metaphors*, AcBib 19 (Atlanta: Society of Biblical Literature, 2004), 63.

47. Ibid., 83.

48. Ibid., 47. Whether or not a history of actual human sacrifice underlies animal sacrifice in most cultures is a point of debate in the scholarly literature on sacrifice.

49. Ibid., 48.

"cultic terms to non-cultic experiences," in a metaphorical way, such as the depiction in 4 Maccabees of the deaths of the Jewish martyrs as bringing about the atonement of Israel, or, in the Pauline literature, Rom 3:25 and 1 Cor 6:19, or Paul's discussion of "true" circumcision (Rom 2:28). In these cases, Finlan says that the important issue is "that the referent be recognized, not that there be unquestioning faith in the cult's literal efficacy."[50] (5) At the fifth and sixth levels, the practice of sacrifice is rejected, and something else comes to replace it. Level Five, characterized by Finlan as "repudiation of sacrifice"[51] is typified by much of the Greek philosophical critique of sacrifice, and is also exemplified in such passages as Amos 5:21–25 and Jer 7:22–23. (6) A spiritually transformed or enlightened life replaces the practice of sacrifice and is seen to be "the real goal of piety."[52]

There are several ways in which Finlan's "levels" do a disservice to interpretation of sacrificial texts. From the outset, the idea of levels evokes the long "evolutionary" conversation once again, and encourages the reader to see level six as the most advanced stage in sacrificial rhetoric. Second, establishing the particular level of an instance of sacrificial discussion masks the way in which a text may manifest different levels simultaneously. Third, most of what Finlan calls "levels" of sacrificial discourse is really just the richness of the conversation itself, drawing out certain themes, and allowing others to recede. Once a text has been assigned to a level, its full meaning may die there, separated from the broader discussion from which it draws its life. The levels conceal the contexts that have provoked these particular interpretations and criticisms.[53]

Finlan describes Paul's use of metaphors of redemption and atonement in relation to the death of Jesus as "anti-types" in relation to the type (sacrifice or payment). He writes, "There is a great difference between Paul's metaphorical appropriation of sacrifice to explain the new way of salvation (thus implicitly replacing the old way), and the revalorization of a sacrificial system that Paul was prepared to abandon."[54] Again he asserts

---

50. Ibid., 51.

51. Ibid., 51.

52. Ibid., 60.

53. Finlan is well aware of critique of his schema. For his rebuttal to Klawans, see ibid., 89.

54. Ibid., 89. Yet he says elsewhere: "The questions of the presence of Level Five spiritualizing (rejection of Jewish cult) in Paul, is complex and difficult. Paul never argues for or against the sacrificial cult. It is certainly not anti-Levitical to use Leviti-

that the "typological interpretation of sacrifice has outlived sacrifice."[55] Ullucci would probably counter such a schema with a single blow: what has been labeled a critique[56] of sacrifice, or spiritualization of sacrifice, is actually a competition among "educated textual specialists"[57] (including Paul) over interpretations and the specialist's status and authority as interpreter. Ullucci's thesis makes far more sense of the biblical evidence: that the people Finlan sees as spiritualizing or replacing sacrifice (e.g., the prophets, Philo, Paul) in fact continued to offer sacrifice. It is more helpful to see the practice of sacrifice remaining relatively stable over time, while interpretations of the practice varied among the specialists. In fact, discussion of proper Temple practice continued and perhaps even intensified after the destruction of the Jerusalem Temple, in the writings of the Mishnah.[58] I also agree with Ullucci that, when discussing Christian writings, chronology is key to understanding the early community's relationship to the Jewish cult, distinguishing pre-70 references to the cult and metaphors drawn from the cult from post-70 rationales for no longer sacrificing.[59] The sacrificial metaphors of Paul that relate to the Jewish sacrificial system draw their rhetorical power precisely from his assumption of the validity of the ongoing sacrificial practices in the Jewish Temple.

Thoughtful presentations and critiques of the wide range of theories on sacrifice are found in many recent treatments of the subject of sacrifice.[60]

---

cal metaphors for the salvation event. To say that Christ is the source of a new blood covenant is to affirm that God was previously working through such a covenant (Ibid., 187).

55. Ibid., 189.

56. In the case of Paul, I am assuming that if it still made sense to portray Paul as participating in the Jerusalem cult by the time Acts was composed, then he most likely did continue to participate in sacrifices when he was in Jerusalem.

57. Ullucci, "Contesting the Meaning of Animal Sacrifice," 58.

58. See the very interesting chapter by Kathryn McClymond, "Don't Cry Over Spilled Blood," in Knust and Várhelyi, *Ancient Mediterranean Sacrifice*, 235–49. There, she argues that "the Mishnah is more than a commentary on the Torah or an explication of the implications of the Torah's instructions. Rather, it establishes a new intellectual system, one that replaces priestly authority and ritual practice with rabbinic authority and ritual argument. Through the shift from instruction regarding priestly ritual practices to debates concerning the correction of priestly error via rabbinic discourse, the axis of Jewish ritual life shifts, reorienting the community to new agents and structures of authority" (244).

59. Ullucci, "Contesting the Meaning of Animal Sacrifice," 67–68.

60. Some examples, in chronological order, are: Douglas, *Purity and Danger*,

The complexity of this scholarly discussion is mirrored in the multiple entailments of sacrificial metaphors in Paul's letters. The preceding sketch offers a variety of themes that may prove helpful in considering Paul's use of sacrificial metaphors in Philippians and 1 Corinthians. Reciprocal gift-giving is the human action that is fundamental to the practice of sacrifice in the Greco-Roman and Jewish contexts. But it is important to distinguish between the fundamental motive of sacrifice (reciprocal gift-giving) and a common element in sacrifices (a festal meal). The communal meal is integral to the Passover sacrifice, which predominates in 1 Corinthians. While the work of some of the scholars mentioned above may not answer the question they were asking (viz., what is the single essential meaning of sacrifice?), their work does give the interpreter an ear for some of the entailments of sacrifice that might otherwise be hard for a nonsacrificer to discern: the potential danger of holiness, the way in which sacrifices serve to order an untidy world, the ordering of gender and social roles in sacrificial practice, relationships of authority and power, the visibility or invisibility of violence, to name a few. When sacrifice is used as a metaphor, these are some of the entailments that will be either heightened or masked in the use of the metaphor.

7–28; de Heusch, *Sacrifice in Africa*, 1–25; Beers, *Women and Sacrifice*, 9–119; Chilton, *The Temple of Jesus*, 3–42. A recent anthology edited by Jeffrey Carter (*Understanding Religious Sacrifice: A Reader* [New York: Continuum, 2003]) makes quick work of getting a sense for the different voices on sacrifice.

5

PHILIPPIANS: SACRIFICIAL GIVING

The relatively brief letter to the Philippians, consisting of only four chapters, offers a chance to try out the theory that attention to metaphors of sacrifice makes sense of the letter as a whole, especially as regards the ethics of life in Christ. The *shelamim* (or sacrifices of well-being) is the name given, in the Jewish tradition, to the basic form of sacrifice in the Hellenistic world, the commensal sacrifice. This sacrifice was often motivated by a spirit of thanksgiving or a desire to celebrate a feast with family and friends. Regarding the letter to the Philippians as a document imbued with metaphorical references to this type of sacrifice helps to clarify some of the thorny issues in its interpretation, such as the letter's unusual juxtaposition of suffering and rejoicing, questions of the document's literary integrity, and issues concerning the ethical import of the so-called Christ Hymn of 2:5–11.

As has been discussed previously in the chapter on metaphor, the foundational metaphors of a culture have a basis in human physicality, such that "up" is connected with life, and with freedom from illness, whereas "down" is connected with illness and death. Consequently, many cultures have developed an "up is good, down is bad" orientation (up is happy, up is honorable, up is rich, etc.). The Christ Hymn of Philippians reverses this very basic set of cultural values, a move that Lakoff and Johnson say will necessarily result in opposition from one's surrounding cultural context. The hymn's downward movement is initiated by a series of choices made by Christ Jesus.[1] All of these choices line up with what was thought

---

1. I agree with White and Schweizer, who interpret μορφή as "condition or 'status,'" as opposed to either 'existence' (ὀυσία) or 'outward appearance' (σχῆμα)" (Michael L. "Morality between Two Worlds: A Paradigm of Friendship in Philippians," in *Greeks, Romans, and Christians: Essays in Honor of Abraham J. Malherbe*, ed. David L. Balch, Everett Ferguson, and Wayne A. Meeks [Minneapolis: Fortress, 1990], 212). Translat-

generally to epitomize "down is bad": slavery, humiliation, death. But it is precisely these choices that bring about God's decision to exalt him, to give him "the name that is above every name." Therefore, ultimately, "up is good" is reaffirmed. But the only way to arrive there is to make the choice to descend in radical obedience to God.

Perhaps most significantly for this particular study, exaltation is visible only with the kind of revelatory sight that can see into heavenly realities. All that is visible of Christ Jesus's earthly life is obedience, slavery, humiliation, and death. It is the revelatory, heavenly view that opens up both his original status and his final vindication and exaltation. The offering of a sacrifice of thanksgiving is a practice that takes concrete elements of this world and translates them into heaven through words, gestures, and smoke. This chapter brings to light the ways in which sacrifices of thanksgiving sound repeatedly and metaphorically throughout the letter to the Philippians, to ground a moral practice of self-offering and debasement, in order to establish the grounds for future glorification by God (3:14, 21).

The Rhetorical Structure of Philippians

Over recent decades scholars have discussed the rhetorical form of Philippians, and in spite of the ongoing question of the unity of the letter, it has been persuasively discussed numerous times as a unitary example of deliberative rhetoric.[2] Here I use the basic structure of Watson and others as a way to locate the metaphors of sacrifice within the letter to the Philippians. The entire letter is the frame in which these metaphors create and receive meaning. Insofar as letters were mainly an oral/aural event in

---

ing μορφή in this way emphasizes the critical reversal of *up* and *down* necessary for understanding the movement of the hymn.

2. See Duane Watson, "A Rhetorical Analysis of Philippians and its Implications for the Unity Question," *NovT* 30 (1998): 57–88, as well as the discussions in Bloomquist (*The Function of Suffering in Philippians*, JSNTSup 78 [Sheffield: Sheffield Academic, 1993]) and Kittredge (*Community and Authority: The Rhetoric of Obedience in the Pauline Tradition*, HTS 45 [Harrisburg, PA: Trinity Press International, 1998]). Watson argues for the unitive view from a *structural* rhetorical perspective. Stowers ("Friends and Enemies in the Politics of Heaven," in *Pauline Theology 1: Thessalonians, Philippians, Galatians, Philemon*, ed. Jouette M. Bassler [Minneapolis: Fortress, 1991]) argues for *thematic* rhetorical unity arising from his characterization of Philippians as a letter of friendship, in which the opening verses of Phil 3 play the important role of contrasting friendship from enmity.

the ancient world, attention must be paid to the ways in which sacrifice sounds, resounds, and harmonizes with other metaphors and themes of the letter. What follows is a simplified map of the occurrence of sacrificial metaphors in Philippians, within the letter's rhetorical framework. Subsequent sections then address how the metaphors function to shape and color the persuasive program of Philippians.

Epistolary Opening (1:1–2): There is only one slight hint of a cultic reference in these two verses, the mention of the "holy ones" (τοῖς ἁγίοις). Holiness is a quality associated with the Jewish Temple, priesthood, and cult, and one of the primary ways for Paul to describe believers in the communities he founded. The word brings to the surface the tension between what Paul's communities had in common with traditional Judaism and what was different about the new gentile communities. It seems that Paul's life-altering "revelation" (Gal 1:16) involved a radically altered interpretation of the cross, from a shameful means of Roman execution to God's instrument for shattering the boundaries[3] between the Jewish community and the rest of the world. Holiness, which had essentially defined the terms of the separation between Jew and gentile, becomes for Paul the characteristic mark of his mostly gentile communities. They are made holy by their manner of life in accordance with their belief in Christ Jesus.

Exordium (1:3–26): A somewhat sacrificial note in this section is sounded in 1:10–11. Here, Paul appears to have in mind an image of the Philippians as a kind of offering, εἰλικρινεῖς καὶ ἀπρόσκοποι, pure and blameless, in the day of Christ. Offerings in the Jerusalem Temple were specifically to be without blemish (ἄμωμος).[4] The additional reference in verse 11 to the "harvest of righteousness" brings to mind the sacrificial calendar of offerings at harvest-time. This vision of the Philippian believers as constituting an offering to God recalls the offering of the gentiles in Isa 66:20, as well as the house of Israel as an offering, in Ezek 20:40–42.

A more complicated sacrificial note is sounded in Paul's discussion of his possible death in 1:20–26. This particular metaphor gains its sacrificial overtones from the accumulated strength of the metaphors that follow it (e.g., 2:8, 17, 27; 3:10). As I will argue subsequently, a letter such as this one was intended to be read many times over, and the metaphors would develop some of their persuasive power in the rereading. Both of these

---

3. This image is expressed most clearly in a second-generation Pauline letter, Eph 2:14.

4. In relation to the sacrifices of well-being in particular, see Lev 3:1, 6.

passages serve rhetorically to cultivate the audience's receptivity and good-will through praise (1:10–11) and pathos (1:20–26).

Narratio (1:27–30): Interestingly, the *narratio*, the succinct statement of the case Paul is making in the letter, contains no sacrificial metaphors. Yet it does contain the image that is the basis for all of the sacrificial metaphors to follow: God's initiating gift that sets all of the rest of the sacrificial gift-giving in motion, "For it has been given to you (ὑμῖν ἐχαρίσθη) on behalf of Christ not only to believe in him, but to suffer for his sake" (1:29). The unnamed giver here is God, who has established this community of believers who are willing to receive even the suffering that comes with the gift of believing. "Conduct your life in a manner worthy of the gospel of Christ" is the leading statement in the *narratio*, a statement that begs the question, "What *is* a manner of life worthy of the gospel of Christ?" Metaphors of sacrifice (principally thank offerings) are central to Paul's creative project of describing unforgettably to the Philippians what it means to live a life worthy of the gospel.

Probatio (2:1–3:21): This section of proof by example is the most dense with sacrificial imagery and overtones. Below it will be seen that the Christ Hymn (2:6–11), the very heart of Philippians, portrays a sacrificial moral pattern of complete self-offering in obedience to God.[5] Following the hymn, there is an inexact echo of 1:10 in 2:15 (ἄμεμπτοι καὶ ἀκέραιοι, τέκνα θεοῦ ἄμωμα). The word ἄμωμα (without blemish) is the technical term that is used in the Septuagint to describe appropriate offerings in the temple. Almost directly following it comes one of the most sharply drawn sacrificial metaphors of the letter: "But if I am being poured out as a libation upon the sacrifice and public offering of your faith, I am glad and rejoice with all of you—and likewise you must be glad and rejoice with me" (2:17–18). This sentence adds an explicit sacrificial note to the examples of self-offering (with the threat of death) that precede and follow it in the stories of Paul, Christ, Timothy, and Epaphroditus.

Peroratio (4:1–20): Gift-giving is one of the major topics of the peroration (4:10–20), and it is toward the end of this discussion of gift-giving that the final explicit sacrificial metaphor is used. Here the gifts the Philippians have sent to Paul via Epaphroditus are likened to "a fragrant offering, a sacrifice acceptable and pleasing to God" (ὀσμὴν εὐωδίας, θυσίαν δεκτήν,

---

5. Pheme Perkins calls the Christ Hymn the "governing metaphor" of Philippians ("Philippians: Theology for the Heavenly Politeuma," in Bassler, *Pauline Theology 1*, 95).

εὐάρεστον τῷ θεῷ, 4:18). As I have said several times before, subsequent readings of this letter would no doubt cause this sacrificial metaphor to sound together with and amplify other instances of gift-giving in the letter.

Epistolary closing: The only sacrificial or cultic language here is "holy" (ἅγιος), as in the letter's opening.

THE LONG-TERM PERSUASIVE POWER OF METAPHOR

In the ancient world, the production and sending of letters was an expensive and time-consuming effort. A letter could cost as much as the week's wages of a skilled laborer[6] and required someone to carry the letter personally to the addressee. The composition and production of a letter like the one from Paul and Timothy to "the holy ones in Christ Jesus in Philippi" (Phil 1:1), was no casual matter. The message of the letter needed not only to convey the significance of the relationship between the two missionaries and the congregation, but also to be persuasive for the moment as well as for the months or years to come. It appears, from the weightiness of the issues addressed in the letter and the care with which they are handled, that the senders intended the letter to provide a focus for moral reflection and deliberation for some time to come. It is within this context, then, that metaphors of sacrifice perform an important rhetorical function.

One of the characteristics of very apt metaphors for the moral life is their predictive power, their ability to suggest patterns of appropriate behavior in circumstances not yet encountered. Janet Martin Soskice says:

> A good metaphor may not simply be an oblique reference to a predetermined subject but a new vision, the birth of a new understanding, a new referential access. A strong metaphor compels new possibilities of vision.... The strong metaphor does not prompt the routine renaming of aspects otherwise identifiable, but suggests new categories of interpretation and hypothesizes new entities, states of affairs, and causal relations.[7]

The metaphor of sacrifice, illustrated by the obedience of Jesus and the actions of Paul and others, provides "a new referential access," giving

---

6. Roughly calculated, according to the information supplied by Bonnie B. Thurston in *Philippians and Philemon*, Sacra Pagina 10 (Collegeville, MN: Liturgical Press, 2005), 25.

7. Janet Martin Soskice, *Metaphor and Religious Language* (Oxford: Clarendon, 1985), 57–58, 62.

coherence to what faithfulness for "holy ones" (Phil 1:1) might entail in various future, unspecified, situations. Sacrifice was a familiar action, a familiar complex of actions, to everyone in Paul's context, pagan or Jew. The Philippians already knew the pattern of offering up in thanksgiving, and then receiving in community, both practically and physically. Every person, gentile or Jew, would have known the pattern of sacrifice from the point of view of the offerer or as a member of the celebrating community.[8] It is this fundamental sacrificial pattern that appears to concern Paul, when he counsels the Philippians, following the Christ Hymn, "therefore," to "work out your own salvation with fear and trembling" (Phil 2:12). With these words, he invites them into a pattern of sacrificial behavior at once literally familiar and metaphorically new.

The word "pattern" is used here deliberately, to signify a set of actions whose basic logic might provide guidance for other actions in quite different circumstances. Stephen Fowl's use of the word "exemplar"[9] functions somewhat similarly, but not exactly. For him the Christ hymn "functions as an exemplar within Paul's argument."[10] I would argue that the *shelamim* sacrifices (sacrifices of thanksgiving) constitute a pattern of offering that Paul applies metaphorically and imaginatively as a guide for the actions of the Philippians. Jesus's choices (to empty, to take the form of a slave, to humble himself, to become obedient to the point of death) embody this sacrificial pattern, a pattern also imitated by Paul, Timothy, and Epaphroditus. Rather than establish the actions and motivations of Jesus Christ as the prime exemplar for the Philippians, Paul actually sets the pattern

---

8. Paul is depending upon a basic level of recognition of sacrificial patterns on the part of all the believers in Philippi, though, as will be demonstrated in the discussion of Phil 2:5–11, it seems that the Levitical preference for the whole burnt offering as the paradigmatic sacrifice (the sacrifice that represents the most complete dedication to God) is operative here. Paul is using metaphors that communicate superficially across the Pagan/Jewish divide, but at a deeper level his communication is colored by his own Jewish experiences and interpretations of sacrifice. Whether the Philippian community was able to sort all of this out is anyone's guess.

9. Fowl (summarizing the view of T. S. Kuhn) defines an exemplar as, "a concrete formulation or experiment which is recognized and shared by all scientists" (*The Story of Christ in the Ethics of Paul: An Analysis of the Function of the Hymnic Material in the Pauline Corpus*, JSTNTSup 36 [Sheffield: Sheffield Academic, 1990], 93). In ethics, one is encouraged to "draw the appropriate analogies" in basing one's actions on those of an exemplar (Fowl, *Story of Christ*, 95).

10. Ibid., 95.

of the *shelamim* as the example, a metaphorical model for an appropriate dynamic and reciprocal relationship with God. Paul himself, Jesus, Timothy, and Epaphroditus are all possible examples of the almost endless number of ways that the pattern might be embodied as the faithful "work out their own salvation" (2:12).

In her commentary on the Gospel of Mark, Mary Ann Tolbert makes the point that the parable of the sower (Mark 4:3–9) functions as a kind of key to the rest of the Gospel, and that this function of the passage has been obscured by the tendency of scholars to read the parables generally as *"parables of Jesus* rather than as *parables of the Gospels.*"[11] Something analogous is true of the Christ Hymn in Philippians. Theologians in particular have shown interest in the Christology implied by the hymn, and biblical scholars have explored the possibilities of the pre-history (if any) of the passage. But the rhetorical function of the hymn as a key to most of the letter's ethical counsels, and the hymn's resonance in the rest of the letter, have not been completely plumbed without more attention to the sacrificial pattern it embodies. It is widely acknowledged that the hymn provides a model of obedience and humility that is mirrored in the actions of Paul (Phil 1:23–26, 3:7–15), Timothy (2:19–24) and Epaphroditus (2:25–30), but it will be seen that the hymn reverberates even more strongly through the letter when it is linked with the sacrificial metaphors related to it.

Metaphors of sacrifice, and of the *shelamim*, or sacrifices of thanksgiving in particular, play an important role in structuring the ongoing moral reflection of the Philippian church, with the so-called Christ Hymn as the central piece in setting forth the sacrificial pattern. Each of the following sections of this chapter will explore how sacrificial metaphors resound with major themes of the letter to shape the community's understanding of their situation (the exigence) and their responses to it (a manner of life worthy of the gospel). As I have said above, the basic commensal sacrifice was carried out all over the Mediterranean in Paul's time. Its elements— offering, libation, meal—can be referred to by Paul without a great deal of explanation to non-Jews.

Moving into discussion of the Christ Hymn, it becomes important to reiterate a point made in chapter 3. Rhetorically, the book of Leviticus

---

11. Mary Ann Tolbert, *Sowing the Gospel: Mark's World in Literary-Historical Perspective* (Minneapolis: Fortress, 1989), 128, emphasis original.

gives prominence to the whole burnt offering, by placing it first, as though it were the most common and basic sacrificial pattern.[12] The offerings of thanksgiving were actually far more numerous, but the prioritization of the holocaust serves an interpretive function toward all of the sacrifices, namely, stressing the costly wholeheartedness of the sacrifier. As a person trained in the Jewish scribal tradition, Paul would very likely have adopted the interpretation put forward in the structure of Leviticus: emphasis on an offering completely consumed by fire, rather than the more typical animal sacrifice that would result in roasted meat for a banquet. Paul imports this interpretation into his understanding of sacrifice in general, whether Jewish or pagan, whether a holocaust or a thank-offering—though his hearers may well not have. For Paul, sacrificial imagery entails a total self-offering. This interpretation of sacrifice may be one of the reasons that the themes of suffering and death are so prominent in Philippians, together with notes of joy and thanksgiving. Paul puts forward a pattern of sacrifice that is familiar to all, but his own experience of it is colored by his Jewish scribal context. Thus, it is this interpretation, derived from Leviticus, that colors his development of sacrificial metaphors, perhaps most specifically the thank-offering pattern portrayed in the Christ Hymn.

SACRIFICE, KENOSIS, AND PHILIPPIANS 2:5–11

The heart of Paul's letter to the Philippians is the "hymn"[13] of 2:5–11. How much of Phil 2:5–11 is traditional and how much is Pauline is the subject of much discussion, but echoes of it reverberate through the language and images of the rest of the letter.[14] Although the hymn contains no explicit sacrificial metaphors, commentators almost always characterize Christ's

---

12. See the discussion of the work of James Watts in chapter 3.

13. The classic discussion of the possibility of Phil 2:6–11 having been a pre-existing piece of Christian tradition, possibly a hymn, that Paul incorporated into the letter, is in Martin's *Carmen Christi* (Cambridge: Cambridge University Press, 1967). A good, more-recent summary of various points of view is in Fee's commentary on Philippians (*Paul's Letter to the Philippians*, rev. ed., NICNT 11 [Grand Rapids, Eerdmans, 1995]); see esp. the notes on 192–94). If the words of Phil 2:6–11 are substantially those of a hymn held in common by Paul and the Philippians, what a pointed choice that would be in a letter focused on issues of harmony in a Christian community. For the sake of simplicity, I have chosen to refer consistently to Phil 2:6–11 as the Christ Hymn, a commonly used designation for the passage.

14. See the chart of "Echoes of Philippians 2:6–11 throughout the Letter" in

actions in this passage as "sacrificial" or "self sacrificial."[15] Given that fact, it is interesting to note as well that Philippians contains some of the most colorful and explicit sacrificial metaphors not related to atonement in the entire Pauline corpus (2:17–18; 4:15–20). Fee has said of the metaphor of libation at 2:17 that "none of this is easy to decipher, in part because of the context and in part because Paul's use of sacrificial imagery is so flexible that usage elsewhere is of little or no help here."[16] In a note to the same verse he writes, "Perhaps we should confess that we are fishing for answers to a very difficult metaphor, on which certainty will be hard to come by."[17]

My purpose here is to ascertain whether there are grounds for describing the actions of "Christ Jesus" (Phil 2:5) in the Philippians hymn as sacrificial, and then to examine the relationship between the hymn and the clear uses of sacrificial metaphors elsewhere in the letter. As has been noted, most commentators use the language of sacrifice when describing both the actions of Christ Jesus in kenosis and the behavior Paul encourages the Philippians to adopt when he counsels them to "do nothing from selfish

Michael J. Gorman, *Apostle of the Crucified Lord: A Theological Introduction to Paul and His Letters* (Grand Rapids: Eerdmans, 2004), 419–21.

15. Gorman, *Apostle of the Crucified Lord*, 423; Fee, *Philippians*, 197, 226; Carolyn Osiek, *Philippians, Philemon*, ANTC 11 (Nashville: Abingdon, 2000), 69; Karl Donfried and Howard Marshall, *The Theology of the Shorter Pauline Letters*, New Testament Theology (Cambridge: Cambridge University Press), 136, among many others. An exception is Hurtado, the nature of whose work on the Christ Hymn requires special care with regard to the language of religious practice. Hurtado also notes that "in the description of Jesus's self-abnegation in vv. 6–8, there is no direct indication of his doing this for the sake of others." He emphasizes, "*the redemptive efficacy of his actions is not in view* in these verses [Phil 2:6–11]" ("A 'Case Study' in Early Devotion to Jesus: Philippians 2:6–11," in *How on Earth Did Jesus Become a God? Historical Questions about Earliest Devotion to Jesus* [Grand Rapids: Eerdmans, 2005], 104). The latter point is important for being clear that, while the death of Jesus might be seen as sacrificial in some way in the Christ Hymn, there is no indication that a sacrifice of *atonement* is being implied. It is the kenotic pattern of Jesus's choices that is being commended to the Philippians, and that might be in some way construed as "sacrificial."

16. Fee, *Philippians*, 251. I am not certain exactly what Fee means by "usage elsewhere" being "flexible." As I am demonstrating here, Paul's use of sacrificial metaphors is flexible, in that the metaphors are tailored to the purposes of the passage at hand and the overall purposes of the letter in which they occur. Deciphering what Paul means with the use of a sacrificial metaphor is best done locally (within a given letter) and not globally (by developing a supposed "theology of sacrifice" in Paul's letters generally).

17. Ibid.

ambition or empty conceit, but in humility regard others as better than yourselves" (Phil 2:3). In the popular sense, of course, sacrifice is taken to be anything that involves giving up something of one's own for a greater good. In this general sense, then, both 2:3–4 and 2:6–8 may be described as sacrificial. There is a pattern of self-offering put forward. But are there any closer linguistic ties with sacrificial imagery in 2:6–8 that might provoke the use of the more explicit metaphors at 2:17–18 and 4:15–20? Does the letter suggest an overarching concern on Paul's part to put forward a pattern of sacrificial behavior as a model for the Philippians, of which Paul (3:4b–11), Timothy (2:19–22), and Epaphroditus (2:25–30) would serve as examples?

Fee points to Isa 53:12 as an important "general" literary background for Phil 2:7.[18] As he puts it, "Just as *harpagmon* requires no object for him [Christ Jesus] to 'seize,' but rather points to what is the opposite of God's character, so Christ did not empty himself *of* anything; he simply 'emptied *himself*,' poured himself out."[19] While the Septuagint describes the "servant of God" (παῖς θεοῦ)[20] as having *handed his life over* to death (ἀνθ᾿ ὧν παρεδόθη εἰς θάνατον ἡ ψυχὴ αὐτοῦ), the Masoretic Text reads that he *emptied, or poured his life out*, unto death (הערה למות נפשו). Retaining Fee's qualified statement, that Isa 45–53 serves as a "general background" to the Christ Hymn, these interesting correspondences of language and concepts between the two texts may open up for the modern reader some of the sacrificial connotations of words like ἐκένωσεν, παρεδόθη, and הערה. One of the differences worth nothing between the passage from Isaiah and the Christ Hymn is the way in which the hymn's use of ἐκένωσεν clearly has incarnation as its purpose,[21] not death (even though

---

18. Ibid., 212.

19. Ibid., 210.

20. This difference in nomenclature between Christ Jesus, the δοῦλος, and the παῖς θεοῦ has been noted. As Fee says, "This linguistic difference is the most frequently given reason for rejecting the idea [of a correspondence between Isaiah 45–53 and Philippians 2:6–11] altogether (e.g. Plummer)" (Fee, *Philippians*, 212 n. 88).

21. See Ernst Käsemann, "Kritische Analyse von Phil 2:5–11," *ZTK* 47 (1950): 313–60; trans. Alice F. Carse, *Journal for Theology and the Church* 5 (1968): 66; and also Fowl, "as the verses to come situate Christ's activity within the human realm, one might think that Christ's taking the form of a slave is a reference to the incarnation, in which Christ became subject to the things to which humanity is subject, including, ultimately, death. This might be further supported by v.8, which further specifies the nature of Christ's obedience. This, however, reflects a misunderstanding of some of the

death is the ultimate result of Christ's self-emptying); while it is said of the παῖς θεοῦ that he clearly παρεδόθη εἰς θάνατον, or הערה למות נפשו. At this point it is worth flagging merely that δίδωμι or παραδίδωμι might point toward a self-giving in either life or death (see esp. Gal 2:20 but also Rom 4:25; 8:32; Gal 1:4).

Martin's frustration with comparisons to Isa 53 underscores just why it is important to sort out which sacrifice is serving as the vehicle of the metaphor. I quote him at some length, because his consternation is so closely linked with the purposes of this study:

> It is strange that, if the author of the hymn had wished to point to the Servant of Isaiah as the prototype of the Church's Redeemer, he should have omitted just those features in His humiliation which give to His sufferings their eternal value, viz., His sinbearing, vicarious work. While the obedience of Christ is mentioned in the hymn, no hint is given as to how this obedience provides a rationale of his redemptive work (as in Romans 5); and no clear statement is made of the interest which sinful men may have in His redemption. There is no allusion to the personal benefits which the Servant's work makes available.... It is singular that, if the author wished to show that Christ was the fulfilment of the Servant, he should have left as implicit only what stands out most clearly in the fourth song—the Servant's atoning ministry.[22]

For Martin, a sacrificial reference means necessarily a reference to an *atoning* sacrifice. But a reference to a sacrifice of atonement would have worked against Paul's purposes in Philippians. The point of the sacrificial metaphors in Philippians is quite different from the reference to atonement in Rom 3:25, where the subject at hand is how God has created a justified community across the Jewish/gentile divide. In Philippians, Paul is using the pattern of a thank-offering to embed the Philippians imaginatively in a cycle of giving and receiving with God, in which their willingness to prioritize their neighbor's good becomes their thank offering to God in

---

older English translations of v.8 which declare the Christ was obedient 'unto death.' The Greek here indicates the extent of Christ's obedience, not the object to which Christ is obedient (hence NRSV's 'obedient to the point of death'). Thus, it becomes clear that in his obedience, even to the point of death, Christ was obedient to God" (*Philippians*, Two Horizons New Testament Commentary [Grand Rapids, Eerdmans, 2005], 97).

22. Martin, *Carmen Christi*, 212–13.

exchange for God's gift to them of believing in Christ and the hope of future glory (salvation).

The pattern of sacrificial self-giving (emptying, pouring oneself out), in obedience to God, is established in the hymn as the central practice of Christ Jesus, and is commended to the Philippians as a template for their own practice (2:3–5). Does this confluence of images account, in part, for Paul's description of his own action in relation to the Philippians as a "libation upon the sacrifice and priestly service of [their] faithfulness" (Ἀλλὰ εἰ καὶ σπένδομαι ἐπὶ τῇ θυσίᾳ καὶ λειτουργίᾳ τῆς πίστεως ὑμων) (2:17a)? Paul appears to see his apostolic actions toward the Philippians as a kind of sacred "pouring out," a libation, added to their own offering of a willingness to suffer (cf. Phil 1:29–30) for their faith. Perhaps his reference here is to his imprisonment. There is no reason to see Paul's libation as consisting only or primarily of his death. He is concerned here with a model for unstinting Christian practice, though death may always remain a possibility when conditions require it.[23] Part of the richness of the metaphor of sacrifice in such instances is its ability to sound notes of both life and death, both joy and relinquishment, in a complex harmony.[24]

Paul's image of sacrifice and libation in 2:17 sets the actions of the Philippians as the primary offering, with his partnership with them forming the accompanying libation, an important element, but not the principal one. In a subtle way, that movement of expressing the work into which he is pouring his life as not the *central* element, but merely the accompaniment to the self-offering of the Philippians, models the ethical move he asks the Philippians to make. As he asks them to put the interests of others (τὰ ἑτέρων) at the center of their concern, pushing their own needs and desires to the side (Phil 2:4), he expresses their faithfulness as the center of his attention, with his work to the side, as the libation. In this gesture, he underscores his role as the slave (δοῦλος) of Christ Jesus (Phil 1:1).

The sacrifices described in Numbers give some indication of the kind of sacrificial imagery that is the reference for Phil 2:17, and also displays verbal connections with 1:10, 2:15 and 4:18:

---

23. In this matter I agree with Osiek, *Philippians, Philemon*, 73.

24. Just how closely death may be associated with the image of pouring out may be seen in the uses of the metaphor at 2 Tim 4:6 (Εγω γὰρ ἤδη σπένδομαι, καὶ ὁ καιρὸς τῆς ἀναλύσεως μου ἐφέστηκεν.) and Ign. *Rom.* 2:2 (πλέον μοι μὴ παράσχησθε τοῦ σπονδισθῆναι θεῷ ὡς ἔτι θυσιατήριον ἕτοιμόν ἐστιν).

Καὶ ἐλάλησεν κύριος πρὸς Μωυσῆν λέγων ἔντειλαι τοῖς υἱοῖς Ἰσραήλ καὶ
ἐρεῖς πρὸς αὐτοὺς λέγων τὰ δῶρά μου δόματά μου καρπώματά μου εἰς
ὀσμὴν εὐωδίας διατηρήσετε προσφέρειν ἐμοὶ ἐν ταῖς ἑορταῖς μου καὶ ἐρεῖς
πρὸς αὐτούς ταῦτα τὰ καρπώματα ὅσα προσάξετε κυρίῳ ἀμνοὺς ἐνιαυσίους
ἀμώμους δύο τὴν ἡμέραν εἰς ὁλοκαύτωσιν ἐνδελεχῶς τὸν ἀμνὸν τὸν ἕνα
ποιήσεις τὸ πρωὶ καὶ τὸν ἀμνὸν τὸν δεύτερον ποιήσεις τὸ πρὸς ἑσπέραν καὶ
ποιήσεις τὸ δέκατον τοῦ οιφι σεμίδαλιν εἰς θυσίαν ἀναπεποιημένην ἐν ἐλαίῳ
ἐν τετάρτῳ τοῦ ιν ὁλοκαύτωμα ἐνδελεχισμοῦ ἡ γενομένη ἐν τῷ ὄρει Σινα
εἰς ὀσμὴν εὐωδίας κυρίῳ καὶ σπονδὴν αὐτοῦ τὸ τέταρτον τοῦ ιν τῷ ἀμνῷ τῷ
ἁγίῳ σπείσεις σπονδὴν σικερα κυρίῳ καὶ τὸν ἀμνὸν τὸν δεύτερον ποιήσεις τὸ
πρὸς ἑσπέραν κατὰ τὴν θυσίαν αὐτοῦ καὶ κατὰ τὴν σπονδὴν αὐτοῦ ποιήσετε
εἰς ὀσμὴν εὐωδίας κυριω. (Num 28:1–10, LXX; common vocabulary or
cognates with Philippians underlined)

Numbers 28 occurs just following the census of the new generation of
Israelites, not those who had rebelled against God in the wilderness,
but those who were born in the wilderness, and who will come into the
promised land without a backward glance at Egypt (Num 26). Joshua is
chosen by God and commissioned by Moses to lead the Israelites (Num
27:12–23), and then God directs Moses concerning the proper offerings to be made when the people come into the land (Num 28:1–29:40).
As can be seen above, this language concerning the sacrifices is echoed
by Paul sporadically in the letter to the Philippians. The effect of this
scattering of sacrificial references is to link the actions of Paul and the
Philippians with the ancient record of God's direction of the Israelites
on their coming into the land, even as the Philippians are called to see
the place where they now live as the ground upon which they will enact
their heavenly citizenship (Phil 3:20). They are fulfilling, in their various
offerings, the most basic requests of God: the supplies they have sent
to Paul during his imprisonment become ὀσμὴν εὐωδίας, θυσίαν δεκτήν,
εὐάρεστον τῷ θεῷ (Phil 4:18); their suffering is perceived as θυσία καὶ
λειτουργία; and their role in the world, when set upon the widest horizon, is a pure offering, εἰλικρινεῖς καὶ ἀπρόσκοποι (Phil 1:10), ἄμεμπτοι καὶ
ἀκέραιοι (Phil 2:15).

Some examples from the writings of Philo may serve to illustrate the
relationship between daily faithfulness and the sacrificial cult that could
form an appropriate context for Paul's thought in Philippians. The essence
of Philo's spiritual teaching on sacrifice might be summed up in the following sentence: "The true altar of God is the thankful soul of the wise person"
(πρὸς ἀλήθειαν τοῦ θεοῦ θυσιατήριαν ἐστιν ἡ εὐχάριστος τοῦ σοφοῦ ψυχή,

Spec. 1.287 [Colson]). Elsewhere he speaks of "that perfect and wholly sound frame of mind of which the whole-burnt-offering is a symbol" (πρὸς ὁλόκληρον καὶ παντελῆ διάθεσιν, ἧς ἡ ὁλόκαυτος θυσία σύμβολον, *Spec. leg.* 1.253). The life of the wise person is the place where heaven and earth meet, the place of daily reconciliation between God and the human being. In a way analogous to Paul's counsel of Rom 12:1–2, this "thankful soul" of the sage (εὐχάριστος τοῦ σοφοῦ ψυχή) is developed by the regular habits of the wise person, as he or she discerns a path of faithfulness: "And indeed though the worshippers (those who "practice holiness," ἀσκηταῖς ὁσιότητος) bring nothing else, in bringing themselves they offer the best sacrifice, the full and perfect sacrifice of noble living (κἂν μέντοι μηδὲν ἕτερον κομίζωσιν, αὐτοὺς φέροντες πλήρωμα καλοκἀγαθίας τελειότατον τὴν ἀρίστην ἀνάγουσι θυσίαν, *Spec.* 1.271–272 [Colson]).

For Paul, what the "sacrifice of noble living" looks like has been reconfigured by the sequence described in the Christ Hymn. The additional examples of Paul (esp. 1:20–26), Timothy (esp. 2:21), and Epaphroditus (esp. 2:30) make the subsequent link from the sacrificial pattern of Christ Jesus to the sacrificial pattern commended to the Philippians. In each case, the sacrifier relinquishes his or her personal desire or best interest for that of another. This downwardly mobile series of decisions constitutes the pattern of living that Paul calls conducting oneself ἀξίως τοῦ εὐαγγελίου τοῦ χριστοῦ (1:27). Fee calls Jesus Christ "the ultimate model of the self-sacrificing love to which he is calling the Philippians,"[25] and underscores the connection between the model and the community by saying that, "Discipleship in the present calls for servanthood, self-sacrifice for the sake of others."[26] But what is so important to grasp in Paul's establishment of this pattern through the interplay of sacrificial metaphors and their entailments is that the pattern of making a sacrificial offering is one that is already deeply, physically familiar to the Philippians. Paul is using that familiarity to suggest moral patterns with which they are not yet familiar, but which he hopes they may come to understand as Timothy and Epaphroditus have. Thus, the church at Philippi may come to be, as Paul says of the Corinthians, a "sweet fragrance," from life to life (2 Cor 2:14–17).

25. Fee, *Philippians*, 226.
26. Ibid., 197.

GIFT-GIVING, FRIENDSHIP, AND SACRIFICE

The overview of interpretations of sacrifice in chapter 4 introduced the early anthropological study of sacrifice done by Edward Burnett Tylor, in which he described the most primitive (in his view) sacrifices as essentially a form of human-divine gift-exchange. The idea of the centrality of reciprocal gift-exchange in sacrifice has resurfaced in the recent work of Stanley Stowers and Daniel Ullucci. If the Christ Hymn, and Paul's counsels developing from it, are to be read as embodying a sacrificial pattern, can they be seen as demonstrating the qualities of gift-exchange? Further, if so, what is the rationale behind such an exchange? What are its rules and expectations? How does it function rhetorically within the letter to the Philippians?

Between ourselves and ancient practices of reciprocity lies a modern philosophical conversation about gift-giving that has posited the logical impossibility of genuine gift-giving. Troels Engberg-Pedersen traces this conversation back to the Kantian ideal of the moral act as completely lacking in self-interest.[27] Hence, a gift, in order to be a true gift, must be completely gratuitous. Such was the point of view of Derrida and Bourdieu, who came by different routes to the conclusion that a true (or "pure") gift is impossible. But this relatively modern conversation does not at all reflect the ancient view of gift-giving, as represented by the work of Seneca, who was roughly contemporaneous with Paul.[28] A comparison of Seneca's *De beneficiis* to the modern philosophical conversation reveals the way in which the modern conversation concentrates upon the inviolability of the gift itself (which must remain untainted by the giver's self-interest), while the ancient conversation focuses more upon human care for the recipient of a gift.[29] The ancient conversation manifests a desirable complexity among the relationships involved in

---

27. Engberg-Pedersen, "Gift-Giving and Friendship: Seneca and Paul in Romans 1–8 on the Logic of God's Χάρις and Its Human Response," *HTS* 101 (2008): 15–44.

28. I agree with Engberg-Pedersen that there is no need to posit that Paul knew of Seneca; the two are drawing upon widely accepted cultural norms relating to giving and receiving.

29. For example, Seneca speaks against a giver's constantly referring to the gift: "Repeated references to our services wounds and crushes the spirit of the other" (*Ben.* 2.11.1 [Basore]). He also chastises the giver for giving out of arrogance or pride, which justly results in ill-will rather than gratitude (*Ben.* 2.11.6, 2.12.13 [Basore]).

gift-giving, above all in the cultivation of reciprocity.[30] In *De beneficiis*, Seneca outlines the three necessary elements in reciprocity: the giving of a gift, the appropriately grateful receiving of a gift, and the return of a gift. Gift-giving is always circular for Seneca, and the benefits of gift-giving permeate the whole circle of giving, receiving, and reciprocating. Self-interest and other-interest are completely intertwined, and friendship is strengthened every time the circle turns again. Using the image of the three Graces, Seneca writes:

> Some would have it appear that there is one for bestowing a benefit, another for receiving it, and a third for returning it.... Why do the sisters hand in hand dance in a ring which returns upon itself? For the reason that a benefit passing in its course from hand to hand returns nevertheless to the giver; the beauty of the whole is destroyed if the course is anywhere broken, and it has most beauty if it is continuous and maintains an uninterrupted succession. (*Ben.* 1.3.3–4 [Basore])[31]

Engberg-Pedersen justifiably questions the modern idea of the "pure" gift as opposed to the "real" gift (the gift implicated in the circle of reciprocity), which was Seneca's concern.

I claimed early on, in agreement with Stowers and Ullucci, that the fundamental sacrificial movement is to enter this cycle of reciprocal gift-giving in an ongoing relationship with God. In a distinctly theological vein, John Milbank also discusses gift-giving in antiquity and now, exploring some of the philosophical and theological ramifications of reciprocity in an essay on the Trinity that may offer some interesting insights into

---

30. "The first fruit of a benefaction is the consciousness of it; a man experiences this from carrying out his gift as he wished; the second and third are, respectively, the glory of it and the things which may be bestowed in exchange" (*Ben.* 2.33.3 [Basore]). While gratitude is all that is strictly owed on the receipt of a benefit, the cycle of giving requires a reciprocal gift at some future date: "Goodwill we have repaid with goodwill; for the object we still owe an object. And so, although we say that he who receives a benefit gladly has repaid it, we, nevertheless, also bid him return some gift similar to the one he received" (*Ben.* 2.35.1 [Basore]).

31. See also the comparison of gift-giving to a ball game in *Ben.* 2.32.1–4. Receiving a gift and being thankful for it is like nimbly catching a ball. Such a person cannot be said not to be a good player, as he or she has just expertly caught the ball, yet the game is deficient if the ball is not thrown back and forth.

Paul's use of the Christ Hymn as a sacrificial moral pattern, a sacrificial exercise of gift-exchange, in Philippians.[32]

Milbank begins by noting the sixteenth-century English phrase "giff-gaff" for the giving and receiving of gifts, a locution that "suggests that taking differs from giving merely by a single vowel."[33] Indeed, "what is crucial is not a distinction of actor and respondent, but the shuttling process of to-and-fro itself."[34] In the ancient period, and in premodern societies generally, gift-giving is understood to be rightly reciprocal, relational, a necessary part of living in community, and not primarily calculated for individual gain. Unspoken rules of reciprocity, which guard against the giving and receiving of gifts becoming a simple contractual arrangement are, first, that there be a delay in the act of reciprocity, and, secondly, that the gift given in exchange must be "different, and although perhaps equivalent, not obviously equivalent."[35] Milbank continues,

> Correct use of a gift always involves in some sense a "giving back," if not to the individual donor then at least to the wider social forces which that individual represents, such that "return" can occur by way of a "giving in turn," or a "passing on" of the original gesture. Non-identical repetition, therefore, includes not only the return of an equivalent but different gift, but also a non-exact *mimesis* (but therefore all the more genuinely exact) of the first gesture in unpredictably different circumstances, at unpredictable times and to unpredictably various recipients.[36]

By contrast, modern notions of gift-giving are remarkably purist, if not puritan. As we have seen, in the modern period there is profound suspicion toward almost any gift, for, in order to be a true gift, it must be a "free" gift, completely devoid of any compulsion in the giving, the receiving, or the return. The modern suspicion of gift-giving, which sees self-deception in almost every attempt to describe a gift as freely given, precisely obscures what was felt as good in the ancient practice of gift-exchange, namely, the

---

32. Milbank, "Can a Gift Be Given? Prolegomena to a Future Trinitarian Metaphysic," *Modern Theology* 11 (1995): 119–61.
33. Ibid., 119.
34. Ibid., 120.
35. Ibid., 125.
36. Ibid.

mutuality that binds people together in community.[37] Milbank calls such purism, "unbiblical for all that it seeks to be super-biblical."[38]

Reciprocal gift-giving is basic to the movements of sacrifice, but gift-giving is also an important element in ancient customs of friendship. A lively twenty-year scholarly conversation has been taking place concerning whether or not Philippians is most appropriately designated a letter of friendship according to ancient rhetorical forms. In his argument *for* this classification, Stanley Stowers enumerates the themes and stock motifs of letters of friendship: expressions of affection and longing while absent; moral exhortation; the ideal of unity among friends, their working together for common goals, their *koinonia* in the practical realities of life; the seeking of the other's advantage; the obligation to be engaged in reciprocal giving; agreement; vilification of enemies.[39] In addition, he notes that ideas of friendship infiltrate the political order, where citizens or whole nations may be encouraged to exercise friendship with one another. In short, he says, "The accumulation of the language of friendship [in Philippians] is unmistakable."[40] Indeed, the quotations he offers from ancient sources echo the language of Philippians in an uncanny way. Stowers's work also helps to make sense of what had been felt to be jarring in Philippians, namely, the shift in tone at 3:2. According to Stowers, the sharp descriptions of enemies in Phil 3:2 and 3:18–19 are part of a "well-known hortatory strategy in its use of contrasting models."[41]

---

37. Two examples Milbank cites in depth are Bourdieu, whose Marxist critique of gift-exchange suggests that "what is going on is a massive pretense by all parties (not, of course, a deliberate or conscious one) that it is not a purely economic, material and self-interested force which drives the system"; and Derrida, who considered all gift-exchange "incoherent" as it is always "contaminated" by "interested contract" (Millbank, "Can a Gift Be Given," 129–30).

38. Ibid., 130.

39. Stanley K. Stowers, "Friends and Enemies in the Politics of Heaven: Reading Theology on Philippians," in *Pauline Theology 1: Thessalonians, Philippians, Galatians, Philemon*, ed. Jouette M. Bassler (Minneapolis: Fortress, 1991). Against Stowers's view, see Todd Still, "More Than Friends? The Literary Classification of Philippians Revisited," *PRSt* 39 (2012): 53–66. Still argues for a mixed classification of Philippians.

40. Stowers, "Friends and Enemies," 112.

41. Ibid., 115. He goes on to say, "The fundamental architecture of the letter is one of antithetical models, most often contrasting Paul and his enemies. The letter urges the reader to emulate one kind of behavior and avoid or oppose another kind."

On the other hand, there are ways in which Philippians does not feel like a "friendly" letter by today's standards. Joseph Marchal has written on the ways in which ancient ideas about friendship were implicated in social distinctions of class and gender, such that women or the lower classes would not be included in conventional discussions of friendship.[42] He speculates that the women and lower class members of Paul's churches would not have felt very friendly toward Paul's coercive language of friendship or his repeated establishment of himself as a moral model. Marchal's critique is not of the designation of Philippians as a letter of friendship, but of a misunderstanding by contemporary interpreters who unwittingly read their own standards of warm personal friendship into a rhetorical form that was embedded in ancient hierarchical structures.

Gift-giving and friendship were deeply intertwined in the ancient world. As Engberg-Pedersen says, "gift-giving presupposes the kind of emotional mutual relationship between giver and receiver that makes it "the *beginning* of friendship."[43]

Seneca discusses the risks that are attendant to both giving and receiving, and the necessity for making a reasoned decision about the people whom you are willing to engage in this way.[44] The giver risks in one way: "So far from its being right for us to give a benefit from a motive of self-interest, often, as I have said, the giving of it must involve one's own loss and risk" (*Ben.* 4.12.2 [Basore]). Furthermore, the receiver risks in another way: "even though there should be no unfortunate consequences…, yet it is grievous torture to be under obligation to someone whom you object to" (*Ben.* 2.18.3 [Basore]). The riskiness of giving and receiving is one of the ways in which gift-giving and sacrifice are related. The risks inherent in gift-giving are increased when the divine is one of the parties. The Jewish sacrificial and holiness codes were a way to minimize the risks: *these are the kinds of gifts God wants, on such-and-such occasions, offered in such-and-such a way.* The Philippians are being invited into a cycle of gift-giving with God that does not have the comfort of these controls.

---

42. Joseph A. Marchal, "With Friends Like These…: A Feminist Rhetorical Reconsideration of Scholarship and the Letter to the Philippians," *JSNT* 29 (2006): 245–55.

43. Engberg-Pedersen, "Gift-Giving and Friendship," 99, emphasis original.

44. "Now [Reason's] first precept will be that it is not necessary for us to receive from everybody…. Let us see, in fact, whether it does not require even greater discernment to find a man to whom we ought to owe, than one on whom we ought to bestow a benefit" (*Ben.* 2.18.2–3 [Basore]).

As I said earlier, the "gift" that initiates the cycle of giving and receiving for the Philippians is God's gift to them, as gentiles, to be believers in Christ (Phil 1:29, in the *narratio*). Through this gift, God initiates a friendship with the Philippians, offering them the potential for holiness, and inviting them into the cycle of giving and receiving. The Christ Hymn, in a metaphorically sacrificial way, illustrates Jesus's offering of himself in obedience to God (his reciprocal gift to God). The Philippians are invited to witness Christ's gift of himself as a paradigm of sacrificial giving, a total gift of the self for the purposes of God. The sacrificial paradigm displays the risks involved in giving and receiving with God: the downward movement, slavery, humiliation, and possibly death—and also the ultimate glory, as God responds lavishly to the gift offered.

L. Michael White has drawn attention to Lucian's *Toxaris* as an important key to understanding how the Christ Hymn might have been heard as a paradigm of friendship by its original hearers. In a contest between two men over who can tell the best story to epitomize the Greek ideal of friendship, one tells the story of a nobleman who befriended his slave. When the slave was wrongfully imprisoned, the nobleman not only cared for him, but eventually "threw away his wealth, status, and freedom" by having himself arrested so that he could join the slave in prison until both were freed. As White summarizes, "in the present form of the Philippian hymn, Christ's 'emptying' and 'humbling' himself to take the 'form of a slave' is being portrayed, at least in part, as an all-surpassing act of selfless love—that is, the supreme virtue of friendship."[45] White's conclusion brings up the possibility that Christ's gift to God was also an initiating act of friendship to gentiles.

The Philippians are being invited to enter the cycle of giving and receiving in patterns of self-offering that are appropriate to their own station and challenges, using the examples of Timothy (2:19–24) and Epaphroditus (2:25–30) to spur their imaginations. What is important in reciprocity is what Milbank called "non-exact mimesis." The "gift" of behavior that Paul asks of the Philippians, via his counsels to them, is doubly mimetic, as they are called to imitate Paul, who is imitating Christ

---

45. Michael L. White, "Morality between Two Worlds: A Paradigm of Friendship in Philippians Morality between Two Worlds: A Paradigm of Friendship in Philippians," in *Greeks, Romans, and Christians: Essays in Honor of Abraham J. Malherbe*, ed. David L. Balch, Everett Ferguson, and Wayne A. Meeks (Minneapolis: Fortress, 1990), 213.

(3:17).[46] This mimesis is non-exact in just the ways that Milbank suggested for proper gift-giving, in that it will occur in "unpredictably different circumstances, at unpredictable times and to unpredictably various recipients" (Phil 2:1–5).[47] Because this circle of gift-giving has part of its circumference in the divine realm with God and Christ Jesus (Phil 2:6–7a, 9–11), and part of it on earth (in Jesus's life as a human being, and also in the actions of Paul, Timothy, Epaphroditus, and the Philippians), such a circle of gift-exchange comes naturally to be conceived as a sacrificial one. As the circle of giving and receiving, described in Philippians, links heaven and earth, so also sacrifices burnt upon the altar ascend into the heavens, in thanksgiving for and assurance of the continual blessings that descend from heaven to earth. Thus, it is no surprise that Paul would describe the partnership of his self-giving service together with that of the Philippians in overtly sacrificial terms: Ἀλλὰ εἰ καὶ σπένδομαι ἐπὶ τῇ θυσίᾳ καὶ λειτουργίᾳ τῆς πίστεως ὑμῶν, χαίρω καὶ συγχαίρω πᾶσιν ὑμῖν (2:17). What distinguishes the sacrificial nature of the life of the Philippians, however, is Paul's understanding that God is not only a giver and receiver in proper turn, but God is a constant, active participant in the whole cycle of appropriate giving and receiving (Phil 1:6, 2:13).

In this regard, it is important to note the word διό in Phil 2:9. God is both the initiator and a responder in the cycle of gift-giving. To say this is not to say that God's goodwill can be manipulated through sacrifice, but simply to say that God is in true relationship with those who make an offering wholeheartedly, and that their faithfulness is honored in the cycle of gift-exchange. To say that the exaltation of Christ Jesus is not related to his humility and obedience would be to sever Phil 2:9–11 from 6–8.

Paul deals most clearly with the sacrificial quality of gift-giving in Philippians 4:15–20. Here the reciprocity of giving and receiving in the ancient world is made plain, using the language of commerce:[48] "no church shared with me in the account of giving and receiving but you alone" (οὐδεμία μοι

---

46. Of course, the most obvious instance of this counsel is outside Philippians, in 1 Cor 11:1, but Paul appears, by contrast to others, to set himself as a "friend of the cross of Christ" when he calls the Philippians to imitate him at Phil 3:17–18.

47. Note the indefinite time frame and the unspecified ἀλλήλους and τὰ ἑτέρων of Phil 2:3–4.

48. The language of this passage is drawn from the world of business, but the exchange of money and goods is fundamentally a subset of gift-exchange, as Milbank also discusses ("Can a Gift Be Given," 147–48).

ἐκκλησία ἐκοινώνησεν εἰς λόγον δόσεως καὶ λήμψεως εἰ μὴ ὑμεῖς μόνοι, Phil 4:15b). Further, as above, the cycle of giving and receiving on earth is also drawn up into its heavenly implications, both in terms of the community's "account," (Phil 4:17), and in terms of God's response (Phil 4:19) to their sacrificial (Phil 4:18) giving. It appears that, in Paul's view, obedient Christian life reverberates across the divide between heaven and earth. Sacrificial gift-exchange is one way for Paul to talk about this constant commerce between heaven and earth. Emptying oneself of "one's own things" (2:4, or the gifts to Paul, 4:18), whether material or immaterial, plays a role in reconciling the world to God. Therefore God, skilled in the practices of giving and receiving, responds (4:19).

While distinct *metaphors* of sacrifice occur at various points in the letter to the Philippians, more broadly conceived *patterns* of sacrifice actually permeate the letter. Gift-exchange between heaven and earth is one of the fundamental patterns of sacrifice, and Paul makes use of a similar pattern of giving and receiving to describe Christian faithfulness, with the Christ Hymn as the preeminent pattern.

APOCALYPTICISM AND SACRIFICE IN PHILIPPIANS

It is well accepted among scholars that Paul's thought is "apocalyptic" or that he has an "apocalyptic worldview."[49] The letter to the Philippians, though not generically an apocalypse, bears out Paul's apocalypticism, and my purpose here is to show how the metaphors of sacrifice used in Philippians function within such an apocalyptic framework.

What I mean by "apocalyptic" or "apocalypticism" in Philippians is best explained with reference to the letter itself. Paul appears to believe that there has developed a disjunction between what God desires for the world and the way that the world is ordered in the present time,[50] a dis-

---

49. In his *Paul the Apostle*, J. Christiaan Beker argued that "Paul's thought is anchored in the apocalyptic world view and that the resurrection of Christ [as seen through Paul's eyes] can only be understood in that setting" ([Philadelphia: Fortress, 1980], 135). Ernst Käsemann, to whom Beker was much indebted, commented upon the influence of Jewish apocalypticism on Paul's thought in his influential commentary on Romans (*Commentary on Romans*, trans. and ed. Geoffrey W. Bromiley (Grand Rapids: Eerdmans, 1973).

50. Some authors refer to this quality of apocalyptic thought as dualistic, to draw attention to the moral valuation of heaven as opposed to earth, or one group of people as opposed to another, or one way of life as opposed to another, etc. In my view, Paul's

junction that he expresses most clearly in terms of the "citizenship in the heavens" (πολίτευμα ἐν οὐρανοῖς) of the Philippians as contrasted with those whose minds are consumed with earthly things (τὰ ἐπίγεια, Phil 3:19–20).[51] Paul is concerned to describe the present reality accurately in its totality (that is to say, including its heavenly dimension), and to suggest a way of living for the Philippians that will be clearly consistent with their heavenly citizenship, while living in the world, perhaps even as citizens of Rome.[52] In doing so, he illustrates Christopher Rowland's point that apocalyptic is concerned not only with eschatology, but is a way to understand the nature of the present time:

> Apocalyptic is as much involved in the attempt to understand things as they are now as to predict future events. The mysteries of heaven and earth and the real significance of contemporary persons and events in history are also the dominant interests of the apocalyptists. There is thus a concern with the world above and its mysteries as a means of explaining human existence in the present.[53]

It is important to maintain clarity about what it means to say that Paul is an apocalyptic thinker or holds to an apocalyptic worldview, while not

---

apocalypticism is an intensification of his view of himself as one of God's prophets. Compare Gal 1:15, the story of his life leading up to the "revelation" (ἀποκαλύπτω) of Christ in him, to Jer 1:5. Paul also refers obliquely to Jer 1 in 1 Cor 3:9.

51. The overtly political language of the heavenly πολίτευμα leads me to believe that Paul is criticizing Roman rule and Roman society in particular.

52. Philippi was a Roman military colony from 42 BCE, and occupied a strategic site on the Egnatian way. Its inhabitants, many of them Roman veterans, were citizens of Rome. It is possible that the pride in their citizenship shown by some members of the church there was the cause for Paul's rhetoric of political allegiance.

53. Christopher Rowland, *The Open Heaven: A Study of Apocalyptic in Judaism and Early Christinaity* (New York: Crossroad, 1982), 2. I agree, however, with DeBoer, who criticizes Rowland for his narrow focus on Paul's mystical experiences in 2 Cor 12 as the chief evidence of Paul's apocalypticism: "This peculiar constriction of apocalyptic in Paul's thought to his personal journey to the heavenly realm in 2 Cor 12—an ecstatic experience Paul recounts only in order to devalue its importance—stands in stark contrast to what is normally understood by apocalyptic, in Paul or elsewhere. It cannot be substantiated by Paul's own use of the language of revelation in a number of other passages. For Rowland, apocalyptic becomes curiously focused on the human experience of the divine world rather than on God's own revelatory action of rectifying a world gone awry" (Martinus C. De Boer, "Paul, Theologian of God's Apocalpyse," *Interpretation* 56:1 [2002], 24).

asserting that Philippians is generically apocalyptic. David Aune distinguishes between the form of an apocalypse as a literary genre ("an autobiographical prose narrative reporting revelatory visions experienced by the author and structured to emphasize the central revelatory message"); the content of an apocalypse ("the communication of a transcendent, often eschatological, perspective on human experience"); and the function of an apocalypse (to "legitimate the transcendent authority of the message by mediating a new revelatory experience for the audience to encourage them to modify their cognition and behavior in conformity with transcendent perspectives").[54] Clearly, none of the above statements would quite describe the letter to the Philippians, though perhaps one might say that revelatory experiences seem to exist just outside the bounds of the letter, or that the Christ Hymn functions as the key revelatory reference, exposing the fullest extent of events not ordinarily perceptible to human beings.

Paul appears concerned to develop the Philippian congregation's awareness of itself from a transcendent perspective *vis à vis* the surrounding culture (1:28, 2:15, 3:7–8, 18–21). He chooses to employ some revelations of the heavenly dimension of reality in order to carry out the persuasive function of apocalypses; according to Aune: "encouraging cognitive and behavioral modifications based on the message communicated from the transcendent world."[55] Notably, Phil 1:6, 9–11; 2:5–11; and 3:14, 19–21 all set the life of the church at Philippi within this full, transcendent context, and encourage behavior congruent with such a context. While the Christ Hymn reveals the story of Jesus in its most transcendent fullness, there is no relating of a vision or heavenly journey as though it were taking place in the present, and no attempt to mediate such a vision for the readers or hearers of the letter. In spite of the material conveyed in the Christ Hymn, the feet of the hearers, and those of the author, remain firmly on the ground. Metaphors of sacrifice work within this construct, as they refer to the ability of material offerings to transcend the divide between heaven and earth, to do the work of reconciling the divine will and human faithfulness.

Paul's apocalyptic, or fully revelatory, view of the state of the world is characterized by a transcendent concern for the present decisions and actions of the communities in his care. In particular, he is concerned that

---

54. David Aune, "The Apocalypse of John and the Problem of Genre," *Semeia* 36 (1986): 65–66.

55. Aune, "The Apocalypse of John," 90.

the Philippians develop the skills of discernment (ἐπίγνωσις and αἴσθησις, εἰς τὸ δοκιμάζειν ... τὰ διαφέροντα, Phil 1:9–10) required to live faithfully in a time when what is approved by the world is abhorred by God, and vice versa.[56] But the eschatological horizon is also important and active upon the present, as is clear in the conclusion of the statement above, ἵνα ἦτε εἰλικρινεῖς καὶ ἀπρόσκοποι εἰς ἡμέραν Χριστοῦ (1:10); or when Paul prays that the one who has begun a good work among the Philippians will bring it to completion ἄχρι ἡμέρας Χριστοῦ Ἰησοῦ (1:6).

While Aune admits that "it is difficult to reconstruct the social situation within which many apocalypses were produced," he nonetheless characterizes much of it as "protest literature."[57] That is, apocalyptic literature typically represents the perspective of an oppressed minority. Collins substantially agrees, while adding that, though

It has been generally assumed that apocalypticism arises from the experience of alienation, or in times of crisis (e.g., Hanson 1987:75), this assumption is defensible [only] if we grant that alienation, and crises, may be of many kinds. Apocalypticism can provide support in the face of persecution (Daniel), reassurance in the face of culture shock (the Book of the Watchers) or social powerlessness (the Similitudes of Enoch), reorientation in the face of national trauma (2 Baruch, 3 Baruch), consolation for the fate of humanity (4 Ezra). What is constant is not the kind of problem addressed but the manner in which it is addressed. In each case the apocalyptic revelation diverts the attention from the distressful present to the heavenly world and the eschatological future. This diversion should not be seen as a flight from reality. Rather it is a way of coping with reality by providing a meaningful framework within which human beings can make decisions and take action (compare the maskilim in Dan 11:32–34).[58]

While we do not know exactly what kind of opposition the "holy ones in Christ Jesus" in Philippi were facing from the wider community, it appears from the letter that their suffering is substantial (1:27–30), and that they need encouragement to stay the course. Paul's own imprisonment and his likening of his situation to that of the Philippians are indications of what

56. See especially the harsh language and strong contrast drawn at Phil 3:17–21.
57. David Aune, "Understanding Jewish and Christian Apocalyptic," WW 25 (2005): 235, emphasis original.
58. John J. Collins, "Early Jewish Apocalypticism," ABD 1:287.

Collins calls "social powerlessness," and some kind of persecution. It is, thus, precisely a "meaningful framework" for their action that Paul is seeking to establish in his letter by setting their experience of suffering within the full spatial context of heaven and earth and the full temporal context of this present moment and the "day of Christ."

Sacrificial metaphors help to carry the rhetorical load, by opening up human behavior in the material world to its full spiritual and cosmic import. Thus, the material gifts provided by the Philippians to Paul during his imprisonment are described as ὀσμή εὐωδίας, then as θυσία δεκτή, and then finally εὐάρεστος τῷ θεῷ (Phil 4:18). The sequence almost seems to describe the ascent of the smoke of the sacrifices, as the reader moves from what can be experienced of them physically (their fragrance), to their ritual acceptability (a human abstraction), and finally to their effect on God (something that cannot be seen at all, but is attested here by Paul). The gifts have, in fact traveled only from the hands of the Philippians to those of Epaphroditus, to those of Paul. But Paul has reinscribed their journey as an ascent to God, a link from earth to heaven at a time when heaven and earth seem to have been rent asunder. By use of this fairly simple sacrificial metaphor, Paul has enlarged the context in which all of the actions of the Philippians are to be interpreted.

Likewise, the sacrificial metaphor at 2:17 plays its role within an enlarged view of the spatial and temporal context of relationships in the Christian community at Philippi. Paul sets the community's refraining from γογγυσμός and διαλογισμός (Phil 2:14) first within the context of the wider human community (τέκνα θεοῦ ἄμωμα μέσον γενεᾶς σκολιᾶς καὶ διεστραμμένης, Phil 2:15), then amplifies that view to include the heavenly realm (ἐν οἷς φαίνεσθε ὡς φωστῆρες ἐν κόσμῳ, Phil 2:15), and then expands the temporal dimension of their actions to its full extent (εἰς ἡμέραν Χριστοῦ, Phil 2:16). It is within this broad setting, then, that Paul's description of the community's positive actions as the θυσία and λειτουργία of their faithfulness (πίστις) makes sense (Phil 2:17). Murmuring and arguing would be not merely unpleasant aspects of their life in community, but would threaten the integrity of their whole offering of faithfulness to God, conceived in the most transcendent terms. The fact that Paul has chosen to pour out his own apostolic life in conjunction with their "offering" of their life together raises the stakes on the people's discernment of appropriate behavior. Anyone accustomed to the offering of sacrifices would see the folly of pouring a costly libation out over an unworthy or impure sacrificial victim.

So, as in the passage at 4:18, the sacrificial metaphor of libation and offering at 2:17 plays a role in reinscribing the context of the daily actions of the Philippians, in relation to an apocalyptic framework. While the surrounding culture takes its cues from earthly powers and customs, the moral life of the Philippians is said to be carried out on a wider stage, and it is in reference to this spatially and temporally wider stage that they are to carry out their work of discerning "what is best … in the day of Christ" (Phil 1:10). By adoption of the path of humility, described in 2:6–8, the Philippians are enjoined to restrain themselves from petty murmuring and arguing. Humility is the ground for faithfulness (πίστις), the quality of daily life that opens the channels between heaven and earth, much as sacrifice does, making faithful human life an acceptable offering to God, and even, perhaps eventually, something glorious (Phil 4:21).

Yet Paul says also that "*even if*" (εἰ καὶ) he is poured out upon the offering of their faith, a costly and possibly painful endeavor, he rejoices. The following section deals with the sometimes confusing combination of suffering and joy in the letter to the Philippians and the role of metaphors of sacrifice in this emotional complexity.

SUFFERING AND JOY

L. Gregory Bloomquist has written on the remarkable conjunction of suffering and joy in Philippians.[59] As he says, "Woven together, suffering and joy create not just a theme but a tapestry that serves as a backdrop for the entire letter."[60] He sets this language in its ancient Mediterranean context, in which death was always a present reality, not only for individuals, but for one's community or even, most terrifyingly, for the Roman Empire itself: "The world—from the struggle of daily life to imperial conquest—was a battleground of social suffering and death in which no one could win."[61] Hellenistic religions and philosophies addressed the issue of death and its attendant suffering in various ways, through magic or ritual, through creating a context in which suffering could be viewed as leading to wisdom, and through counseling equanimity in all situations. But none

---

59. L. Gregory Bloomquist, *The Function of Suffering in Philippians*, JSNTSup 78 (Sheffield: Sheffield Academic, 1993), and "Subverted by Joy: Suffering and Joy in Paul's Letter to the Philippians," *Int* 61 (2007): 270–82.

60. Bloomquist, "Subverted by Joy," 270.

61. Ibid., 271.

of these means could enable a person to conquer death, the prime cause
of suffering in the first place. "For this reason," writes Bloomquist, "we
should not be surprised that in antiquity joy is rarely mentioned, except
as an illusion."[62]

Against this backdrop, then, Bloomquist remarks upon Paul's surprising emphasis on joy in the letter to the Philippians, a letter written while
Paul himself was imprisoned and cognizant of the possibility of his own
death (Phil 1:20–24).[63] Bloomquist says that "Joy was ... something that
Paul appears to have thought that he could offer to those willing to accept
his message."[64] Bloomquist goes on to explore Paul's "rhetorical reconfigu-
ration of suffering and joy."[65] He attributes only a part of Paul's reinterpretation of suffering to the fact that Paul appears to have little fear of death.
What he finds more significant is that "in Paul's very *experience* of suffering, he has found the impossible joy."[66] He credits Paul with "invent[ing]
a new discourse for a new culture."[67] The new culture was inaugurated
in Christ who met death fearlessly, and thus consequently brought about
the "death of death."[68] Bloomquist links the glorification of Christ in Phil
2:9–11 to the joy that Paul himself is experiencing and toward which he
points the Philippians: "In such a new world, joy would not be found in
resisting or avoiding suffering and death—both of which were impossible—but in accepting suffering and eventual death as a vehicle to advance
the life-giving work of Christ."[69]

Bloomquist offers a helpful clue to the overall literary pattern of Philippians when he uses the metaphor of the tapestry to describe its structure,[70]
for the letter is characterized by a weaving in and out of certain repeated
themes. But an important set of threads is missing from his account, that
of the sacrificial metaphors. For it is they that truly bring together most
coherently the contrasting but ultimately harmonious colors of suffering
and joy that mark the letter. In sacrifice, and particularly in the *shelamim*

---

62. Ibid., 274.
63. Bloomquist describes the conditions of ancient prisons in ibid., 274–75.
64. Ibid., 274.
65. Ibid., 275.
66. Ibid., 280, emphasis original.
67. Ibid., 280.
68. Ibid., 282.
69. Ibid., 282.
70. Ibid., 270.

or commensal sacrifices, the relinquishing of something of value (the animal victim) is grounded in joy from beginning to end. The sacrifice is occasioned by thankfulness and joy, and results in the compounded joy of the shared feast.

The narratives of sacrifice in Genesis provide some clues to the emotional content of the sacrifices, on which Leviticus is silent. Taken together, the significant sacrifices, such as the offerings of Cain and Abel (4:3–7), Noah's burnt offerings (8:20–22), the covenant sacrifice between God and Abram (15:7–21), the near–sacrifice of Isaac by Abraham (22:1–19), and Jacob's offering of oil at Bethel (28:18), depict a spectrum of motivations for sacrifice, together with a variety of accompanying emotions. While the value of what is offered is almost always at issue, the emotional cost of sacrifice becomes most terrifyingly clear in the Akedah, or binding of Isaac. The substitution of the ram given by God for the son, also given by God, does not slow the heartbeat of the reader/hearer of the story and grants insight into the personal costliness of all the sacrifices. Yet the outcome of the sacrifices is not suffering, but increased life. In all the sacrifices in Genesis there is a drawing near of God and human beings for the flourishing of human life. The pattern of costly offering that ushers in human flourishing is the same pattern Bloomquist has mentioned in speaking of the relationship between Paul's suffering and the well-being of the Philippian community, above: "in Paul's very *experience* of suffering, he has found the impossible joy, because in suffering and inevitable death and because of them, he has found men and women, like the Philippians, coming to life in Christ."[71] This is the sacrificial pattern.

The self-offerings made by Christ Jesus in his descent into slavery and the cross,[72] by Paul in his imprisonment for the gospel, by Timothy in the genuineness of his concern for the Philippians, by Epaphroditus in his risking death to care for Paul, all participate in this sacrificial pattern, the pattern that transforms suffering into joy. When Paul then links that pattern of self-giving behavior to the pattern of the *shelamim* (Phil 2:17–18;

---

71. Ibid., 280, emphasis original.

72. In the Christ Hymn, the pattern is slightly different. There Christ Jesus's emptying out of himself, taking the form of a slave, and following the path of obedience and humility all the way to death on the cross results not in his own rejoicing but in his exaltation and glorification. Yet his glorification becomes a ground for the rejoicing of the Philippians. Perhaps earthly joy, even in situations of suffering, anticipates eschatological glory (3:21).

4:18), he does not have to *persuade* the Philippians to be joyful; he merely *invites* them to rejoice, for rejoicing is the natural accompaniment to a sacrifice of thanksgiving.

The natural conjunction of suffering and joy in the offering of a sacrifice is seen most clearly in Philippians at 2:17–18, where Paul's being poured out as a libation over the offering of the Philippians ushers in four uses of the verb χαίρω, "to rejoice": Ἀλλὰ εἰ καὶ σπένδομαι ἐπὶ τῇ θυσίᾳ καὶ λειτουργίᾳ τῆς πίστεως ὑμῶν, χαίρω καὶ συγχαίρω πᾶσιν ὑμῖν. Τὸ δὲ αὐτὸ καὶ ὑμεῖς χαίρετε καὶ συγχαίρετέ μοι. But the other instances of the verb χαίρω also occur in circumstances in which one person's self-offering for others or for the gospel results in an increase in life and, thus, joy. At 1:15–18, Paul's selfless interpretation of the benefits of the gospel being preached, no matter the motivation of the preacher, causes him to rejoice; 3:1 follows the recounting of the self-offering of Timothy and Epaphroditus; and at 4:4, the repeated injunction, Χαίρετε ἐν κυρίῳ πάντοτε; πάλιν ἐρῶ, χαίρετε, comes just after Paul's addressing of the possible cause of "murmuring and argumentation" in the community, the dispute between two important figures, Euodia and Syntyche.

Fee chooses to see 4:4 and following as the beginning of a new section of the letter, rather than a consequence of 4:1–3. Thus, he characterizes Paul's call to rejoice at this point as an aspect of Jewish piety (along with prayer and thanksgiving), as well as "the distinctive mark of the believer in Christ Jesus."[73] But *why* should rejoicing be "the distinctive mark of the believer"? When one observes the imperative to rejoice in the context of Paul's acknowledgment of the very real struggles the community is facing in order to reconcile its leaders (4:2–3), to "stand firm in the Lord" even while under pressure from the outside (4:1), to trust that the Lord is near even in the most anxious times (4:5–6), one can see that the sacrificial pattern is at work here, even when not explicitly mentioned. The sacrificial pattern of a costly offering being occasioned by and also resulting in joy is the very shape of faithfulness in Philippians, and the shape of Paul's consolation as well.

A close look at the Christ Hymn reveals, interestingly, that the ground for the community's rejoicing is not the joy of Christ Jesus, but his glorification. By the "ground" of their rejoicing, I mean the situation that prompts their grateful self-offering, their sacrificially patterned way of life. The par-

---

73. Fee, *Philippians*, 404.

allel between Christ's experience and that of the believers is not exact, but is, rather, anticipatory. Christ's emptying out of himself, taking the form of a slave, and following the path of obedience and humility all the way to death on a cross, results not in his own rejoicing, but in his exaltation and glorification (2:9–11). The response of the believers to his glory is thankful joy and self-offering according to his pattern. Glory is an eschatological reality, as Paul says of his expectations for himself and other believers at 3:21.

A similar pattern is observable in 2 Cor 8:1–15, where the traditional material (γινώσκετε γάρ) quoted or paraphrased in verse 9 echoes the Christ Hymn: τὴν χάριν τοῦ κυρίου ἡμῶν Ἰησοῦ Χριστοῦ, ὅτι δι᾽ ὑμᾶς ἐπτώχευσεν πλούσιος ὤν, ἵνα ὑμεῖς τῇ ἐκείνου πτωχείᾳ πλουτήσητε. The abundance of the Corinthians (8:14) rests upon Christ's self-impoverishment for their sakes. The churches of Macedonia are put forward as an example of appropriate mimesis of Christ's generosity and its effects (8:2). While, strictly speaking, the Macedonians did not *choose* their affliction and poverty, they did choose their free response to that state of affairs: abundant joy (ἡ περισσεία τῆς χαρᾶς αὐτῶν). It appears that their affliction and poverty are the outward signs of their faithfulness to Christ (as in Phil 1:28). Though Paul does not compare their behavior to sacrifice, it follows that pattern. Their faithfulness is their offering, and it has cost them dearly. But, in the logic of sacrifice, that very cost results in an overflowing of joy and even further generosity, perhaps akin to the banquet that follows a commensal sacrifice. One of the interesting elements of the reciprocity of sacrifice that becomes very clear here is its generous messiness. The giving-and-receiving of sacrifices is not limited to the sacrifier and the god. Christ begins the offering in 2 Corinthians, and both the Macedonians and the Corinthians are receivers. The Macedonians consequently give generously to Paul's collection for Jerusalem, and their giving becomes a motivation for the giving of the Corinthians (2 Cor 8:3–6). The two believing communities are related not only through Christ, but through their shared practices (ἡ κοινωνία τῆς διακονίας, 2 Cor 8:4) of costly faithfulness and generosity; and they are also in a balanced relationship of giving and receiving, of cost and rejoicing, with the saints in Jerusalem (2 Cor 8:13–15).

In relation to an apocalyptic worldview, metaphors of the *shelamim* link what can be seen with what cannot be seen. This capacity of sacrificial metaphors to reinterpret experience is also an aspect of their function with regard to suffering and joy. What can be seen in any sacrifice is loss and death, the loss of an animal whose raising or procurement has been costly, and the pouring out of its blood. But what is unseen is how the death of the animal brings life to the offerer, and reconciliation with God and neighbor. Likewise, in the case of the Philippians, what can be seen is their suffering, and their struggles to stand firm and united as a community. In his letter, Paul sets out multiple examples to train them to see in their suffering itself the outward sign of their future glory. The sacrificial pattern reframes their experience, and gives them cause for rejoicing in the present.

CONCLUSIONS

Skillfully chosen metaphors are a powerful way in which to shape a community's ongoing moral reflection, as they may be applied in analogous circumstances not yet encountered. In the center of the letter to the Philippians, Paul sets forth a description of the descent and glorification of Christ Jesus (Phil 2:6–11) that establishes a metaphorically sacrificial pattern of living. The moral pattern characterized as sacrificial is marked by a willingness to shift one's concern from one's own needs or desires to the well-being of one's neighbor (Phil 2:1–5), a pattern seen in its fullness in Christ's kenotic descent and humble obedience to God, even at the cost of death on a cross. The glorification of Christ serves as a promise to the Philippians that sacrificial behavior in the present will lead, ultimately, to glory.

Sacrifices of thanksgiving (the Jewish *shelamim*), culminating in a festal meal, were the most basic sacrificial pattern in the ancient Mediterranean, known across all of the cultures of the people in Paul's communities. The belief that offerings were pleasing to God, and that they assured God's favor toward the offerer, is fundamental to the Christ Hymn and to the sacrificial metaphors of Philippians. There is a cycle of reciprocity between God and humankind that is set in motion through sacrifices of thanksgiving that can be depended upon for human well-being. The sacrificial pattern set forth in Phil 2:6–11 reverberates through the rest of the assessment of the condition of the Philippians and Paul's consequent counsels to them, and assures them that what can be seen, namely, their current suffering, is not the whole story.

In order to interpret Philippians adequately, it is crucial to identify with accuracy the type of sacrifice being referred to in the letter's metaphors. For example, the various themes and connections supported by imagery relating to the dedicatory sacrifices of well-being (*shelamim*) in Philippians are negated if one applies the entailments of propitiatory sacrifices. Entailments of sacrifices for sin do not support the moral counsels of Philippians in the way that metaphors related to the *shelamim* enhance the themes of reciprocity, friendship, joy, and courageous generosity. Where Paul does employ an explicit metaphor of atonement, in Rom 3:21–26, he prepares for the metaphor extensively in the preceding chapters, and underscores it in the summary statement concerning reconciliation at 15:7.

By tracing the sacrificial language in Philippians as it appears within the various rhetorical divisions of the letter, the metaphors of sacrifice appear repeatedly, but not in any formal pattern. They appear as a kind of ongoing rumination that colors the moral counsels and other themes of the letter, such as gift-giving, friendship, unity, other-regard, rejoicing, and citizenship. It is this sporadic repetition in the use of the metaphor that reveals it not as a rhetorical flourish, but as a tool of active thought. The givens of the situation: the crucifixion of Jesus, and Paul's imprisonment and possible death, draw forth these sacrificial metaphors to claim agency in the face of opposition, and to structure the common life of the Philippians along patterns of self-offering. In the letter to the Philippians, the present-day reader has a chance to see sacrificial imagery at work in a lively and ad hoc way, before sacrifice became a commonplace way to speak of Christian life. One of the properties of metaphor, when used to grasp something not yet fully known, is that the metaphor actually begins to *create* similarities where they were not seen before. Paul's gradual linking of the sacrifices of thanksgiving, the cross, and the moral life of Christians is a creative move that gives the letter's recipients a way to predict what behavior is appropriate to them as believers and to continue in that course of action, even if all they can observe in their immediate environs is opposition.

It may be that the use of metaphors of sacrifice to speak of everyday patterns of living was a fearsome prospect to some. The actual Jewish sacrificial system had many formal features that guarded against the chance that a sacrifice might be offered wrongly. Sacrifices could be offered only by particular people, prepared in particular ways, in particular places at particular times. When people are encouraged to *live* sacrificially, they do so without any of these formal protections. This fact alone puts them at risk of offending God by being unprepared, or making an unsuitable offering. Sacrificial metaphors, used to describe daily moral decisions, gave guidance in otherwise uncharted territory.

Metaphors have the propensity both to hide and to reveal aspects of the tenor and the vehicle as they interact. In writing to the Philippians, Paul uses explicitly sacrificial metaphors to speak of the relationship of his efforts to those of the Philippians (2:17), and gifts sent from the Philippians to Paul during his imprisonment (4:18). Furthermore, he uses sacrificial language and patterns to speak of the community itself as an offering on the "day of Christ" (1:8, 2:15); of his possible death in prison (1:18b–26); of the descent, death, and glorification of Christ (2:5–11); of the self-effacing service of Timothy (2:19–24); and of Epaphroditus's risk-taking (2:25–30). What is hidden in the narrative of the Christ Hymn is the agency of Rome in the death of Jesus. Within the confines of the hymn, the only agents are Christ Jesus and God. The other sacrificial metaphors and patterns then continue to inscribe the life of the Philippians within a narrative that places their decisions in the light of the power and presence of God. Sacrificial metaphors heighten a hearer's awareness of God, while minimizing the power of all that is not God, namely, Roman authority, or any other local opposition. The examples of extreme risk-taking for the Gospel by Paul and Epaphroditus make sense within such a dramatic and sharply drawn frame.

Metaphors of sacrifice, which call for a person to relinquish his or her own best interest, in service to another person or goal or value, are what we have called earlier a "high stakes" metaphor. As Christian Eberhart says of sacrificial language generally, it "serves the purpose of assigning importance to gestures or actions along widely accepted categories of a religious value system. Whether in religious contexts or not, this terminology is implicitly recognized as rhetorically authoritative."[74] A sacrificial metaphor may be coercive, and is difficult to contradict, because it places at issue one's relationship with God. In the letter to the Philippians, Paul uses metaphors of sacrifice to undergird his reflections on self-interest and unity, on risk-taking on behalf of the community, on obedience to God, and on the significance of generosity. The connection with sacrifice intensifies the consequences of these human decisions and actions. Besides the ability of sacrificial metaphors to reassign agency, something that they hide is Paul's own possible self-interest in any of these areas. We do not have enough information about the recipients of the letter to know what they made of Paul's use of sacrificial metaphors, but we can see that Paul chose a highly persuasive way to interpret and respond to their situation.

A dedicatory sacrifice (such as the Jewish *shelamim* or any of the basic Greco-Roman commensal sacrifices) is a complex event that suggests a

---

74. Eberhart, "Sacrifice? Holy Smokes," 21.

whole series of entailments, as it brings together a community's under-standings of holiness, friendship, morality, reciprocal gift-giving, the relationship between suffering and joy, and commerce between heaven and earth. As we have seen, the sacrificial metaphors in Philippians offer Paul a nuanced array of tones to structure his reflections upon the community's life in the face of inner divisions and outward opposition. These metaphors illustrate Lakoff and Johnson's discussion of complex metaphors that employ "one highly structured and clearly delineated concept to structure another."[75] Once such metaphors come into play, they begin to create a new reality for those who live by them, enabling them to live in ways that run counter to the culture around them. The sacrificial metaphors in Philippians structure a moral life comprised of seeking the lowest status, the other's well-being, and perhaps even death itself.

---

75. Lakoff and Johnson, *Metaphors We Live By*, 61.

6

1 Corinthians:
The Community That Keeps the Feast

In 1 Cor 16:8, Paul says that he plans to stay in Ephesus until Pentecost (ἕως τῆς πεντεκοστῆς). It is unclear how long before Pentecost he was writing,[1] but the number of metaphorical references to the Passover in 1 Corinthians suggests that that festival was near, and provided a background to his thinking about the situation in Corinth. In any case, just as metaphors of the sacrifices of thanksgiving (*shelamim*) appear to underlie much of Philippians, metaphors relating to the Passover appear to bring together a number of Paul's counsels in 1 Corinthians, and to offer a set of associations to guide the community's ethical reflection in the future. Paul imaginatively reinscribes the whole complex of actions associated with the preparations for and celebration of the feasts of Passover and Unleavened Bread by the Jewish community as a moral pattern for the assembly at Corinth, primarily with regard to unifying the fractured church. I am not suggesting that metaphors of the Passover are the only overarching metaphors of the letter,[2] but that they, and their entailments, work in concert with other images to establish and reinforce the guiding counsel of 1 Corinthians, "that there be no divisions among you" (1:10). What follows is not a thoroughgoing interpretation of 1 Corinthians, but a study of how one particular family of metaphors plays a consistent role in supporting the principal paraenesis of the letter.

---

1. How long before Pentecost one might assume this letter was written depends, in part, on one's understanding of ταχέως in 4:19. The reference to Pentecost at all, without any explanatory remarks, would appear to indicate that the community at Corinth could be expected to have at least a basic acquaintance with the Jewish ritual calendar.

2. One thinks immediately of metaphors of the temple, the body, the *logos* of the cross, etc.

Several strong metaphors in 1 Corinthians have proven to have "staying power" in Christian thought, such as that of the community as a body, the community as a building, the body as a temple, and the physical body as a seed of the resurrection body. Tracing the recurrence of metaphors of the Passover must be done with some attention to the whole network of other images that Paul is weaving to create the letter. I will first discuss the quality of metaphors in 1 Corinthians in a general way, and then turn to the mapping of metaphors of the Passover in particular within the rhetorical structure of 1 Corinthians.

LAYERING OF METAPHORS IN 1 CORINTHIANS

In his discussion of the rhetoric of 1 Corinthians, John Lanci says, as others have doubtlessly thought before, "Following the reasoning of 1 Corinthians is difficult."[3] He continues:

> Paul evokes images and ideas and manipulates them in a way best visualized not as a straight line but as an oscillation: first he presents an image, he then drops it and turns to another image, then he either returns to the first image or presses the second one into a different context. The cross of Christ, for instance, appears as the "power of God" in 1 Cor 1:18, then disappears; but allusions to the death of Christ, and to power, mingle throughout the rest of the letter.[4]

"Oscillation" is one way to describe the appearance and reappearance of imagery in 1 Corinthians, but perhaps it does not capture fully the way in which metaphors resonate with one another, overlap, and sometimes even seem to conflict with one another. So, to Lanci's term, "oscillation," one should add some sense for the interplay, or layering of imagery that Paul achieves.

The complexity of Paul's use of image and metaphor causes me to turn to a different medium of expression altogether for comparison. Like the themes of a musical composition, the strongest metaphors of 1 Corinthians sometimes sound at the same time, and are often related to one

---

3. John Lanci, *A New Temple for Corinth: Rhetorical and Archeological Approaches to Pauline Imagery* (New York: Lang, 1997), 46.

4. Ibid.

another. For example, the Temple[5] and the Passover are obviously not the same thing, but they have overlapping entailments. Taking the whole letter into account, when one is sounded, and then the other, the meaning that gradually develops is more complex than simply how either Temple or Passover functions in its immediate context. The principal metaphors of 1 Corinthians are often not presented singly, and not used once to make a point and then discarded, but rather are used multiple times over the course of the letter in various harmonious or discordant combinations and relationships to one another, and some of them resonate implicitly across long stretches of the counsels and arguments of the letter. Ultimately, there is a kind of layering effect of some of the strong metaphors in 1 Corinthians, as they resound across the entire letter, even in passages in which they are not being used explicitly.

It is this layering that makes possible the kind of quick turn of imagery such as we find at 1 Cor 6:19–20, where Paul moves dizzyingly from temple to purchase price without any warning. A shift that might be jarring in its immediate context makes sense within the complex layering of images that occurs throughout the letter. Both temple (3:17; 6:19) and purchase (6:20; 7:23) appear more than once, and both are used in relationship to other images and vocabulary. The Temple plays a recurring role in the imagery of the Passover and of construction, as we shall see; and the phrase "you were bought with a price" relates to several of Paul's counsels concerning slavery, freedom, and belonging (obviously 7:21–24, but also perhaps a passage like 3:23). The first major appeal of the letter (1:10–17) establishes the fact that one of the central problems at Corinth is the community's misunderstanding concerning to whom they truly belong, and so the fact of their having been "bought" already by God is important

---

5. As noted earlier, I have adopted a system of capitalizing "Temple" when the referent is the Jewish Temple in Jerusalem and using the lowercase "temple" when the referent appears to be temples more generally. The system breaks down at points when, though Paul's own image may be of the Jerusalem Temple, he may be leaving open the possibility that his hearers are imagining the temples they are familiar with in Corinth. Because it is the Jewish Temple that is related to the activities of the Passover, I capitalize the "T" when I speak of Passover and Temple together, as here. The very question of the referent is, however, one of the points of this work: Paul and his addressees are potentially bringing very different sets of entailments to bear on their comprehension of sacrificial metaphors. Exclusive use of imagery and entailments of the Passover would seem to indicate previous teaching and exposure of the Corinthian church to the Passover narrative and practices.

throughout the letter.[6] What we see are not so much *mixed* metaphors, in the sense of a clumsy error, as *layered* metaphors, sounding effectively, if sometimes startlingly, in concert.

The strongest metaphors of 1 Corinthians have become almost normative for speech about Christian community: the Christian community as a planting (3:5–7), as a building (3:9–15), as a temple (3:16–17), as a body (12:12–31). Further, as Lanci has convincingly shown, Paul increases the resonance of some of the strong metaphors by using language related to them even where he is not using the metaphor explicitly. For example, as Lanci argues, the word-group οἰκοδομέω is instrumental to Paul's arguments for "the submission of individual rights for the sake of the common good," as an aspect of his concern for the community's factionalism.[7] Paul uses οἰκοδομέω both literally, when speaking of construction (3:9, 10, 12, 14), and metaphorically (8:1, 10; 10:23; 14:3, 4, 5, 12, 26), to speak of the edification of the community, and the two uses amplify one another: "The imagery and vocabulary together sustain a single theme describing the creation of the Christian community in terms of a building."[8]

The layering of images is an important concept to retain when turning to consider metaphors relating to the cult in general (1:8; 3:16–17; 4:1; 5:7–8; 6:19–20; 10:16–18; 11:23–26), and to the Passover (3:16–17; 11:23–26), in particular. The strength of Passover imagery occurs not merely in its explicit use, but in its resonance with all of the cultic metaphors and with language related to some of their entailments, such as eating, freedom and slavery, covenant, cleanness, belonging, holiness, and community.

---

6. For a full exposition of the importance of the theme of "belonging" to God, to Christ, and to one another in 1 Corinthians, see Victor Paul Furnish, *Theology of the First Letter to the Corinthians,* New Testament Theology (Cambridge: Cambridge University Press, 1999), especially chapters 2–4. As he says, succinctly, "Indeed, when we have come to terms with what Paul is saying about knowing God and belonging to Christ, we shall be very close to the theological center of 1 Corinthians, and with that, very close to the heart of his gospel as it finds expression here" (*Theology of the First Letter,* 29). See also Furnish, "Belonging to Christ," *Int* 44 (1990): 145–57.

7. Lanci, *A New Temple for Corinth,* 53.

8. Ibid., 60.

CULTIC METAPHORS AND MITCHELL'S
RHETORICAL PLAN OF 1 CORINTHIANS

Because 1 Corinthians is a longer and more complex letter than Philippians, it can be difficult to get a sense of the whole, and to see how recurrences of a metaphor or motif relate to the structure of the letter. An overview of the role of cultic metaphors in 1 Corinthians may be achieved by mapping the incidence of the metaphors in relationship to a compositional analysis, such as that provided by Margaret Mitchell.[9] Using her rhetorical scheme as a kind of scaffolding, one is able to see the roles that cultic metaphors play in supporting some of Paul's principal arguments. Not all of the metaphors invoke the Passover specifically, but by looking at all of the cultic metaphors, one can gain a sense for how they work together in the letter, as well as what is contributed more uniquely by metaphors relating to the Passover. The discussions to follow integrate a study of metaphors of the Passover into the four introductory rhetorical sections of the letter as outlined by Mitchell, the epistolary prescript (1:1–3), the thanksgiving (1:4–8), the πρόθεσις, or thesis statement (1:10), and the διήγησις, or statement of facts (1:11–17); as well as the first three sections of the proof (1:18–4:21; 5:1–11:1; 11:2–14:40). Metaphors of the Passover and its entailments cease to be employed after the third section of the proof, though there are a few sacrificially related metaphors (15:3, a reference to atonement; 15:20, 23, references to the offering of "firstfruits").

1 CORINTHIANS 1:1–3, EPISTOLARY PRESCRIPT

While the language of holiness is not particularly pronounced in 1 Corinthians, there are a few places where it is used pointedly and significantly, and one is at the very beginning of the letter, as a description of the role and purpose of the Corinthian church. After designating himself as κλητὸς ἀπόστολος, Paul addresses the community as κλητοὶ ἅγιοι, those who are ἡγιασμένοι ἐν Χριστῷ Ἰησοῦ. The word group ἅγιος/ἁγιάζω shows up again with the most frequency in 1 Cor 6 and 7 (6:1, 2, 11, 9; 7:13, 14 (three times), 34), where the boundaries of the community are most at issue.[10]

---

9. Margaret M. Mitchell, *Paul and the Rhetoric of Reconciliation* (Tübingen: Mohr Siebeck, 1991), 184–294.

10. Such as whether or not it is appropriate for members of the church to sue one another in courts of law; whether or not it is permissible for members of the church

Interestingly, it is also in chapter 6 that Paul likens the "body" of members of the Corinthian assembly to a "temple of the Holy Spirit" (6:19). While there has been much debate over whether Paul intends by his metaphor a replacement of the Jewish Temple at Jerusalem, or whether he is drawing upon the more immediate experience of pagan temples in Corinth,[11] in this wide-angle overview, the metaphor appears to play a role in the definition of the community in relation to its neighbors. Holiness is a kind of boundary marker between the *ekklesia* at Corinth and the city around them. Because holiness is not the central issue in the *prothesis* of the letter, it appears that discussions of holiness are instrumental to Paul's overall project of building up the community's sense of itself as a coherent body with a distinct "call" by God.

1 Corinthians 1:4–8, Epistolary Thanksgiving

The phrase "so that you may be blameless on the day of our Lord Jesus Christ" (ἀνεγκλήτους ἐν τῇ ἡμέρᾳ τοῦ Ἰησοῦ Χριστοῦ, 1 Cor 1:8) recalls the similar "so that in the day of Christ you may be pure and blameless" (ἵνα ἦτε εἰλικρινεῖς καὶ ἀπρόσκοποι εἰς ἡμέραν Χριστοῦ) in the thanksgiving in Phil 1:10, although the word ἀνεγκλήτος does not have the same history of cultic use as ἀπρόσκοπος. In fact, its biblical use is primarily in the New Testament, where it refers mainly to qualifications for church office (1 Tim 3:10, Tit 1:6, 7). Its use in Colossians (παραστῆσαι ὑμᾶς ἁγίους καὶ ἀμώμους καὶ ἀνεγκλήτους κατενώπιον αὐτοῦ, 1:22) ties it to cultic language (ἅγιοι, ἄμωμοι), but the NRSV translation of its use in 3 Maccabees gives perhaps the best sense of the word: "giving no ground for complaint" (3 Mac 5:31). There it refers to the blamelessness of the Jews, who have given the king no cause to bring a charge against them. The speaker in 3 Maccabees uses the primary meaning of ἐγκαλέω as a legal term, meaning to bring a charge against someone. Thus, ἀνεγκλητός, being above reproach, appears to have more moral than cultic overtones.

This slight difference may not be significant in 1 Cor 1:8, but it does point to an important distinction between the use of the sacrificial metaphors in 1 Corinthians and Philippians. In Philippians, the self-empty-

---

to engage in sex with prostitutes; sexual issues relating to marriage; marriage to an unbeliever; circumcision and membership in the community; slavery and membership in the community.

11. See Lanci's summary of these debates in *A New Temple for Corinth*, 7–23.

ing—or sacrificial—pattern of Jesus, portrayed in the Christ Hymn, is imitated by Timothy, Epaphroditus, and Paul, and is recommended as a model to the Philippians. They are to live self-givingly toward one another, and this willingness to live sacrificially is reflected in the language of offering in the very beginning of the letter (Phil 1:10). Paul prays that they may be like a spotless offering in the day of Christ. But in 1 Corinthians, as we shall see, Jesus Christ is the Passover lamb, but the people of the Corinthian church are to take as their moral model not the lamb, but the faithful Jewish community that prepares for the Passover by cleaning out the leaven, and that celebrates the feast in unity and covenant fidelity to God. Thus, Paul's prayer in the beginning of the letter is that they may be beyond reproach (in their actions as the community of the Passover), not that they be a spotless offering.

1 CORINTHIANS 1:10, ΠΡΟΘΕΣΙΣ,
THESIS STATEMENT TO THE DELIBERATIVE ARGUMENT

Παρακαλῶ δὲ ὑμᾶς, ἀδελφοί, διὰ τοῦ ὀνόματος τοῦ κυρίου ἡμῶν Ἰησοῦ Χριστοῦ, ἵνα τὸ αὐτὸ λέγητε πάντες καὶ μὴ ἐν ὑμῖν σχίσματα, ἦτε δὲ κατηρτισμένοι ἐν τῷ αὐτῷ νοῒ καὶ ἐν τῇ αὐτῇ γνώμῃ.

In the most general way, metaphors of the Passover relate to the *prothesis* of 1 Corinthians by supplementing three aspects of Paul's counsels in the letter as a whole. First, the Passover was unique to the Jewish people, and was, in fact, the defining celebration of the people of Israel. Jewish identity centered on the common experience of deliverance and salvation commemorated in the yearly Passover sacrifice. Metaphors of the Passover, applied to the Christian community at Corinth, may thus be used to emphasize the members' distinctive identity by virtue of what God has done among and through them (e.g., 1 Cor 5:7b–8). Metaphors of the Passover unite this gentile community to the historical people of God, the people for whom God has done marvelous things. This identification is important not only for defining the community in relation to outsiders (e.g., 10:14–22), but for establishing defining principles within the community as well (e.g., 1 Cor 5:9–13).

Second, the celebration of the Passover was, as we have seen in the writings of Josephus, understood as a time when much of the *nation* of Israel gathered together as a body. Josephus's inflation of the numbers of people gathered in Jerusalem for the festival only underscores the point

that it was symbolically important that his readers imagine the entire
Jewish people gathered as one (*Ant.* 11.4.8.109–112; 17.9.3.213.). Thus,
metaphors of the Passover in 1 Corinthians play a role in Paul's counsels
to unity (e.g., 1 Cor 11:28–29). The Passover as a *national* holiday seems to
fit in, as well, with the customary, political use of deliberative rhetoric. By
the mid-first century, God's nation has expanded to include gentiles, such
as the assembly in Corinth.

Third, the Feast of Unleavened Bread, with its ritual cleaning out of the
old leaven, lends itself to images of separation from defilement (e.g., 5:6–7,
and perhaps lingering through the arguments to follow, such as 6:15–19).
My point is not only that metaphors of the Passover undergird discrete
arguments for the community's distinctive identity, its unity, and its definition, but that the repetition of this family of images at various points in the
letter creates a resonance that is heard or felt throughout the letter, as Paul
takes up various issues relating to the threat of division and factionalism.

1 Corinthians 1:11–17, ΔΙΗΓΗΣΙΣ, Statement of Facts

The facts Paul exhibits concern mainly a misplaced understanding of
"belonging" at Corinth. There are factions among the members of the
community, as they divide the community along the lines of the different
teachers who have come through to guide them: Paul, Apollos, Cephas, and
"Christ" himself (!).[12] They have lost a sense for the belonging that unites
them, belonging to God through Christ, which results in their belonging to
one another as a community in Christ. Those who belong to one another are
people who are willing to give up what they might rightfully claim, in order
to bring about the well-being of another. As an example, Paul describes his
own relinquishing of eloquent wisdom for the good of the Corinthians, a
faithful presentation of the strange power (1:18) of the cross.[13]

1 Corinthians 1:18–4:21, First Section of the Proof, Censure of Corinthian Factionalism and the Need for Paul's Advice

Paul lays out the moral grounding of 1 Corinthians in 1:18–2:16 with
extended reflections on the λόγος τοῦ σταυροῦ, or, as I will refer to it, the

---

12. For consideration of what might be meant by "I am Christ's," see Furnish,
Theology of the First Letter, 30.
13. See the discussion of 1 Cor 11:24, τὸ σῶμα τὸ ὑπὲρ ὑμῶν, below.

"logic of the cross."[14] The NRSV translates λόγος τοῦ σταυροῦ as the "message about the cross," but this characterization of the λόγος as a spoken proclamation of some kind misses its active, moral function.[15] Rather than speech about something, this λόγος is an enacted pattern of behavior. The synecdoche of the cross (including the resurrection of the crucified one) reveals the counterintuitive, countercultural wisdom of God, who raises up what the world despises. For Paul, Jesus's death on the cross functions as a moral paradigm of selfless concern for the well-being of others, especially the lowest or weakest of others, a pattern of life that he commends to the community at Corinth (8:11–12).[16] This moral pat-

---

14. I have chosen the English cognate "logic" to translate λόγος as a way to emphasize the pattern of moral calculation that Paul is encouraging for the church at Corinth. The "logic of the cross" is a way of calculating (λογίζομαι) one's actions with the well-being of others as the focus of one's concern.

15. Philippians also exhibits this "logic" of the cross as a moral paradigm (Phil 2:5–11), but without the precise language of the λόγος τοῦ σταυροῦ. Thiselton translates ῾λόγος τοῦ σταυροῦ as the "proclamation of the cross" (*The First Epistle to the Corinthians: A Commentary on the Greek Text* [Grand Rapids: Eerdmans, 2000], 147); Furnish translates it as the "word" of the cross, but as a kind of shorthand for the wisdom of God, as opposed to that of the world (*Theology of the First Letter*, 39–40). A very interesting light might be shed upon what Paul means by considering Nussbaum's reflection on the word *logos* in relation to her discussion of the therapeutic dimension of Hellenistic philosophy: "As soon as there was an expert art of medicine that could, by some precise and teachable procedures, bring relief to the suffering body, it was natural to ask whether there might not be some other art that could in a parallel way handle "diseases" of thought, judgment, and desire. It was also very natural, thinking about experiences of persuasion, consolation, exhortation, criticism, and calming, to feel that the art or arts in question would be arts of speech and argument, of *logos* somehow understood. In fact, an analogy between *logos* and medical treatment is extremely old and deep in ancient Greek talk about the personality and its difficulties. From Homer on we encounter, frequently and prominently, the idea that *logos* is to illnesses of the soul as medical treatment is to illnesses of the body" (Martha C. Nussbaum, *Therapy of Desire: Theory and Practice in Hellenistic Ethics* [Princeton: Princeton University Press, 1994], 48–49). The relationship between healing and *logos* is especially intriguing as regards 1 Cor 1:18, where the λόγος τοῦ σταυροῦ is used in conjunction with the verb σώζω. What Paul means is that the saving power of the cross is released when one lives into a pattern of action consistent with its "logic," namely, giving up what one might be entitled to, for the advantage of the (weaker) neighbor. One's own process of healing, or salvation, is experienced in this pattern of self-giving (τοῖς δὲ σῳζομένοις ἡμῖν [ὁ λόγος τοῦ σταυροῦ] δύναμις θεοῦ).

16. It is *God's* pattern of self-giving and God's intentions that are carried out in Jesus's dying "for the weak" (1 Cor 8:11).

tern serves as a consistent logic, uniting God's calling of the Corinthians
(1:26–29); Paul's self-description of his behavior among the Corinthians
(2:1–5), his sufferings on their behalf (4:8–13), and the rights he gives
up for their good (9:3–23); the counsels of chapter 8 and 11:17–34; the
pattern of love put forward in chapter 13; and the insistence, in chapter
14, that prophecy is not for the one who speaks out, but for the building
up of the community, and thus silence is sometimes called for (14:30).
Metaphors of the Passover function in concert with the logic of the cross,
not to describe the actions of the Corinthians as their "Passover sacrifice,"
but to suggest that this pattern of behavior can guide them into becoming
the community that is unified and prepared to gather properly around the
Passover table (11:34).

In chapter 3, metaphors of joint labor on a building yield to the first
metaphor of a temple. Paul describes himself and Apollos, the other principal teacher of the community, as διάκονοι δι᾽ ὧν ἐπιστεύσατε (3:5), and
then as συνεργοί (3:9), who have labored within the community, described
first as God's field, then God's building.[17] At 3:10, Paul compares himself
to the initial ἀρχιτέκτων of this building, the one charged with laying the
foundation. At 3:16 he turns the metaphor slightly, and what has been an
undefined building becomes God's temple (ναός θεοῦ). While the image
of the temple is not linked to the Passover in the narrative traditions,
by the first century Passover was celebrated in and around the Temple
in Jerusalem, and was coordinated by the priests (see m. Pesah. 5:5–7.).
Metaphors of the Temple sound together with those of Passover, adding
to the conception of the ἐκκλησία of gentile believers as a place of God's
focused presence.

Subsequently, in what may be a continuation of the imagery of the
temple, Paul uses language sometimes related to the service of the temple
to describe his, Apollos's and Cephas's roles toward the community: οὕτως
ἡμᾶς λογιζέσθω ἄνθρωπος ὡς ὑπηρέτας Χριστοῦ καὶ οἰκονόμους μυστηρίων
θεοῦ (4:1). The noun ὑπηρέτης is first found in classical Greek literature as
a descriptor for Hermes, as messenger to the gods (θεῶν ὑπηρέτης, Aeschy-

---

17. I have previously drawn attention to the possible background of Jer 1:10 to
1 Cor 3:9, in the quick shift of imagery from field to building: "See, today I appoint
you over nations and over kingdoms, to pluck up and to pull down, to destroy and to
overthrow, to build and to plant." Paul also echoes the first chapter of Jeremiah in his
autobiographical narrative in Gal 1:15. These references may give some insight into
Paul's view of himself as carrying forward the lineage of God's prophets.

lus, *Prom.*, 954). Likewise, the men of Delphi are described as ὑπηρέται of Apollo, as they are the mediators of the god's oracles (Sophocles, *Oed. tyr.* 712). But the term also had wide usage in the military, governmental, medical, and judicial spheres to describe the role of all kinds of relatively high-level assistants, such as aides-de-camp, quarter-masters, medical assistants, notaries, secretaries, executioners. The common ground is that the ὑπηρέτης serves by willingly carrying out the orders of a superior. Obedience is the primary characteristic of the faithful ὑπηρέτης. The ὑπηρέτης is not a δοῦλος, as the obedience is freely rendered. The term is witnessed rarely in the Septuagint, but appears in the writings of Philo and Josephus, both literally (to describe assistants of rulers and high-ranking officials), and also metaphorically, as in Philo's description of smell as the ὑπηρέτης of taste (*Sacrifices* 44). Josephus uses the term to describe the work of the Levites in their assistance of the priests in the Temple (*Ant.* 3.11.1.258; 3.8.1.189). Josephus's use is the kind that may color Paul's employment of the term at 1 Corinthians 4:1. Ὑπηρέτης is also the word used to describe the attendant who takes the Torah scroll from Jesus in the synagogue in Nazareth (Luke 4:20). Like much of the imagery of 1 Corinthians, ὑπηρέτης functions in both the sphere of the Jewish Temple and in the sphere of the mundane. The complexity of possible contextual references for the term is consistent with what we will come to see increasingly as a blurring of the lines between the clearly holy and set apart (in time, space, or persons) and the ordinary (in time, space, or persons).

John Lanci's context for the imagery of the temple is the archeological evidence of the many construction projects taking place in Corinth in the mid-first century.[18] Indeed, in chapter 3 Paul moves very naturally from the imagery of construction (3:9–15) to the metaphor of the temple (3:16–17). According to Lanci, "a building project presented a number of challenges to its workers which were similar to the challenges Paul saw confronting a fragmented Christian community."[19] Thus the metaphor of the temple-as-building is a part of Paul's strategy for rebuilding community at Corinth. Drawing together some of the themes of 1 Corinthians, he notes that "[a]ncient construction projects offered people with many different skills the challenge of working on a single project," that "the work of the individual had to be accomplished in concert with others for the

---

18. John Lanci, *A New Temple for Corinth.*
19. Ibid., 77.

sake of the common task," that itinerants from many different countries
and backgrounds had to learn to work together, that "both slaves and
free people worked together," and that the complexity of building projects often required the skills of an ἀρχιτέκτων, or construction supervisor.[20]
Because the temples under construction that Paul's audience would have
been familiar with were all pagan temples, Lanci asserts that the referent
of temple imagery in 1 Corinthians is therefore not the Jewish Temple in
Jerusalem, but those close at hand in Corinth.

However, the complexity of Paul's use of metaphors should lead one to
ask, rather, whether Paul may be purposely leaving the precise referent of
the temple ambiguous. Lanci's description of the processes of construction
at Corinth in the first century brings depth and liveliness to his explication of the metaphor of the temple as it relates to the imagery of construction, and therefore as it relates to the arguments against factionalism.
But simultaneously, the metaphor of the temple also reverberates through
the metaphors of Passover (5:6–8), through discussions of holiness (most
obviously at 6:19, but also at 1:2; 6:1, 2, 9, 11; 7:13, 14, 34), and the practice of sacrifice (10:18–22). This context of references to Jewish practices,
Jewish sacrifices, and Jewish holy days, together with the qualifier θεοῦ,
establishes the *principal* referent of the ναὸς θεοῦ of 3:16 as the Temple at
Jerusalem, the only place where God's spirit (τὸ πνεῦμα τοῦ θεοῦ) could
truly be said to dwell, while *at the same time* the proximity of the image
to the discussion of construction may provoke visions of the immediate
context of the temples being built in Corinth.[21] It is Paul's evocation of
such a density of experience through his imagery that, no doubt, rendered
his images memorable and powerful when his letters were read in their
original setting (2 Cor 10:10a).

Given the comparisons to the temple and the possible reference to
temple personnel (ὑπηρέται Χριστοῦ), then, it is especially intriguing to
see the use Paul makes of the phrase ὡς περικαθάρματα τοῦ κόσμου (1 Cor
4:13) as a descriptor for himself and the other apostles. Thiselton translates
περικαθάρματα τοῦ κόσμου as "the world's scum," noting also its technical
use in the Septuagint as a synecdoche to refer to the scapegoat (περικάθαρμα

---

20. Ibid.

21. Paul would perhaps have had in his own mind memories of the ongoing construction of Herod's temple in Jerusalem, which continued almost until the date of its
destruction in 70.

δὲ δικαίου ἄνομος, Prov 21:18).[22] Like some of the other imagery of 1 Corinthians, περικαθάρματα has both a meaning within the sphere of the Jewish cult and a meaning in the wider Hellenistic culture (such as, ὑπηρέτης or ναός). Thiselton notes the origin of the word in the action of scouring out a pot to remove the filthy scum that clings to the surface. It is precisely this tone of revulsion that gives the word its power when used to describe what is placed upon the scapegoat before it is sent into the wilderness. At 1 Cor 4:13 Paul compares himself and the other apostles to such "offscourings," perhaps intending a reference to what is placed upon the head of the scapegoat on Yom Kippur.[23] This is the sort of imagery that tips one off to the fact that Paul is not literally reinscribing the community at Corinth as a temple, even less as *the* Temple or the *true* Temple. There is no simple replacement of the Jerusalem Temple by the ἐκκλησία θεοῦ happening here, since the ὑπηρέται Χριστοῦ are simultaneously the περικαθάρματα τοῦ κόσμου. These terms are evidence of the upside-down interpretations that are characteristic of an apocalyptic worldview. From one perspective, Paul and his fellow apostles are the scum of the world; from another perspective, they are the servants of God. Apocalyptic imagery does not change the world; it changes how the world is *seen*. The clearly metaphorical use of the term περικαθάρματα is an indication of the imaginative purpose of the cultic metaphors, as they serve to reinterpret reality after the crucifixion of God's Messiah.

The apocalyptic dimension of changing how people *see* things is underscored by 4:9, where God is the subject who "exhibits" (ἀποδείκνυμι) the apostles as "last of all," allowing them to be a "spectacle" on a stage that includes heavenly and earthly beings together. God's visible demonstration here anticipates the cognate noun ἔνδειξις in Rom 3:25, where God puts forward the cross of Christ as visual proof (ἔνδειξις) of God's justice at work. The power of both statements is that they leave events as they are

---

22. Thiselton, *First Epistle to the Corinthians*, 364.
23. See the discussion of the scapegoat by Stephen Finlan above, ch. 5; and Finlan, *The Background and Content of Paul's Cultic Atonement Metaphors*, AcBib 19 (Atlanta: Society of Biblical Literature: 2004), 97–98. Andreas Lindemann, in weighing the possible cultic vs. noncultic interpretation of περικαθάρματα and περίψημα, decides for the noncultic interpretation: "Da also beide Worte auch kultische Bedeutung haben können (das, was kultisch "abgewischt" bzw. "zusammengekehrt" wird), wäre hier etwa die Bedeutung "Sündenböcke" o.ä. möglich…. Da aber beide Worte umgangssprachlich eine verwerfliche Person bezeichnen … liegt diese Auslegung doch wohl näher" (*Der Erste Korintherbrief* [Tübingen: Mohr Siebeck], 110).

(Jesus is crucified, Paul is beaten and imprisoned), but they completely
alter the interpretation of the event. In the case of Romans, the cross
becomes the mercy seat in the holy of holies; in the case of 1 Corinthians,
the scum of the world are seen to be God's emissaries. In both cases, what
is truly remarkable is that it is God who is said to be making the metaphors, changing how believers interpret and live in the world.

First Corinthians 4 is bracketed by language that will lead directly
into images of the Passover, the verb φυσιόω (4:6, 18–19). Φυσιόω is the
koinē Greek equivalent of the Attic Greek φυσάω, to blow or puff, as with
a bellows, or to blow or puff up in the sense of distending something. By
extension, it means to puff oneself up with arrogance or conceit. Philo
makes this connection in explaining why leavened dough is not permitted
as a grain offering (Lev 2:11, 6:17): "Leaven [is forbidden] because of the
rising (ἔπαρσιν) it produces. Here again we have a symbol, that none as he
approaches the altar should be uplifted (ἐπαίρηται, "risen") or puffed up by
arrogance (φυσηθεὶς ὑπ'ἀλαζονείας)" (*Spec Leg* 1.53.293). This is clearly the
direction in which Paul begins to takes the word in 5:6, as we shall see in
the next section. "Puffing up" is an important connector between the first
and second sections of the proof, and is a recurring charge that Paul issues
against some in the Corinthian community (1 Cor 4:6, 18, 19; 5:2; 8:1; 13:4).

1 CORINTHIANS 5:1–11:1, SECOND SECTION OF THE PROOF,
THE INTEGRITY OF THE CORINTHIAN COMMUNITY
AGAINST OUTSIDE DEFILEMENT

At 5:2 Paul repeats the charge that the community is "puffed up," this
time over an incident of what Paul considers sexual immorality: καὶ ὑμεῖς
πεφυσιωμένοι ἐστέ! Paul's solution to the problem makes this use of the term
particularly interesting—that the offending person be removed from the
community, as yeast is removed before the Passover: ἵνα ἀρθῇ ἐκ μέσου ὑμῶν
ὁ τὸ ἔργον τοῦτο πράξας (5:2). Here, the use of the metaphor has clearly suggested actions congruent with it. Once yeast has been detected in the household that expects to celebrate the Passover, the yeast must be cleared out.

"Boasting" (καύχημα) is the term Paul next links to the idea of being
puffed up, and sums up its danger by saying, οὐκ οἴδατε ὅτι μικρὰ ζύμη ὅλον
τὸ φύραμα ζυμοῖ; (5:6b).[24] While the force of this statement is most likely

_____

24. Note that "puffing up" (φυσιόομαι) and boasting (καυχάομαι) are also linked at

directed to the understanding that a small amount of corruption may have a great effect,[25] the move to the metaphor of yeast leads Paul directly into more explicit metaphors of the Passover: ἐκκαθάρατε[26] τὴν παλαιὰν ζύμην, ἵνα ἦτε νέον φύραμα, καθώς ἐστε ἄζυμοι. Καὶ γὰρ τὸ πάσχα ἡμῶν ἐτύθη Χριστός. ὥστε ἑορτάζωμεν μὴ ἐν ζύμῃ παλαιᾷ μηδὲ ἐν ζύμῃ κακίας καὶ πονηρίας ἀλλ᾽ἐν ἀζύμοις εἰλικρινείας καὶ ἀληθείας (5:7–8). Furthermore, perhaps with the language of the feast still in his mind, Paul counsels at 5:11 not only not to "mix with" (συναναμίγνυσθαι)[27] such a person but not even to eat with such a one (μηδὲ συνεσθίειν).

In comparing this with the biblical instructions concerning the Passover (Exodus 12:1–13:10; Lev 23:5–8; Numbers 9:1–14; 28:16–17; Deut 16:1–8), there is very little correspondence of language,[28] except for the essential concepts (πάσχα, θύω, ἄζυμοι), and yet the *actions* described for the community correspond to the whole complex of the actions of preparation for the Passover, together with the Feast of Unleavened Bread: careful attention to what yeast there may be in the house, removal of the yeast, the sacrifice of the Passover lamb, the gathering of the those who have prepared themselves appropriately (and *only* those) to enjoy a common meal. Paul's reference appears to be not a text, but his own actual experiences of celebrating the Passover.

The metaphor of leaven actually shifts between 5:7 and 5:8, with the sacrifice of the paschal lamb, Christ, as the hinge-point. Verses 5:6–7a depict the community as a batch of unleavened dough. This single loaf

---

4:6–7. In 2 Corinthians, language related to "puffing up" is rarer (φυσιώσεις, 12:20), but the language of boasting increases exponentially (2 Cor 1:12, 14; 5:12; 7:4, 14; 8:24; 9:2, 3; 10:8, 13, 15, 16, 17; 11:10, 12, 16, 17, 18, 30; 12:1, 5, 6, 9). It appears that arrogance remains an issue for Paul in Corinth, but he does not always address it with the imagery of "puffing up," as he does in 1 Corinthians.

25. As is the sense in Gal 5:9.

26. Thiselton writes, "The imperative ἐκκαθάρατε is the first aorist active imperative of ἐκκαθαίρω, in which the compound ἐκ signifies both motion and intensity, and the effective aorist signifies the summons to perform a specific act. It is not too much to perceive in the Greek compound and syntax an implicit urgency about effectively completing this action with thoroughness, especially in its ritualistic context" (*First Epistle to the Corinthians*, 405).

27. Thiselton, "not to mix indiscriminately with" (*First Epistle to the Corinthians*, 409).

28. Furnish remarks upon the surprising paucity of scriptural citations used by Paul in 1 Corinthians to support his ethical counsels ("Belonging to Christ," 148).

appears to anticipate the statement of 10:17, "Because there is one bread, we who are many are one body, for we all partake of the one bread." 5:7b describes the death of Christ as a Passover sacrifice. Then, at 5:8, the hearers shift metaphorically from bread to become the people who celebrate the Passover together, with their unleavened bread "of sincerity and truth." The quick shift of referent in this passage reveals the way in which metaphors serve as active tools of thought for Paul. There are two traditional sayings here, the first having to do with the power of a grain of yeast (μικρὰ ζύμη ὅλον τὸ φύραμα ζυμοῖ), and the second the Christian teaching (τὸ πάσχα ἡμῶν ἐτύθη Χριστός), but around them Paul has woven ad hoc the two harmonious, but not identical, images of the community as unleavened loaf and as Passover celebrants. These verses clearly illustrate the cognitive usefulness of metaphors, to bring to speech a hunch about the relationship between two things, and then to suggest actions in accordance with the new comparison.

The explicit, but unexplained, references to the Passover in 5:6–8 cause one to inquire about the composition of the community with regard to the Jewish or Greco-Roman cults.[29] For whom would these images and the memories they evoke be most powerful? Fee writes, "[Paul] clearly assumes that his Gentile readers will understand this thoroughly Jewish imagery."[30] Fee speaks as though there were a hard boundary between gentile and Jew, and perhaps also between a traditional Jew and a "believer" in Jesus. Across this boundary, understanding would be difficult to obtain. But perhaps Paul's use of imagery of the Passover calls us to see a more fluid situation in which Paul and other followers of Jesus, whatever their previous background, continued to observe many of the Jewish practices, as we have seen above,[31] even if they have added a new dimension to their understanding of the meaning of their actions.[32]

---

29. As noted above, Paul also makes reference to Pentecost (16:8), without seeming to think that the reference needs any explanation. Lindemann says of the Passover, "darüber sind die korinthischen Christen also durchaus informiert" (*Der Erste Korintherbrief*, 128), but he does not support the notion that the community either observes a yearly Passover or perceives the weekly "Herrenmahl" as a Passover celebration (129).

30. Fee, *First Epistle to the Corinthians*, 218.

31. See chapter 4, concerning Paul's relationship to the Jewish sacrificial cult.

32. Clearly, there is new interpretation that has been applied to the Passover by early believers, as the crucifixion of Jesus Christ appears to have been likened to the

On the comparison of Jesus's death to the Passover sacrifice, Fee writes, "the slaying of the lamb is what led to the Jews' being 'unleavened.' So too with us, Paul says. Our Lamb has been sacrificed; through his death we have received forgiveness from the past and freedom for new life in Christ."[33] To say that the slaying of the lamb is what makes the people unleavened, and that what its death achieves is forgiveness of the past, is an eccentric reading of the story of the Passover and its subsequent reenactments. The people prepare unleavened cakes or clean out the leaven by their own efforts; and the death of the lamb is an act of obedience that initiates God's deliverance of the people from oppression, not forgiveness of past sins. Thiselton's interpretation of 5:7 is more accurate to the inner logic of the metaphor of the Passover:

> Just as the Passover festival embraces a series of aspects and events, so the whole work of Christ, including his death and resurrection, includes many aspects. But *the death of Christ* corresponds to the death of the Passover lamb. Here, for Paul, the old is abolished and the blood of the Passover lamb ratifies the promises of redemption *from* bondage (where "Egypt" symbolizes the bondage of human existence without Christ) *to* a new purity and freedom *by* a costly act. This is not to read *into* Paul any "theory of the atonement," for the transparently clear reference here to *sacrifice* (θύω) is complemented by the language of redemption (ἀγοράζω) in 6:20, and *covenant promise, identification,* and the shedding of *Christ's blood* in 11:25–26. The blood of the Passover lamb, splashed upon the lintel of the door of the redeemed household *marks the identity* of those who are about to enter a new freedom from bondage to a new purity of service as God's own holy people.[34]

When paying close attention to sacrificial metaphors, one needs to ask, what is the *most likely* content of metaphors of the Passover? While atonement is

---

sacrifice of the Passover lambs prior to the writing of 1 Corinthians. This passage is one of those that begin with οὐκ οἴδατε ὅτι.

33. Fee, *First Epistle to the Corinthians*, 218. Later in the same discussion of 1 Cor 5:8, Fee says, "The death of Christ has freed us from sin; thus we are to live as those who have been set free" (219). Clearly, the connection between Passover and freedom has caused him to connect the passage at hand with Rom 6:15–23. But the reader needs to be very careful not to import elements of the Yom Kippur sacrifice where they are not present. Doing so causes one to miss the exact purpose of this particular cultic metaphor.

34. Thiselton, *First Epistle to the Corinthians*, 405–6, emphasis original.

almost always heard as an overtone of Jewish sacrifice, atonement is not one of the *principal* entailments of the Passover. So when Paul says that "our paschal lamb, Christ, has been sacrificed,"[35] what role is the metaphor playing in the counsel at hand? What arguments does it support, and how? Metaphors drawn from the Passover are used primarily to support the *prothesis* of 1 Corinthians by calling this church to the same kind of unity that properly characterizes those who keep the Passover feast. As an aspect of that unity, and to strengthen it, Paul is also calling the Corinthians to greater care in the conduct of their common moral life, which he compares to careful preparations for the Passover.

Paul has suggested that the community's boasting, its "puffing up," is evidence that it has not been scrupulous in cleaning out all the "old leaven." The "old leaven" is presumably both the behavior of the man who is living with his father's wife *and* the community's unworthy handling of his case (ἐν ζύμῃ κακίας καὶ πονηρίας). This "old leaven," though perhaps insignificant in its beginning, has corrupted the entire lump of dough, so that they no longer perceive how their actions miss the mark. Their boasting is the outward show of the yeast that infects them. The metaphor deepens as Paul says, somewhat ambiguously, καθώς ἐστε ἄζυμοι.[36] It would appear that, whatever they were before, incorporation into Christ has made them "unleavened," sincere, true (5:8). Ritually, this kind of purity would mean that they were a people prepared to be in proximity to God.

As we have seen before, the metaphor is being used to redescribe the community's reality. What they "really" are is unleavened. Now what will they do? "Let us celebrate" (ὥστε ἑορτάζομεν). The celebration of the Passover had long been an act of resistance for the Jewish community under foreign domination. The feast was eaten in a reclining position in the first century, a sign that all who ate it were free, not slaves, as they had been in Egypt.[37] No matter that in their current political situation, Israel was under the domination of Rome. They were free people in the deepest sense, and confirmed their freedom by their posture at the Passover and by their keeping of the covenant with the God who freed them. Likewise, the church in Corinth (now a part of Israel by virtue of being incorporated

---

35. I agree with Thiselton's preference for translating πάσχα as paschal *lamb*, or Passover lamb, as the lamb is properly the object of the sacrifice.

36. The NRSV adds the intensifier "really" ("just as you really are unleavened").

37. See Joachim Jeremias, *The Eucharistic Words of Jesus*, trans. Norman Perrin (New York: Scribner's Sons, 1966), 48 (and nn. 4, 5), on reclining at the Passover.

into the people of God) is being invited to live into the reality opened up by the metaphor of the Passover: purity (being unleavened), sincerity, and truth.

It appears that God's forgiveness is *assumed* here, for all who will again go carefully about the work of finding and eradicating the destructive behaviors that represent the old leaven, but forgiveness is not the principal force of the metaphor, "Christ, our Passover." Rather, it is a call to careful conduct of community life, a call to live as people worthy of the freedom and fullness of life they have been brought into by the cross of Christ. It would appear that the saving image Paul has used with the community at Corinth is that of the Passover. The crucifixion of Jesus by Rome has been appropriated by God as a Passover sacrifice, to achieve the deliverance of the gentiles and to bring them into a place where they may live rightly with God and their fellow believers.

The gathering of the whole nation of Israel for the celebration of the Passover is not merely the gathering of a tribe, but the gathering of those who have prepared themselves for the festival. The use of a metaphor of Passover, in a letter devoted to rebuilding true community among the congregation at Corinth, undergirds arguments against divisiveness by focusing on behavior within the community that Paul regards as corrupting. The community that celebrates the Passover is united not only in the sense that they get along with one another, but in the sense that they have undergone a common practice of preparation for the feast, in this case a feast that is always ongoing. Philo says, in his discussion of the Passover and the Feast of Unleavened Bread, that "the whole life of a good person is the equivalent of a feast (ἑορτή) held by one who has expelled grief and fear and desire and the other passions and maladies of the soul."[38] Paul appears to have something similar in mind, in connecting ἑορτάζωμεν (5:8) with the ongoing moral life of the community.[39]

This sense of proper preparation continues at 6:11, when Paul contrasts what the community used to be (ἄδικοι) with what has happened to bring them into the ἐκκλησία τοῦ θεοῦ at Corinth: ἀλλὰ ἀπελούσασθε,

---

38. ἅπας ὁ τοῦ σπουδαίου βίος ἰσότιμος ἑορτῇ νομίζηται λύπην καὶ φόβον καὶ ἐπιθυμίαν καὶ τἄλλα πάθη καὶ νοσήματα τῆς ψυχῆς ἐληλακότος (Philo, *Spec. Laws* 2.157).

39. Thiselton notes, "The continuous present tense offers grounds for Godet's comment that 'Our Passover feast is not for a week, but for a lifetime.' This reflects Chrysostom's observation: 'It is a festival, then, the whole time in which we live'" (*First Epistle to the Corinthians*, 406).

ἀλλὰ ἡγιάσθητε, ἀλλὰ ἐδικαιώθητε ἐν τῷ ὀνόματι τοῦ κυρίου Ἰησοῦ Χριστοῦ καὶ ἐν τῷ πνεύματι τοῦ θεοῦ ἡμῶν. Being washed, made holy, and made just ("rectified"[40]) is consistent with being appropriately prepared to celebrate the Passover. For instance, m. Pesah. specifies that "one who has suffered a bereavement of a close relative *immerses* and eats his Passover offering in the evening" (8:8a, emphasis added). Washing renders the person who is cultically unclean properly prepared to join the community for the feast. It is not necessary to imagine a more complicated sacramental background to the statement than a reference to ritual immersion that cleans a person before participating in a sacrifice.[41]

The metaphor of the body (σῶμα) as a temple of the Holy Spirit (ναὸς τοῦ ἐν ὑμῖν ἁγίου πνεύματος), "which you have from God" (1 Cor 6:19–20), is one of the strong cultic metaphors of the letter that have developed currency in Christian teaching and preaching far beyond reference to this particular use. Yet for understanding the constellation of metaphors of the Passover in 1 Corinthians, it plays a supporting role, not a central one. In a variety of ways, this passage resonates with the imagery of the Passover. The first is, simply, that Passover was celebrated in and around the Temple in Jerusalem in Paul's day, and so mention of the Temple naturally amplifies the motif of the Passover in the letter. Secondly, though the Passover lambs were slaughtered in the Temple precincts in the first century, the meat was consumed in homes, if possible.[42] Philo describes how the sanctity of the Temple extends to the homes in which the feast is consumed: "At that time, every house is clothed with the appearance and dignity of a temple."[43] At Passover, the lines between the everyday and the holy, between the familiar and the awesome, are blurred. For a time, home becomes Temple. Paul uses this extension of holiness to speak of the daily moral life of the church at Corinth, and clearly has done so previously (οὐκ οἴδατε ὅτι).[44]

---

40. So Leander Keck, *Romans*, ANTC 6 (Nashville: Abingdon, 2005), 101; and Furnish, *Theology of the First Letter*, 55.

41. Fee agrees that it is unlikely, on both theological and grammatical grounds, that ἀπελούσασθε is an allusion to baptism (*The First Epistle to the Corinthians*, NICNT 7 [Grand Rapids: Eerdmans, 1987], 246–47).

42. For a fuller description of how pilgrims to Jerusalem celebrated the feast, see Jeremias, *Eucharistic Words of Jesus*, 42–43; m. Pesah. 7.

43. ἑκάστη δὲ οἰκία κατ'ἐκεῖνον τὸν χρόνον σχῆμα ἱεροῦ καὶ σεμνότητα περιβέβληται (*Spec. Laws* 2.148).

44. This is the eighth time Paul has used the phrase, οὐκ οἴδατε ὅτι (3:16; 5:6; 6:2, 3, 9, 15, 16, 19), and two more follow (9:13, 24).

The third and fourth points I want to make are connected. The body that Paul is calling a temple of the Holy Spirit is simultaneously the body of any believer and the common body of the community (τὸ σῶμα ὑμῶν). The ambiguity that has sent scholars to their Greek grammars to solve the problem of the singular noun and its accompanying plural pronoun is more than likely intended by Paul as an important conundrum for the Corinthians to consider.[45] Is there one body at issue here, or many? Isn't that precisely the question that Paul wants the community to ask? What Paul said of "the whole lump" at 5:6 remains true: that, as with a lump of dough, any corruption in a portion of the body of the community will affect the whole. Moreover, this common body is defined overall by belonging: it belongs, individually and corporately, to God (οὗ ἔχετε ἀπὸ θεοῦ καὶ οὐκ ἐστὲ ἑαυτῶν), who has bought it at a price (ἠγοράσθητε γὰρ τιμῆς).

The question of the σῶμα will arise pointedly again, at 11:24, 27, and 29, where Passover imagery is more explicit. In relation to the Passover, then, 6:19–20 amplifies the themes of the holiness of the prepared community, their unity as both a reality and a call, and the fact of their belonging, to God and, consequentially, to one another. Paul remonstrates with the community for their not having prepared for the celebration of the feast[46] as they ought. First Corinthians 6 and 7 contain a sustained list of directives for cleaning up the community's life. The tenor of many of the counsels is a combination of scrupulosity and realism similar to what is evidenced in m. Pesahim. For instance, m. Pesah. 3:7 deals with the kinds of ordinary calamities that can occur in the middle of one's attempt to prepare for the festival properly, such as the person who has set out to observe

---

45. Hans Conzelmann writes, "What was said in 3:16 of the community, that it is the temple of God, that the Spirit of God dwells in it, is here transferred to the individual" (*1 Corinthians: A Commentary on the First Epistle to the Corinthians*, Hermeneia [Philadelphia: Fortress, 1975], 112). Thiselton writes, in a slightly more nuanced way, "The corporate aspect of the community as the Spirit's temple in 3:16 receives a more individual application here, which arises in the context of the personal lifestyle at issue in this chapter" (*First Epistle to the Corinthians*, 474). Thiselton also comments in a note on the text that "the singular with the genitive plural ὑμῶν may seem awkward, while classical Greek sources offer evidence of the distributive use of the singular where a plural meaning might be suggested" (474).

46. It appears that the celebration of the Passover of Christ is conceived by Paul as a daily reality, much like the recurring proclamation of his death at every Lord's Supper, as he says at 11:26. As Lindemann says, the church lives daily in a "quasi Passa-situation" (*Der Erste Korintherbrief*, 129).

the feast at his father-in-law's house, and then realizes along the way that he has some leaven left in his own house. If he can reasonably turn around, remove the leaven, and still arrive at his father-in-law's house in time for the feast, he should do so. But if he can't, "let him nullify it in his heart." Similarly, if he has had to leave his home, with the leaven still in it, to save someone from drowning, or from thugs, or from fire or a collapsed house, then he may nullify the leaven in his heart. But if his journeying is merely "a pleasure jaunt" on the festival, and he remembers that he has some leaven left in his house, then by all means he must return and clear out the leaven.

Attentiveness and realism also characterize Paul's counsels to those who are married to unbelievers (1 Cor 7:12–16). Like many of the situations presented in m. Pesahim, the situation here is not ideal. Some members of the Christian community—those who, as we have seen above, are explicitly "called to be holy" (1:2)—are married to people who are not a part of that community. So what becomes of the holiness of the believer? For Paul, the dynamism of the believer's holiness sanctifies his or her spouse, because if this were not so, then their children would be unclean (ἀκάθαρτος), but as it is, the couple's children are holy (ἅγιος) (7:14).[47] There is a limit to scrupulosity with regard to holiness, and in this case it is reached in the discussion of children. The children are clearly clean, clearly holy. In the Mishnah, limits are likewise reached when a principle is stretched to the point at which it becomes absurd, as in m. Pesah. 1:2. Once a family has cleaned out the leaven as well as they can, "They do not scruple that a weasel might have dragged [leaven] from house to house and place to place. For if so, [they will have to scruple that a weasel has dragged leaven] from courtyard to courtyard and from town to town, [so,] there is no end to the matter." Paul's comparisons to the preparations for the Passover and the Feast of Unleavened Bread are intended to help his community chart a course that is careful, but balanced; otherwise, there would be "no end to the matter."

An interesting problem faces Paul in the discussion of slavery and freedom at 7:17–24. Freedom from bondage in Egypt is obviously one of the principal entailments of the Passover narrative, and yet, perhaps in part because he is addressing some whose favorite slogan is πάντα μοι

---

47. I hold the so-called "optimistic" interpretation of this passage. See the discussion of the optimistic and pessimistic views in Thiselton (First Epistle to the Corinthians, 537–38).

ἔξεστιν (6:12, twice; and πάντα ἔξεστιν, 10:23), Paul does not contrast the social experience of slavery with a state of complete freedom in Christ. Rather, the fact of one's having been "purchased" (τιμῆς ἠγοράσθητε, 7:23) renders one not ἐλεύθερος (a free man), but ἀπελεύθερος κυρίου (a freedman of the lord). As Dale Martin writes,

> When Christ buys a person, the salvific element of the metaphor is not in the movement from slavery to freedom but in the movement from a lower level of slavery (as the slave of just anybody or the slave of sin) to a higher level of slavery (as the slave of Christ).... By calling the slave a "freedman of Christ" rather than a "free man *in* Christ," Paul stresses precisely what Conzelmann denies: that the status of the person is the issue, not eschatological freedom.... The slave's real status is determined by his or her placement in a different household entirely: the household of Christ. The slave is a freedperson of the Lord and shares in the benefits, status, and obligations that relationship brings.[48]

Placing Paul's choice of the phrase ἀπελεύθερος κυρίου within this study of entailments of the Passover sharpens one's awareness of how deftly Paul is attempting to handle the issue of freedom in Corinth. The situation there is shown to be different from the one that prevails in Galatia and Rome, where Paul uses metaphors that more directly evoke imagery of deliverance from bondage (Gal 4:1–9, 24–26; 5:1; Rom 8:12–17, 21–23). The metaphors in Galatians, in which life before Christ is described explicitly as enslavement to the "elemental spirits of the world" (ὑπὸ τὰ στοιχεῖα τοῦ κόσμου ἤμεθα δεδουλωμένοι, Gal 4:3) are actually of the kind that one would expect to accompany so much Passover imagery in 1 Corinthians. The same is true of Romans 8:21. The claim "Our Passover lamb, Christ, is sacrificed for us" (1 Cor 5:7) has the ring of a slogan, much like the supposed slogans that are quoted in 8:1, 4. Perhaps it is the case, as in much of chapter 8, that Paul is in the position of needing to soft-peddle some of his previous, memorable statements. Some members of the church in Corinth may have a tendency to take Paul's counsels to extremes, and so he is more nuanced in speaking with them about freedom, just as he is in speaking about knowledge in 1 Cor 8 (a kind of "yes, but").[49]

---

48. Dale B. Martin, *Slavery as Salvation* (New Haven: Yale University Press, 1990), 63–65, emphasis original.

49. See, for example, his handling of the possible slogans at 7:1; 8:1, 4, 8. Some of these may have been teachings of Paul that the community has taken to extremes. See

Chapters 8–10 of 1 Corinthians have long been the subject of debate concerning whether or not they illustrate a disunity in the letter.[50] In particular, the question arises as to whether Paul's counsels concerning the eating of εἰδωλόθυτα in chapter 8 are contradictory to his counsels in chapter 10, and what the role of Paul's description of his own behavior in chapter 9 might be, sandwiched as it is, between two discussions of εἰδωλόθυτα. Willis summarizes the scholarly consensus that has developed, namely: that 8–10 are a unity, and that rhetorical study of their interrelationships and their role in the letter as a whole have contributed to the consensus; and that chapter 9 functions as an *exemplum* for both chapters 8 and 10. There continues to be disagreement concerning the nature and location of "religious" meals, or meals at which sacrificial meat is served, and therefore there is disagreement concerning the motivation of those who want to continue to eat εἰδωλόθυτα. I agree with Willis that it is "likely they had experienced the cultic dining as predominantly a convivial occasion with others (although surely acknowledging the presence of the deity in appropriate ways and with due piety)."[51]

Perhaps it is most helpful to return to the language of "belonging" to characterize the difficult situation in which members of the fledgling Christian church at Corinth are finding themselves. "Belonging" is certainly implied in the language of κοινωνία in chapter 10 (1 Cor 10:16 (twice), 18, 20). Of special significance to the discussion of κοινωνία is 1 Cor 1:9, where the proof of God's faithfulness to the Corinthian church is the fact of God's having called them into κοινωνία with "his son, Jesus Christ, our Lord." The statement of God's faithfulness (πιστὸς ὁ θεός) is the ground for the appeal to unity that is the *prothesis* of the letter (1:10).

The Corinthians' choice to belong to the body of Christ is not confined to what they do when they gather as ἐκκλησία but is now causing a painful separation from the social fabric to which they have belonged up to now. Paul's arguments reroot them in two kinds of belonging: (1) belonging to the community that includes both those sophisticated enough to understand that the many gods do not have any real power, as well as those who

---

Thiselton's summary of views on the origins of 7:1 (*The First Epistle to the Corinthians,* 498) and 8:1 (*First Epistle to the Corinthians,* 620). In any case, it would appear that Paul is well advised to take care to avoid hyperbole with the Corinthians.

50. The debate is well summarized in Wendell Willis, "1 Corinthians 8–10: A Retrospective after Twenty-Five Years," *ResQ* 49 (2007): 103–12.

51. Ibid., 112.

are confused when they see a fellow believer eating εἰδωλόθυτα (8:1–13); and (2) belonging to Christ himself, at whose table they enjoy the Lord's supper (10:14–33).

In chapter 8 Paul returns to the language of "puffing up" that he has used before in imagery that he connected with the Passover (5:2, 6–8). Here, what does the puffing up is not arrogance over behavior, but over the possession of knowledge: οἴδαμεν ὅτι πάντες γνῶσιν ἔχομεν. ἡ γνῶσις φυσιοῖ (8:1). Here Paul adds another layer to a set of linked concepts that he is setting in opposition to one another. On the one hand are the problems he has diagnosed in the community: the invisible, but yeast-like corrupting power of boasting, arrogance, moral laxity, and now a certain kind of knowledge,[52] all of which need to be removed like the leaven before the Passover. On the other hand are the remedies that need to be encouraged: building up the community and a commitment to holiness (which are both connected to images of the temple), and love. For love builds up (ἀγάπη οἰκοδομεῖ, 8:1), and does not "puff up" (ἡ ἀγάπη … οὐ φυσιοῦται, 13:4). In making his case against a spurious "knowledge" (εἰ τις δοκεῖ ἐγνωκέναι),[53] Paul relies upon this set of related metaphors to do much of the work for him by triggering recollections of the ways he has used them previously in the letter.

It is here that Paul does a very surprising thing with the cultic metaphor of leaven. It would be expected that a metaphor referring to the cleaning out of leaven before the Passover would be used to support arguments for establishing a firm boundary toward outsiders. This way of thinking would be consistent with Mary Douglas's term, "high group," in her group/grid schema.[54] The question that has been put before Paul[55]

---

52. Margaret Mitchell states, "This γνῶσις is one of the precious commodities claimed as an exclusive possession by some, contributing to community division, both in itself and in the justification it provides for certain controversial actions, one of which is eating meats which have been sacrificed to idols" (*Paul and the Rhetoric of Reconciliation*, 126).

53. See Thiselton's interesting discussion of the use of the perfect infinitive here, and what it means for a Christian process of "coming to know" (*First Epistle to the Corinthians*, 624).

54. The concept of "group" refers to how closely knit a community is, how significantly the members are bonded with one another. "High" group would indicate very strong bonds within a community. The concept of grid refers to hierarchy or differentiation of roles within the group. High grid would indicate a great deal of differentiation among roles, or a very clearly articulated hierarchy.

55. Presumably in writing; see 7:1.

presumably has to do with whether or not is it appropriate for a Christian to eat εἰδωλόθυτα. Paul begins with that question (8:1), and then moves immediately to speak of the corruption (the "puffing up") in the community that has entered in via the attitudes of those who profess to have certain γνῶσις. Only then does he return to the initial subject, to say, περὶ τῆς βρώσεως οὖν τῶν εἰδωλοθύτων (8:4). The primary threat of corruption in the community, according to Paul, comes not from social intercourse with outsiders, but from the conduct of one's relationships within the community. Paul's use of a Passover metaphor in this regard is not straightforward, but ironic. Leaven is not tracked into the community from outside, but seems to be arising from attitudes within the community itself, and Paul is concerned to eradicate the behaviors and attitudes that the corrupting "leaven" (here, certain types of γνῶσις) feeds on. Whatever he may counsel later concerning the eating of sacrificial meat (10:14–33), the issue of arrogance is, for Paul, more critical than the setting of boundaries. Ridding the community of the corrupting effect of arrogance, boasting, "knowledge" is the proper way to "keep the feast" in Christ.

The tone of "Christ our Passover" in chapter 5 is still resounding in the background here, as is the "logic of the cross" from the first chapter of 1 Corinthians. While both make sense of the death of Jesus, they spin out into complementary—not synonymous—metaphors and counsels. In chapter 9, Paul will put himself forward as an example of one who does not make full use of the ἐξουσία that he might rightfully claim, an example of the kind of behavior he calls for in 8:9–13, and that illustrates the foolish-seeming logic of the cross (1:18). The image of the corrupting tendency of γνῶσις plays a counterintuitive supporting role here, not defining the "clean" community from the "polluted" outside world, but pointing out where corruption begins from within.

When Paul puts his own life forward as an example in chapter 9, he compares his work to service in the Temple: "Do you not know that those who are employed in the Temple (οἱ τὰ ἱερὰ ἐργαζόμενοι) gain their subsistence from the Temple offerings (τὰ ἐκ τοῦ ἱεροῦ ἐσθίουσιν),[56] and those who serve the altar (οἱ τῷ θυσιατηρίῳ) have a share in what is offered on the altar (παρεδρεύοντες τῷ θυσιατηρίῳ συμμερίζονται)? (9:13). Paul maintains the image of the community as Temple, and himself in service to

---

56. See Thiselton, *First Epistle to the Corinthians*, 692.

the Temple (as at 4:1), even when Temple-like qualities of the community
are not the primary issue. He appears to have a consistently cultic view
of his work and of the gentile ἐκκλησία, not because these things replace
the Jerusalem Temple, but because they are metaphorical extensions of
it, places where God is consistently present to those who are prepared to
come into proximity with the divine.

Chapter 9 also presents one of the most explicit instances of Paul's
modeling the pattern of centering one's moral reflection not around one's
own freedom and privilege, but around the need of the other: Ἐλεύθερος
γὰρ ὢν ἐκ πάντων πᾶσιν ἐμαυτὸν ἐδούλωσα, ἵνα τοὺς πλείονας κερδήσω
(9:19). This is the pattern of moral reflection he has encouraged among
the Corinthians in the discussion of εἰδωλόθυτα in chapter 8 (8:9–11), and
that he will put forward in his key counsel of chapter 10 (10:23–24). When
one's actions are "for" others (as Christ's in 11:24), then one's own authority (ἐξουσία) will be tempered, so that it does not become a "stumbling
block for the weak" (8:9). Or, positively, the Corinthians are pressed to ask
themselves, what will "build up" (οἰκοδομέω, ἐποικοδομέω, 3:9, 10, 12, 14;
8:1, 10; 10:23; 14:3, 4, 5, 12, 26) or "profit" (συμφέρον 12:7) the entire community the most.

According to Ellen Aitken, chapters 10 and 11 are a unity in that
together they are concerned to describe for the Corinthian church what it
means to celebrate a cultic meal properly or improperly. Within Mitchell's
rhetorical framework, this thematic unity means that concern with the
cultic meal will cross over from the second to the third proof, just as "puffing up" crossed over the rhetorical divide between the first and second
proofs. Aitken holds that chapter 10 "reenacts the foundational legend of
the cult of Israel in such a way that the Corinthian community is located
in the wilderness, where it must choose between a cultic meal properly
performed and one gone awry. This narrative move provides the framework for understanding the cultic practices discussed in 1 Cor 11:17–34."[57]
If she is correct, then Paul has made a dramatic move, in these two chapters, to locate the Corinthians within the story of the Passover–exodus–
Sinai covenant as well as within the narrative of Jesus's Passover. The tension between "is" and "is not" in metaphors of the Passover is heightened,
as the story of the Israelites in the wilderness becomes the story of the

---

57. Ellen Bradshaw Aitken, "τὰ δρώμενα καὶ τὰ λεγόμενα: The Eucharistic Memory
of Jesus' Words in First Corinthians," *HTR* 90 (1997): 366.

Corinthians living amid a pagan society. To use Aitken's term, Paul "actualizes" the "foundational narrative of Israel" by explicitly describing the incidents he draws from the wilderness experience as τύποι for the moral discernment of the Corinthians (ταῦτα δὲ τύποι ἡμῶν ἐγενήθησαν, 10:6).

Aitken argues that the scriptural background for 1 Cor 10:1–13 is not only Exod 32, from which the quotation is taken at 10:7 (Exod 32:7), but perhaps even more importantly Exod 24, which tells of the rituals involved in the ratifying of the covenant at Sinai. Thus the "cloud" of 10:1 is more likely the cloud of Exod 24:15, not the cloud that protected the people during their wanderings.[58] The significance of Aitken's argument is that Exod 24:8 (ἰδοὺ τὸ αἷμα τῆς διαθήκης, ἧς διέθετο κύριος πρὸς ὑμᾶς περὶ πάντων τῶν λόγων τούτων, LXX) is widely agreed to be the background of 1 Cor 11:25 (τοῦτο τὸ ποτήριον ἡ καινὴ διαθήκη ἐστὶν ἐν τῷ ἐμῷ αἵματι). Thus, she draws chapters 10 and 11 together by virtue of some of their shared scriptural foundation. Aitken summarizes her exegesis of 1 Cor 10 by saying that, "At the heart of this homily, then, is a contrast between two cultic meals, one eaten in the presence of the Lord and one in the presence of an idol.[59] This opposition is precisely that which Paul makes in 1 Cor 10:19–21, namely, between the table of the Lord and the table of demons."[60]

Interestingly, Meeks's summary of the significance of chapter 10 reiterates some of the points that are linked to Passover imagery in chapter 8:

> The result of the argument leaves the issue of the Christian group's boundaries—and that is the policy question behind the immediate concern about eating meat—somewhat ambiguous. On the one hand, social intercourse with outsiders is not discouraged. Paul desacralizes the mere act of eating meat, in order to remove a taboo that would prevent such interaction. It is thus not "idolatry;" in this respect Paul agrees with "the strong." On the other hand, any action that would imply actual participation in another cult is strictly prohibited. Thus the exclusivity of the cult, which had been a unique mark of Judaism, difficult for Pagans in the Hellenistic cities to understand, would remain characteristic also of Pauline congregations. The emphasis in Paul's paraenesis, however, is not upon the maintenance of boundaries, but upon the solidarity of the

---

58. Ibid., 363.

59. Ibid., 364. The first is the meal eaten in Exod 24 as part of the ratification of the Sinai covenant. The second is the meal eaten in Exod 32 in the presence of the golden calf.

60. Ibid., 365.

Christian community: the responsibility of members for one another, especially of the strong for the weak, and the undiluted loyalty of all to the one God and one Lord.[61]

What is especially significant for this study is the consistency with which Paul continues to map the experiences of the Corinthian community onto those of the Israelites who were delivered from bondage in Egypt on the night of the first Passover sacrifice, wandered in the wilderness, and then kept the Passover immediately upon entry into the land (Josh 5:10–12).

1 CORINTHIANS 11:2–14:40, THIRD SECTION OF THE PROOF, MANIFESTATIONS OF CORINTHIAN FACTIONALISM WHEN "COMING TOGETHER"

At 11:17 Paul picks up the second thread of what he began at 11:2 with his words of commendation, by beginning with what he *cannot* commend (οὐκ ἐπαινῶ). I have called 1 Cor 11:17–34 the "center" or the "heart" of the letter and, as such, it is interesting to see that at this point Paul recalls the *prothesis* by repeating the key word σχίσματα, to begin the important discussion of the conduct of the community at the Lord's Supper. Note that the echo of the *prothesis* is amplified by the ironic introduction, οὐκ εἰς τὸ κρεῖσσον ἀλλὰ εἰς τὸ ἧσσον συνέρχεσθε (11:17). As 1:10 was followed by evidence of factionalism in the community (whether Paul is using their own words against them or is creating slogans that represent what he believes to be their point of view: ...ἐγὼ μὲν εἰμι Παύλου, ἐγὼ δὲ Ἀπολλῶ, ἐγὼ δὲ Κηφᾶ, ἐγὼ δὲ Χριστοῦ, 1:12), 11:17–18 is followed by observable evidence of divisions at the Lord's Supper: ἕκαστος γὰρ τὸ ἴδιον δεῖπνον προλαμβάνει ἐν τῷ φαγεῖν, καὶ ὃς μὲν πεινᾷ ὃς δὲ μεθύει (11:21). These formal similarities to the thesis statement and "statement of facts" of the letter as a whole are clues to the significance of what is to follow.

Aitken's discussion of the "actualizing" capacity of cultic language, in her consideration of 1 Cor 11:23–26 is an important one,[62] though I do not agree with her final conclusion about the point of Paul's argument in these verses. Aitken rightly calls verses 23–26 "marked speech": "an event

---

61. Wayne A. Meeks, "'And Rose up to Play': Midrash and Paraenesis in 1 Corinthians 10:1–22," *JSNT* 16 (1982): 74–75.

62. Here she is informed by the work of Roman Jakobson and others of the Prague School of Linguistics (Aitken, "τὰ δρώμενα καὶ τὰ λεγόμενα," 367).

in language set apart from ordinary speech.[63] I would suggest that, as
marked speech, the quotation of this tradition functions as an enigmatic
but authoritative utterance in this context."[64] Like the narrative that is a
required part of a proper celebration of the Passover (m. Pesah. 10), this
narrative about the supper has the power to place the hearers within the
setting it describes. What is so complex about what Paul is doing in chapters 5, 10, and 11 is that he is placing the Corinthians, imaginatively, in a
cluster of related historical settings all at once. Simultaneously, they are the
community prepared to flee Egypt, with their unleavened loaves still warm
and the blood still wet on the lintel (Exod 12; 1 Cor 5:7; 11:26); they are
wandering in the wilderness, powerfully claimed by God and identified
as a people bound to God and to one another, and yet confused, anxious,
still capable of idolatry (Exod 32; 1 Cor 10:1–13); they are gathered at the
supper table (a Passover feast?) of the Lord ἐν τῇ νυκτὶ ᾗ παρεδίδετο (11:23);
they stand together to ratify the Sinai covenant (Exod 24; 1 Cor 10:1–13)
and the "new" covenant (Jer 31:31, 38:31 LXX) "in Christ's blood" (1 Cor
11:26); they are poised there, "until he comes" (ἄχρις οὗ ἔλθῃ, 1 Cor 11:26).
It is as though the people "on whom the end of the ages has come" (εἰς οὓς
τὰ τέλη τῶν αἰώνιων κατήντηκεν, 10:11) are witnesses to the collapse of time
in a heap upon them. Why this complexity? Paul is attempting to locate the
Corinthian church imaginatively in such a way that they can understand
both the promise inherent in the pivotal nature of their time and place,
and the dangers attendant to being *where* they are, and *when* they are.

Each of the historical locations evoked by Paul is fraught with tension:
the night of the exodus, the wilderness wanderings, the sacrifices around
the golden calf, the ratifying of the covenant, the exile and the dream of
a new covenant, the night before the handing over of Jesus. Each of these
moments is characterized simultaneously by enormous opportunity and
enormous danger. From each of these places one can see what might be:
the promised land where the covenant might be fully embodied; the resurrection, in which one might live fully to God. But those promises are not
yet entirely fulfilled.

---

63. She also says, "Moreover, the utterance [11:23–26] is familiar to the community; it must have influence as part of their cultic treasure horde" (ibid., 368). In
this way, 1 Cor 11:23–26 may function analogously to Phil 2:5–11, if both were part of
preexisting traditions.

64. Ibid., 366.

It is a similar tension that Paul calls into being by suggesting that the night of the Passover feast is ongoing (5:7), and that in eating and drinking in a particular way, the Corinthians "proclaim Christ's death until he comes" (11:26). Paul is calling for extraordinary care and attentiveness in everyday actions.[65] Ironically, Bendlin notes that, cultically, "contrary to what usually is claimed, the opposite of pollution is not purity: with regard to both purity and pollution, the opposite is normality."[66] Paul is relocating his community within imaginative settings that are cultically charged, removed from the normal, and then he tells them to live there every day. However, the cleanness he calls for is more moral than physical, as he demonstrates through the things he chooses to compare to "leaven": boasting, arrogance, inattention to sexual immorality, and a spurious "knowledge" that sets one person over against another. The primary dangers to the church are internal to the community rather than external.

In Aitken's view, what Paul is trying to establish with the drama of the narrative of the Lord's Supper is proper observance of the Christian cult.[67] That is true as far as it goes, but Paul is actually using the poignancy of improper cultic observance to illustrate what has gone wrong in the people's everyday relationships with one another. Aitken does acknowledge that

> The cultic meal felicitously performed is that which is successful in its re-enactment of the cultic legend. In the Corinthian meal, the foundational legend of the covenant is the death of Jesus. This memory, as an event in ritual and narrative, *as well as the ethic and koinonia of the people,* becomes for Paul the criterion for the successful performance of the cult.[68]

Faithfulness in everyday life (the "ethic and *koinonia* of the people") is the *primary* object of Paul's cultic metaphors, rather than the special times

---

65. Of course, Paul is not entirely unique in this regard; Philo also encouraged a similar attentiveness to daily life as the place of encounter with God. What is different about Paul is his sense that he and his churches are living in a pivotal age (10:11).

66. Anreas Bendlin, "Purity and Pollution," in *A Companion to Greek Religion,* ed. Daniel Ogden (Oxford: Blackwell, 2007), 178.

67. As she writes, "1 Cor 10:1–13, I suggest, sets the stage by defining what is at stake in 'getting' what this marked utterance is about, namely, the proper performance of the cultic meal" (Aitken, "τὰ δρώμενα καὶ τὰ λεγόμενα," 367). The "marked utterance" to which she refers is 1 Cor 11:23–26.

68. Ibid., 370, emphasis added.

and places of Christian cultic activity. The distinctions being drawn in the Lord's Supper are emblematic of distinctions being drawn in other areas of the community's life, as Paul has made clear in the "statement of facts," at 1:11–17.

In attending to the particularity of cultic metaphors, 11:26 is a crossroads of sorts. The mention of the θάνατος τοῦ κυρίου brings into view the long meditation on the moral implications of the cross in 1:18–2:16, which is largely consistent with the counsels Paul develops from Phil 2:5–11;[69] it recalls the phrase τὸ πάσχα ἡμῶν ἐτύθη Χριστός at 5:7; and, to a lesser degree, it anticipates the traditional material quoted by Paul at 15:3, Χριστὸς ἀπέθανεν ὑπὲρ τῶν ἁμαρτίων ἡμῶν. As Finlan says of Rom 3:25,[70] it is very important to maintain clarity with regard to the different interpretations of Christ's death that are overlapping, or amplifying one another here. At issue is, in particular, how we are to interpret the words over the bread, Τοῦτό μού ἐστιν τὸ σῶμα τὸ ὑπὲρ ὑμῶν, and thus the important counsels and warnings concerning discernment of "the body" (11:27–29).

Conzelmann downplays the role of any significant connection with the Passover, saying that, "in contrast to the Synoptics, the Supper in the Pauline version is not characterized as a Passover meal. The point of this historical note is that the historic institution of the sacrament is the ground of its present validity."[71] He goes on to develop the view that the connection with a sacrifice for sin is more relevant:

> To the specifically sacramental interpretation of the working of the meal, there is added a further interpretive element in wholly different terminology: the death of Christ was (!) a sacrifice "for you." This can mean an atoning sacrifice or a vicarious sacrifice. Either way the fruit of this sacrifice is the removal of the guilt of sin ("for our sins," 15:3).[72]

---

69. Thus David E. Garland's interpretation, "Paul views these divisions [in the Corinthian observance of the meal] as nullifying the very purpose for gathering together for worship in the name of Christ. It contradicts what the Lord's Supper proclaims as the foundation of the church: *Christ's sacrificial giving of his life for others*" (*1 Corinthians*, Baker Exegetical Commentary on the New Testament [Grand Rapids: Baker Academic, 2003], 22, emphasis added).

70. Finlan, *Background and Content*, 123, 178.

71. Conzelmann, *1 Corinthians*, 197.

72. Ibid., 198.

Conzelmann's own discussion leads him to muse upon whether atonement or covenant is the primary sacrifice at issue here: "A linguistic analysis leads to the conclusion that one of the two interpretations of the sacrifice (atonement or covenant) is secondary. But which? Did the words of interpretation originally speak of an atonement sacrifice? Or of a covenant sacrifice? Or neither?"[73] Conzelmann's dismissal of the connection with the Passover causes him to lose sight of what Paul is saying through precisely that metaphor, which he has been unfolding steadily in his counsels up to this point. The covenant initiated by the Lord's Supper and his blood entails a practice of living for others, and, thus, preparing adequately for this feast implies a consistent moral practice of putting the needs of others first by cleaning out the yeast of boasting and self-aggrandizement (3:21, 4:6, 8:1), and promoting the "unleavened" practices of love (13:4). The body that is "for" others is the one that needs to be discerned (11:28–29) and practiced (11:33–34).

Like Conzelmann, Horsley specifically denies that the meal being remembered in 1 Cor 11:23–25 is a Passover meal: "While Mark (14:12–15), followed by both Matthew and Luke, sets the Last Supper into the context of a Passover meal, Paul's tradition, along with the context in chapter 11, suggests no connection with a Passover meal (the notion of Christ as the Passover lamb in 5:7 was apparently not connected with the Lord's Supper)."[74] Why Horsley chooses to see a strict separation between what is said at 5:7 and 11:23, he does not say. His refusal to read the meal in 11:23 as a Passover causes him some trouble when he reaches the remembrance called for in 11:24 and 25:

> Although Paul's tradition does not view the Lord's Supper as a new Passover, the biblical tradition of such memorials as ritual reenactments of Israel's founding events is surely the background from which the celebration of the Lord's Supper as a ritual enactment in remembrance of Jesus's action, in the meal and on the cross, must be understood (cf. Exod 12–13).[75]

Note that the passage Horsley has referred to is the very description of the Passover in Exodus. Having denied a connection with the Passover, then,

---

73. Ibid., 200.
74. Richard A. Horsley, *1 Corinthians*, ANTC 7 (Nashville: Abingdon, 1998), 160.
75. Ibid., 161.

Horsley goes even further afield to find a context for the remembrance that is called for: "the Corinthians and others socialized into Hellenistic culture, and with little acquaintance with the Jewish Scriptures, may well have understood the supper more in terms of Greek memorial feasts for dead heroes."[76] Yes, it is difficult to know what context Paul's *audience* would have brought to his words, yet why should one assume that they had no knowledge of the Passover, when Paul has already referred pointedly to a Passover tradition at 5:7? It seems perverse to continue to deny connections with the Passover sacrifice. The Corinthian community's understanding of the experience of a Passover celebration may well have been amplified by their experiences of Greco-Roman cultic meals, and yet it also appears that Paul has done a considerable amount of teaching about the history and meaning of the Passover.[77] Complexity and density of reference would appear to be Paul's strategy in dealing with abuses at the Lord's Supper in Corinth.

So, is there, or is there not, a reference to the Passover in 1 Cor 11:23–26? The tradition that Paul has received begins with a meal, ἐν τῇ νυκτί. The Passover is the only sacrifice that is set distinctly for the nighttime. Haran describes the practice of the Passover:

> Suffice it to point out that the very eating at night is the complete reverse of the customary procedure in the biblical times (even with regard to secular slaughtering). And of all the various categories of sacrifice there is not a single oblation that must be eaten just at night-time, save the Passover—just as there is not a night in the whole year on which it is obligatory to eat sacrificial flesh except the one that begins on the fourteenth of the first month at twilight.[78]

Thus, the very fact of Paul's beginning with the introduction, ἐν τῇ νυκτί would have been the first clue that there is a reference to the Passover.[79]

---

76. Ibid.

77. As we have seen, at least the theme of deliverance from slavery appears to have been familiar to the churches in Galatia and Rome. It seems logical that the metaphor of Christ as Passover lamb was a part of very early Christian tradition, whether begun by Paul or received by him.

78. Menahem Haran, "The Passover Sacrifice," in *Studies in the Religion of Ancient Israel*, VTSup 25 (Leiden: Brill, 1972), 89.

79. See Ben Witherington III, *Conflict and Community in Corinth: A Socio-rhetorical Commentary on 1 and 2 Corinthians* (Grand Rapids: Eerdmans, 1995). Withering-

Given that fact, together with the correspondence between this passage and the synoptic witness, and Paul's use of Passover imagery elsewhere in the letter, a Passover feast appears to be the most likely occasion for Jesus's words over the bread and the cup, as Paul uses them here.

The narrative remembrance called for in 1 Cor 11:24–25 is also an important aspect of celebration of the Passover,[80] as Horsley acknowledges. As Collins says, "Reminiscence, as a motif of the Passover celebration, was particularly significant. In the celebration of Passover a Jewish family not only recalled the saving events of the Exodus experience but also reminded God of those events and themselves became participants in the salvific experience of their ancestors."[81] What they remember is what God has done for them, namely: "He brought us forth from slavery to freedom, anguish to joy, mourning to festival, darkness to great light, subjugation to redemption, so we should say before him, Hallelujah" (m. Pesah. 10.). So, whatever other sacrifices are sounding here, there is at first the Passover, and the stipulation that the community that gathers for the Passover is one that is prepared (by cleaning out the old leaven) and unified.

In Jewish lore, there was an intimate connection between the Passover and the covenant at Sinai. The Passover and the subsequent covenant ratified through a sacrifice at Sinai are not two unrelated events in Jewish history. According to Aitken, "The phrase 'in my blood'" (11:25) recalls the events of Exod 24 that form the background to 1 Cor 10:1–13, and "locates Jesus, and in particular his death, within the reenacted narrative

---

ton writes, "The Lord's Supper stands out from Passover in that it celebrates a human person and his final deeds on earth, while the Passover celebrates divine action—the exodus-Sinai events. Jesus broke the bread after giving thanks. But this does not prove that he was celebrating a Passover meal, since thanksgiving over bread was part of every Jewish meal" (Witherington, *Conflict and Community*, 251). Here he footnotes Jeremias, but Jeremias himself says that the later meal of the day was customarily eaten in the afternoon, not at night (Jeremias, *Eucharistic Words*, 44–46). That fact is part of Jeremias's case for seeing the "Last Supper" as a Passover.

80. See, for example, Exod 12:14, "This shall be a day of remembrance for you" (καὶ ἔσται ἡ ἡμέρα ὑμῖν αὕτη μνημόσυνον καὶ ἑορτάσετε αὐτὴν ἑορτὴν κυρίῳ εἰς πάσας γενεὰς ὑμῶν νόμιμον αἰώνιον ἑορτάσετε αὐτήν, LXX).

81. Raymond F. Collins, *First Corinthians*, Sacra Pagina 7 (Collegeville, MN: Liturgical Press, 1999), 428. See also m. Pesah. 10: "In every generation a person is duty-bound to regard himself as if he personally has gone forth from Egypt, since it is said, *And you shall tell your son in that day, saying, It is because of that which the Lord did for me when I came forth out of Egypt* (Exod 13:8)."

as the offering that ratifies the covenant."[82] Conzelmann says, in speaking of 11:25, "The mention of blood again of course contains the idea of sacrifice. If above the thought was that of atonement and/or substitution, here it is that of the covenant and the covenant sacrifice. But here, too, of course, no sharp distinction is to be made."[83]

Horsley picks up on the significance of the metaphor of covenant sacrifice in his comparison between 1 Cor 11:23–26 and Mark 14:22–24: "While Mark's words have the more explicit citation of 'blood of the covenant' from Exodus 24:8, Paul's 'new covenant in my blood' suggests more that 'the Lord Jesus's' constituted the sacrifice that generated the blood by which God and the people were bound, by analogy with the covenant ceremony in Exodus 24:5–8."[84]

Once again, however, failure to be attentive to actual sacrificial practice and its contemporary description has caused some readers to miss the connection between the new covenant in Christ's blood (11:25) and Paul's interpretation of what is happening to the community in 11:29–32. Horsley connects the κρῖμα of 11:29 with ἄχρις οὗ ἔλθῃ, of 11:26:

> When Paul applies the tradition in 11:27–32 he makes immediate use of the eschatological reminder about the (imminent) *parousia*. In a sequence of events dominated by "judgment," he invites the Corinthians to "examine" themselves and to "discern," in the face of God's "judgment," what behavior is appropriate at the Supper.[85]

But the ground for God's judgment of the community is not the *parousia*, but the fact of the church's having broken the purpose of the covenant (ἡ καινὴ διαθήκη ... ἐν τῷ ἐμῷ αἵματι) with their factionalism. As Kitts has shown, covenantal sacrifices contain within them "deadly ramifications of violating the cosmic principles behind oaths and kindred commitments."[86]

---

82. Aitken, "τὰ δρώμενα καὶ τὰ λεγόμενα," 369.

83. Conzelman, *1 Corinthians*, 199. He adds in a footnote on the same page, "The synthesis of atonement sacrifice and covenant sacrifice underlies the pre-Pauline formula which is contained in Rom 3:24, ff." (n. 71).

84. Horsley, *1 Corinthians*, 161.

85. Ibid., 162.

86. Margo Kitts, "Sacrificial Violence in the *Iliad*," *JRitSt* 16 (2002): 31. Schottroff, while acknowledging the significance of the inauguration of the "new covenant," sees the illness and death that have befallen some of the Corinthians as the result of their having, like Ananias and Sapphira, "'misappropriated' something consecrated to God

The covenant in Christ's blood contains expectations for the conduct of the church, some of which Paul has made clear through his comparisons to the community that keeps the Passover, and some of which are established by the "logic of the cross," which comes into play in chapter 11 through the phrase, τὸ σῶμα τὸ ὑπὲρ ὑμῶν (11:24). At 11:29, Paul charges the Corinthian community with not having "discerned the body." But what body are they supposed to have discerned?

Τὸ σῶμα τὸ ὑπὲρ ὑμῶν constitutes the moral center of 1 Corinthians. It is the point of Paul's discussion of the logic of the cross in 1:18–2:16. Τὸ μωρὸν τοῦ θεοῦ (1 Cor 1:25) is the willingness to give up a right, or even to suffer, for the benefit of another. Paul illustrates the principle with reference to his own willingness to put away rhetorical wizardry and flashes of wisdom when he came to Corinth with his proclamation of Christ crucified (2:1–2). He describes himself as trying to discover a language and demeanor low enough to be in keeping with the strange divine wisdom of the cross, and at the same time appropriate for this community, few of whom are sophisticated or wise. (1:26). The pattern of the cross is behavior that is ὑπὲρ ὑμῶν, conduct shaped by the needs of the other.

Because the statement "This is my body that is for you" occurs in such a dramatic setting, and because it is so clearly relevant to the central moral injunctions and models of the letter, it seems odd that interpreters go to 15:3 (Χριστὸς ἀπέθανεν ὑπὲρ τῶν ἁμαρτιῶν ἡμῶν) for its interpretation. Paul's use of the traditional material at 15:3 indicates his awareness of the interpretation of Jesus's crucifixion as an atoning sacrifice, but he does not choose to use that reference in 11:23–26. Atonement is simply not the issue in chapter 11. Paul's metaphors drawn from the Jewish sacrificial system are drawn purposefully. The model of the "body that is for you" carries the same message that Paul has been trying to convey in multiple ways since the beginning of the letter, namely, that divisions in the community are jeopardizing their very life, and that they need to be more scrupulous in analyzing their actions with reference to the needs of the other, especially the weaker other. Metaphors drawn from the model of the Jewish community, appropriately prepared to celebrate the Passover,

---

(Acts 5:2), thereby risking illness and death.... Sharing in the meal signifies sharing in justice, holiness, and fellowship (κοινωνία) both among themselves and with Christ. Wounding the integrity of a community presumes a break between the human being and the divine" (Louise Schottroff, "Holiness and Justice: Exegetical Comments on 1 Corinthians 11:17–34," *JSNT* 79 [2000]: 54).

have been sounded through many of Paul's arguments up to and through chapter 11. The phrase ὑπὲρ ὑμῶν in 11:24 does not signal the addition of a new sacrificial reference here (i.e., atonement), but rather adds depth to what it means really to remember "our paschal lamb, Christ," and the new covenant initiated in his blood. Consequently, appropriate proclamation of the death of this Christ occurs precisely in *how* the community eats and drinks together (11:26), and whether or not all of their actions are "for" (ὑπὲρ) one another.

The capstone is set on this argument when Paul says, within his "hymn" to love in chapter 13, that "Love is *not* puffed up" (οὐ φυσιοῦται, 13:4). Love, spelled out in all of its actions, perfectly characterizes the unleavened community.

1 CORINTHIANS 15:1–57, FOURTH SECTION OF THE PROOF, THE RESURRECTION AS THE FINAL GOAL; UNITY IN THE ΠΑΡΑΔΟΣΕΙΣ

In the fourth section of the proof, the frequency and intensity of metaphors of the Passover drop off sharply. As we have noted, in 15:3 Paul quotes a significant tradition he has received regarding an interpretation of the death of Jesus: ὅτι Χριστὸς ἀπέθανεν ὑπὲρ τῶν ἁμαρτιῶν ἡμῶν κατὰ τὰς γραφάς. The reference here is clearly to a sacrifice of atonement, but that fact only makes Paul's more frequent use of the Passover metaphors in 1 Corinthians appear even more strategic. At 15:20 and 15:23, the language of "firstfruits" is a possible reference to the celebration of the "sheaf," which falls on the second day of the seven days of the Feast of Unleavened Bread (see Philo, *Spec. Laws* 2.162, 2.171). But in the main, the work of the Passover metaphors is complete after chapter 13. The epilogue (15:58) and the epistolary closing (16:1–24) do not contain any significant metaphors of the Passover.

CONCLUSIONS

While developing clarity with regard to Paul's use of metaphors of the Passover in 1 Corinthians does not completely undermine most previous interpretations of the letter, it does sharpen our senses for perceiving the power of this group of related images to give the members of the church at Corinth a steady pattern for the conduct of their moral life. The image of the Jewish community that has prepared appropriately for the feast and gathered as a unity to celebrate it is an imaginative model for the Christian community's discernment of what constitutes corruption (leaven) in their own setting, for the high standards to which they are now held as people of the new covenant, and what it means to be κλητοὶ ἅγιοι. As we have seen, using Mitchell's rhetorical scheme of the argument of 1 Corinthians, metaphors relating to the Passover are explicitly evident in three of the four sections of the "proof," and also resound implicitly through other cultic metaphors, and even, ultimately, in the λόγος τοῦ σταυροῦ through the dense connections drawn at 11:23–26.

As in the case of the metaphors drawn from the *shelamim* in Philippians, it is clear that the proper frame for considering the metaphors of the Passover in 1 Corinthians is the letter as a whole (not the individual sentences in which they occur), even though the imagery is clustered up through chapter 13. The Passover imagery helps to establish a basic narrative in which the Corinthians may find their place and act accordingly.

One of the salient qualities of a metaphor is that, as Ricoeur said, a metaphor stretches the verb "to be" to its limits, to the place where *is* and *is not* actually touch each other. Jesus of Nazareth was not a Passover lamb, and the gentile community of Christ-believers in first-century Corinth is not Israel. But by the sleight-of-hand of Passover metaphors, the crucifixion of Jesus becomes the night that the Jewish slaves fled from Egypt, and a group of gentiles in Corinth becomes the Israelites looking for their way in the wilderness. Paul uses the strength of Passover metaphors to reinscribe the ἐκκλησία of Corinth within the narrative of the deliverance of Israel from slavery in Egypt. By setting the community within this imaginative framework, he is equipping them not only to hear the counsels he gives in the letter concerning their need to unify but also to improvise on the narrative in situations as yet unanticipated.

The Passover is a highly structured metaphorical complex that Paul chooses to map upon the equally complicated moral life of the Christians in Corinth. One of the features of the regulations for the Passover is that, though it is formally one of the *shelamim* (in that it is a commensal sacrifice for which an animal is slaughtered ritually and then shared in a festive meal), it is described in Lev 23 among the calendric feasts, such as First-fruits, Pentecost, and so on. Within the Jewish system of sacrifices, the Passover is one of those feasts that honor and sanctify time. In Paul's use of the metaphor, Passover likewise structures the Corinthians's apprehension of themselves as living at a particular time in history. The first Passover (like the day of Jesus's crucifixion) was a day of terror for the community, but the subsequent commemoration of the seminal event is a day of festivity. An aspect of Paul's use of Passover imagery appears to be to heighten the Corinthian community's awareness of the seriousness of the original event that created their community, the death of Jesus (5:7; 11:26). The terrifying event should have created a community unified by loyalty to God and to one another. Something has caused the Corinthians to forget that their present status as "freed people of the Lord" (7:22) came at a cost (6:20; 7:23), and to forget that the purpose of their new status is to be a community where they live for (ὑπὲρ) one another.

The Passover imagery also serves to locate the Corinthians within a certain narrative space, perhaps the wilderness in which the Israelites were formed as a people in covenant with God, and made ready to enter the land they had been promised. This may be one of the principal roles of chapter 10, to structure the community's sense of the liminal quality of the place in which they find themselves. Like the community in the wilderness, the Corinthians are trying to discern paths of faithfulness where there are no well-worn paths. One of the advantages of using metaphors to locate people in time and space is, again, the is/is not quality of metaphors. They can be employed as long as they are useful, and then abandoned and replaced with others when necessary. To say that Paul uses metaphors drawn from the Passover in 1 Corinthians is not to say that he imagines that community *always* in that light. The hearers are free to use the metaphors to help guide their moral reflection for as long as the metaphors serve them, but they may be replaced just as easily if a more apt image will serve them better.

While Philippians and 1 Corinthians have much in common in terms of the self-giving moral pattern[87] that Paul is promoting, the different cultic metaphors used in the two letters relate in very different ways to the moral pattern. In Philippians, use of the thank-offering served as an analogy of self-offering for the advantage of the community. Members of the community were enjoined to see their lives of courageous care for one another as their offerings to God. This imagery was used to define what it means to "conduct your life in a manner worthy of the Gospel of Christ" (1:27). In 1 Corinthians, Christ is imagined as the Passover Lamb, whose sacrifice makes possible the deliverance of the people and their gathering as a holy and united people of God. The Corinthians are simultaneously

---

87. I am referring to the Christ Hymn of Philippians and the *logos* of the cross in 1 Corinthians.

the Israelites gathered for the feast (having cleaned out all the leaven) *and* a single unleavened loaf (5:7). Here, the metaphors serve to counter the factionalism that apparently provoked the letter (1 Cor 1:10). In 1 Corinthians, the community is not the sacrifice itself; it is the accompanying loaf of bread and the people of God gathered properly to keep the feast.

Entailments of metaphors of the Passover (leaven, holiness, unity, freedom, wilderness, blood, covenant, remembrance) challenge the church at Corinth to become a community of belonging, to God and to one another, by imaginatively placing themselves both within the exodus narrative and within the ongoing community of commemoration. The λόγος τοῦ σταυροῦ underscores the personal costliness of engaging in the actions that are required for this true κοινωνία: "discerning the body" (1 Cor 11:29) that is for others. This is how holy ones "keep the feast" (5:8).

7

Conclusions, Romans, and a Look Ahead

Much of this work has concerned the *resonance* of metaphors and the importance of developing an *ear* for how it is that metaphors of sacrifice function in particular Pauline letters. So it is perhaps not out of line to make a comparison between Paul's complex use of metaphors and something else that creates a very complicated, multi-layered sound.

In the late 1920s the American philanthropist Charles R. Crane made a trip to Russia on which he was exposed for the first time to the sound of the ringing of Russian church bells. Russian bells are neither made nor rung like Western European bells: "Whereas Western European bells are tuned on a lathe to produce familiar major and minor chords, a Russian bell is prized for its individual, un-tuned voice, produced by an overlay of *numerous partial frequencies*, with only approximate relations to traditional pitches.... Where Western European bells play melodies, Russian bell ringing consists of rhythmic layered peals."[1] Crane and his friend Byzantologist Thomas Whittemore were captivated by the sound of these Russian bells. When the Soviets prohibited the ringing of church bells, and then began the systematic destruction of the bells and the reuse of the metal for armaments the great bells of the Danilov monastery were removed. Crane and Whittemore heard about the Danilov bells and arranged to purchase them and have them brought to Lowell House, Harvard, in 1930.

The inaugural ringing of the bells was not exactly a "resounding" success. "The official public concert ... was a huge failure. 'At once the horrid truth became apparent,' the Lowell tutor wrote. 'This ... was no carillon ... on which each note could be played independently with some sem-

---

1. Elif Batuman, "Onward and Upward with the Arts: The Bells Harvard Helped and a Russian Legacy," *The New Yorker* (April 2009): 23, emphasis added.

blance of a tune.' 'GIFT CHIMES PROVE WHITE ELEPHANT,' a local headline read."[2]

Soon after the installation of the bells, a Russian bell-ringer, Konstantin Saradzhev, who was said to be "Moscow's most famous bell-ringer,"[3] arrived in Cambridge and began playing the bells. He had what he called "true pitch," the ability to distinguish not just the twelve tones of an octave but 1,701 tones in the space of an octave. For this reason, he delighted in the complex overtones of the Russian bells: "Each bell sounds a unique cloud of untempered frequencies, producing intervals unplayable on any twelve-tone keyboard."[4]

The response of modern readers to Paul's use of metaphor reminds me to some extent of the first concert played on the Danilov bells at Harvard. Paul does not obey the rules of current English usage. He mixes his metaphors remorselessly for the person who is trying to make sense of his imagery; worse still, it appears that this mixing is not completely the result of haste or lack of forethought, for, as this study has shown, the meaning of a single metaphor in a given letter is subject to the way in which it is layered with others and the way in which its entailments reverberate through different sections of the letter. Where one is looking for something like the simple clarity of a classical piano (what Saradzhev called, disdainfully, "that well-tempered nitwit"[5]), one is met, in Paul's metaphors, by something more like the complexity of untempered Russian bells.

From the Vantage Point of Two Letters

The study of sacrificial metaphors in Philippians and 1 Corinthians was undertaken as a test case, to observe the use of these metaphors in relation to the structure and principal counsels of those letters, to see whether or not attention to *specific* sacrificial references (rather than a supposed general sacrificial theology) would yield greater understanding of Paul's rhetorical strategies. What became clear in each case was that Paul employed several references to a single sacrifice and its entailments to organize a complex of moral counsels, so that the community could

---

2. Ibid., 26.
3. Ibid., 25.
4. Ibid., 26.
5. Ibid.

respond faithfully and imaginatively to the situations they had inquired about, and could even anticipate how to respond faithfully in situations that had not yet arisen. For the Philippians, the comparison to the *shelamim* served to model a pattern of obedient self-offering for God's purposes and for the good of the neighbor; served to make sense of the mixture of suffering and joy that they were experiencing; and served to tie their experience of sacrificial congress between the earthly and heavenly realms to Paul's apocalyptic teaching on their "true" citizenship. For the Corinthians, on the other hand, metaphors of the Passover and its entailments served to undergird Paul's teaching on guarding the holiness of the covenanted community, the ethical implications of the Lord's Supper, and what it means to belong to one another as a community in Christ. In both letters, the comparisons to particular sacrifices brought to the surface the delicate interplay between God's graciousness and the community's faithfulness.

The choice of Philippians and 1 Corinthians as test cases was based, in part, on the fact that the most prevalent sacrificial metaphors used in those letters do not have sacrifices of atonement as their reference. Because atonement has historically dominated Christian interpretations of sacrifice, it was important to choose letters that made use of nonatonement metaphors of sacrifice, in order to highlight how attention to other specific sacrifices allows a more nuanced interpretation of Paul's persuasive strategies. But, having seen how the nonatonement metaphors of sacrifice function in Philippians and 1 Corinthians, it may be of interest to pose some questions and make some preliminary remarks about similarities and differences between the use of sacrificial metaphors in Philippians and 1 Corinthians and their use in Romans. What follows is not a full study of the sacrificial metaphors in Romans, and certainly not a serious engagement with the extensive scholarly work on Romans, but more of a wide-angle view of the letter from the stance of the particular study of Philippians and 1 Corinthians above. What I am proposing is that the use of cultic metaphors in Romans is as contextually specific and rhetorically strategic as those of Philippians and 1 Corinthians.

"Numerous Partial Frequencies": Romans 1:9; 3:25; 5:2, 9–10; 8:3, 23, 32; 11:16; 12:1; 15:16, 27

The first thing one notices, in simply cataloguing the sacrificial metaphors in Romans, is the wide variety of sacrifices referred to: the Yom

Kippur sacrifice (3:25), the Akedah (8:32), the firstfruits (8:23; 11:16),[6] the *shelamim* (12:1). Then there are the less obvious (and less universally acknowledged) partial references and allusions, such as the Yom Kippur scapegoat (8:3), the possible reference to Yom Kippur at 5:9–10, or the cultically charged language of approach at 5:2 (προσαγωγή) and the use of cultic language at 1:9 and 12:1 (λατρεύω, λατρεία), 5:16 (λειτουργός and ἱερουργέω) and 15:27 (λειτουργός). The story of the Russian bells at the beginning of this chapter speaks of the "overlay of numerous partial frequencies" that characterizes the Russian bells, in contrast to the tempered tones of Western European bells. This description is very apt for the sacrificial metaphors of Romans as well: there are numerous partial cultic frequencies.

One way to make order of the cultic metaphors is to repeat the method we used in 1 Corinthians, to map their occurrence within a rhetorical schema of the letter. And, as in both 1 Corinthians and Philippians, it is also important not only to note where the images fall within the arrangement of the letter, but also to take an account of how clearly and forcefully they sound; in doing so, two images come to the fore as primary, those of Rom 3:25 and 12:1. Each comes at a clear shift in the conversation, both use very vivid cultic metaphors, and both are key dramatic points in the development of the argument toward the exhortation, Διὸ προσλαμβάνεσθε ἀλλήλους, καθὼς καὶ Χριστὸς προσελάβετο ὑμᾶς εἰς δόξαν τοῦ θεοῦ (Rom 15:7). Jewett calls Rom 15:7 "the climax of the letter" in which "the actions of Christ in behalf of Jews and Gentiles draws [sic] together the themes of the fourth proof and provides a 'coda' for the entire preceding argument of the letter."[7]

What follows is a brief consideration of each of these two strong metaphors. The presence of the other "partial frequencies" is a reminder of how provisional all metaphors are. Metaphors serve a purpose, they suggest action congruent with them, they may stay in the mind for a long time, but they are always bound by the *is/is not* quality of metaphor.

---

6. The mention of "firstfruits" at 8:23 and 11:16, and the possible reference to the Akedah (or binding of Isaac) at 8:32 constitute "*very* partial frequencies" of sacrificial metaphors.

7. Jewett, *Romans: A Commentary*, Hermeneia (Minneapolis: Fortress, 2007), 362, 887.

YOM KIPPUR AND ROMANS 3:21–26 (6:5–6; 8:3)

In this section I address most particularly Stanley Stowers's discussion of Rom 3, because there is so much that I agree with in his treatment, though at the same time he makes a very compelling argument *against* the presence of a sacrificial metaphor in 3:25.[8] Engaging his work is a way to counter the traditional interpretation of substitutionary atonement, while maintaining a sense for the contextual rhetorical power of a sacrificial metaphor.

When one hears (or reads) the letter for the first time, 3:21–26 comes after Paul's two-pronged approach to express the common predicament of both the Jews and other nations. As Stowers summarizes Rom 1–3, "At the present historical moment both Israel as a whole and the other nations stand equally before God as disobedient peoples (not every individual member)."[9] I agree with Stowers that the issue is not the universal question, "How can the sinner be saved?"[10] but rather the need to describe what God has chosen to do, as a response to the Messiah's crucifixion, to put all people, gentiles and Jews, in right relationship with God and with one another. The sacrificial metaphors work to describe how something that cannot be seen can yet be powerfully effective. When the letter is reread, 15:7, the exhortation to "Welcome one another" is anticipated through all of the argumentation of the first fourteen chapters, and sounds along with the cultic metaphors. Jewett speaks of the setting for the language of welcome in 15:7 as the setting of hospitality and meals.[11] Though the Yom Kippur sacrifice was not connected with a meal, the rest of the sacrifices were. The language of sacrifice that reverberates from Romans 3:25 may have set up an image of the hospitality connected with meals that readers today are no longer sensitive to, an image that anticipates the

---

8. Stanley Stowers, *A Rereading of Romans: Justice, Jews, and Gentiles*, (New Haven: Yale University Press), 194–226.

9. Ibid., 197.

10. Ibid.

11. Jewett, *Romans*, 888. Perhaps what he means, in part, is that this letter would have been read in the context of an *agapē* feast: "In the context of early Christian literature, the home in view is the house or tenement church and the occasion is most likely the love feast, since this was the format of the assembly that turned the secular space of a house or portion of a tenement or shop into an arena of sacred welcome" (Jewett, *Romans*, 888.) We have seen already, in chapter 7, how the comparison to a Passover meal affected the tenor and expectations of Christian communal meals.

exhortation to "welcome one another as Christ has welcomed you, to the glory of God" (15:7).

At 3:21, Paul heralds the announcement of what God has done in Christ at this particular point in time to deal effectively with sin and separation: Νυνὶ δὲ. The passage closes with a repetition: ἐν τῷ νῦν καιρῷ (3:26).[12] As in Phil 2:6–11 and 1 Cor 11:23–25, at the mention of the crucifixion the hearer appears to enter a different kind of time, in which something that has already happened is either dramatically or grammatically made present *now*. In this case, it is as though Paul were narrating an event of such significance that it cannot slip easily into the past tense. Further, as with the narratives in Philippians and 1 Corinthians, this one may consist of a combination of hymnic and traditional material,[13] woven in with Pauline additions.

It is clear in 3:21–26 there is one subject, God, who is motivated to act at this time out of the demands of God's own justice (δικαιοσύνη) and God's *desire for justice* (justification, δικαιόω) among humankind. Jesus Messiah and his faithfulness are the *means* for the manifestation of God's justice (διὰ πίστεως Ἰησοῦ Χριστοῦ, ἐν Χριστῷ Ἰησοῦ, ἐκ πίστεως Ἰησοῦ) and Christ is the *object* of God's work (ὃν προέθετο ὁ θεὸς) toward justice. The people of the world, both Jews and gentiles, may join themselves to this manifestation of God's justice by joining their confidence and faithfulness (πίστις) to that of Jesus Christ. The cosmic vision expressed here is of the opening of a way for all people to be in right relationship with God and their neighbor and thus to be a part of the community of the people of God (YHWH). Words built upon the stem *dik-* are heard seven times in these six verses, forming the structure of the whole discussion. The stem *dik-* means "just" or "right," an extension of its basic, physical meaning: smooth or flat or straight. It suggests being in right and constant relationship with another.

---

12. According to Jewett's schema, Rom 3:25 falls roughly at the center of the first proof, as the solution to the problem of universal sin that he has been describing up to that point (viii). What follows afterward, in chapter 4, is an expanded midrash on Abraham in support of the faith/faithfulness described in 3:21–26. The centering of 3:21–26 within the first proof is a sign of its importance, as will be borne out by the ways it reverberates through the rest of the letter. Stowers captures the sense of a cosmic turning point in his translation, "But at this time in history" (and elsewhere, "at the present crisis in history," "at this crisis in history") (Stowers, *Rereading Romans*, 194–95).

13. Jewett references many of the studies; see *Romans*, 270 n. 11.

I agree with Stowers that the Jewish sacrificial system (as well as most of the Greco-Roman cults) was about life, not death, and that the modern preoccupation with the death of the victim is misplaced. The few interpretative statements in Leviticus are clear that it is the *life* of the animal that is signified by its blood. I disagree with Stowers, however, when he says that Paul is diverting from this view by drawing attention to Christ's blood: "By referring to Jesus' death through 'blood,' Paul underlines the violent nature of his death."[14] The blood mentioned here carries the same connotation as the blood mentioned in Leviticus: life. This fact would actually lend credence to Stowers's interpretation of the "Messiah who delayed," with its emphasis upon Jesus's faithfulness to God's ultimate mission of the justification (bringing into right relationship) of all. It is more likely that, rather than drawing attention to Jesus's violent death, Paul is creating aural links to Lev 16 (LXX), with its repeated interlacing of ἱλαστήριον (seven times), αἷμα (ten times), and ἁμαρτία (eleven times). The blood of Jesus in this case is his life, his faithful manner of life, fully revealed in his willingness to endure the cross. God freely chose to receive the blood of Jesus on the cross as a means of opening up relationship to all people. As has been mentioned above, Paul uses a sacrificial metaphor to remove agency from Roman authorities and to give it to God.

Stowers argues that it is unlikely that first-century Jews, let alone first-century gentiles, would recognize the reference to the ἱλαστήριον. But we have seen in Philippians and 1 Corinthians that Paul expected a high degree of recognition of Jewish cultic practice, that his references probably depended upon previous teaching, and that many of his references had a scriptural basis. The confluence of αἷμα, ἱλαστήριον, and ἁμαρτάνω in Rom 3:23–25 creates a forceful echo of Lev 16. This is the point at which it is most important to underscore the fact that we are in the realm of metaphorical speech, because the power of Paul's imagery relies upon the fact that there is absolutely nothing in common *in a literal sense* between the brutal death of Jesus and the Jewish sacrificial cult.

An obvious clue that Paul has begun to metaphorize is the fact that he actually mixes his metaphors. In 3:24, he describes (the death and resurrection of) Christ Jesus as a means of release or ransom. Then, with scarcely a breath, Paul moves into the Yom Kippur image. The imagery is intended to be shocking in the extreme. Crucifixion was a terrifying way

---

14. Stowers, *Rereading Romans*, 210.

to die, as the Gospels witness. Knowing the images that must be in his hearers' minds, Paul stays completely away from language of violence and death, choosing instead the language of the cult. In this way, the hearers' expectation of horror meets holiness; expectation of terror comes face to face with faithfulness; brutal injustice meets the very source of justice; and the violent blood of the cross meets the blood of life. From the literal point of view, there are only grit, grime, violence, brutality, and death. But God proposes (προέθετο) a different view: a display of God's gracious justice, as the blood of life splashes upon the ἱλαστήριον within the holy of holies. In effect, Paul makes God a creator of metaphor, as God "puts forward" a different way of interpreting Jesus's death, an interpretation that grounds the Messiah's vindicating resurrection.

The metaphor does nothing to threaten the importance of the Jerusalem Temple. In fact, it depends upon the Temple for significance. From Paul's point of view, the sacrifices will continue to be offered, and presumably God will continue to enjoy their fragrance. What is different is that *for gentiles* God has opened a way of justification, a way that began at the heart of all that was opposed to God, on the spot where the Messiah was crucified. The necessary large-scale purification that was needed, a Yom Kippur for the nations, happened at the time of the crucifixion because God chose to see it that way. The metaphor does nothing to undercut the strength of Stowers's depiction of what was accomplished by Jesus's faithfulness:

> In foregoing his messianic prerogatives, Jesus was allowing Jews and gentiles an opportunity to repent and trusting that God would delay his mission until God's righteousness could be effected. Jesus' refusal to take the easy way out was an act of faithfulness to God's commission and God's purposes. He died on behalf of others. God vindicated Jesus by raising him and making him the pioneer of the world's renewal. Jesus, like Abraham, was not just a passive object of faith but one whose faithfulness actually effected the merciful justice toward the world's peoples that God intended.[15]

The sacrificial metaphor, as Paul has used it, keeps God as the principal agent in bringing about the justification of the peoples. Stowers's telling takes a small step away from Paul's emphasis on the sovereign power of God, by suggesting that it is Jesus's faithfulness alone that "effected the

---

15. Ibid., 214.

merciful justice toward the world's peoples that God intended." The Yom Kippur metaphor establishes *God* as the one who made the decision to regard Jesus's faithfulness as an action as effective as those in the Temple. God did not *need* a sacrifice. God did not need a death. God freely chose to regard the otherwise senseless death of Jesus as effective for the world in the same way that the Yom Kippur sacrifices were effective for the Temple and the people of Israel: as a purification that could usher in a clean slate, and a chance to begin again at living by God's norms of justice.

Like the other sacrificial metaphors we have encountered, this one suggests a way of life congruent with it. Those who choose to join their faithfulness to that of Jesus[16] are to live in a community that manifests right relationship with God and neighbor. The squabbling over practices that seems to be going on among the Roman house churches makes a lie of the newness of life the people have been given. While, as we have noted above, Leviticus gives us very little access to the emotional *timbre* of the sacrifices, one can perhaps get a hint from other literature. The reconciling sacrifice in the first book of the *Iliad*[17] resulted in right relationships between human beings and the god who was honored in the sacrifice, and also right relationships among the people who had been at odds with one another. The emotion that follows on the sacrifice is one of complete peace on earth, and between heaven and earth. One must assume that the Yom Kippur complex of sacrifice and scapegoat likewise resulted in the sense

---

16. With great reluctance I wade into the controversy over the translation of πίστις Χριστοῦ. As we saw following the Christ Hymn in Phil 2:12–13, the confession that the "Lord is Jesus Christ" (Phil 2:11) is both a confession of faith and a commitment to faithfulness (2:12) that is grounded in the exposition of the faithfulness and faith of Jesus (2:6–8), in God's faithfulness to Jesus (2:9) and also grounded in confidence in God's faithfulness to all those who "work out their own salvation" by the pattern of Jesus's self-offering, "for it is God who is at work among you" (2:13). The translation of πίστις, then, in all of its guises, is probably more accurate to Paul's intention when all those layers of meaning are allowed to stay intact, as they do in the Greek. Faith and faithfulness are completely intertwined with one another, as are God's πίστις, Jesus's πίστις, and the believer's πίστις. That messy knot of meanings and persons seems to be a part of Paul's gospel and is especially important to recognize in relation to the sacrificial metaphors, especially when they are combined, as at Rom 3:24, with δωρεά and χάρις. As we have seen in the study of Phil 2, gift-giving in the ancient world was not a way of saying that something had come to you entirely without obligation to respond. On the contrary, a gift was a sign of a desire for an ongoing relationship marked by reciprocity.

17. See chapter 3.

that all, in heaven and on earth, had been set in right relationship. The distinction that develops in English translations, when one makes the choice to translate δικαιοσύνη as *either* justice *or* righteousness[18] does not exist in Greek, and is, like the wordplay on πίστις, part of Paul's verbal sleight of hand in Rom 3:21–26. What God has done, by manifesting the crucifixion of Jesus as blood on the ἱλαστήριον, is to set Jewish and gentile believers in right relationship with God and also with one another.

As I have shown repeatedly, metaphors have the ability to function as a vehicle of thought, to propel the mind to concepts previously unthinkable. The language of "manifestation" (πεφανέρωται, Rom 3:21), "putting forward" (προέθετο, Rom 3:25), and "display" or "proof" (ἔνδειξιν, Rom 3:25, 26) all witness to the essentially metaphorical nature of all of the images used in Rom 3:21–26. The images—of God vindicated in the courtroom, of an imprisoned or enslaved people ransomed, and of a people reconciled with God and their neighbor through the Yom Kippur sacrifice—are intended to transfer the Roman community from its customary habits of divisive thought and action to the freshness of a new day, where they stand free and in right relationship with God and their fellow believers. According to Paul, even God uses metaphor to provoke human transformation.

The metaphor of the ἱλαστήριον gains strength from its shocking strangeness, a strength that is amplified by the fact that it has to be sorted out from the other images that surround it, and by the fact that the passage that contains it is dense with wordplays on a limited vocabulary and has to be read and reread, heard and reheard, for comprehension. For all of these reasons, the image of the mercy seat sticks in the mind during the rest of the letter. It reverberates in Rom 5:1–2,[19] where "access"[20] to the holy place of God's grace is combined again with the language of πίστις and δικαιοσύνη. From there, Rom 5:8–11[21] picks up the theme of Christ's death

---

18. Attempts to give a sense for the play on words by using English terms like "rightwise" or "rectify" and their cognates, or the traditional "justify," are abstractions, and lack the actual experience of human well-being that Paul was trying to evoke with the mixture of metaphors he concocts in Rom 3:21–26.

19. Jewett designates 5:1 as the beginning of the second proof. He calls 5:1–11 the "introduction" to the second proof, which is concerned with the establishment of "life in Christ as a new system of honor" (*Romans,* viii).

20. προσαγωγή, a term that may describe approach to a king, but probably refers here to "unhindered access to the sanctuary as the place of God's presence" (Käsemann, *Commentary on Romans,* 133).

21. I am leaving 5:6–7 out of the discussion, as a probable interpolation (see Keck,

as something that is ὑπὲρ ἡμῶν, and reiterates some of the vocabulary from 3:21–26 (αἷμα, ἁμαρτία, δικαιόω), as well as a concept implicit in 3:21–26, but not mentioned there explicitly, reconciliation (καταλλάσσω).

There may be other "partial frequencies" of Yom Kippur at 6:5–6 and 8:3–4. Where the concept of sin is present in Romans, there is, to some extent, the resonance of Rom 3:21–26. It has been shown, through the study of cultic metaphors in Philippians and 1 Corinthians, that Paul is likely to repeat references to a particular sacrifice, in order to establish an analogy powerful enough to guide a community's moral reflection over time. Since the ἱλαστήριον and αἷμα of 3:25 seem to be a clear reference to Yom Kippur, we might expect to find more references to that sacrifice or to its entailments. On the surface of it, it would appear that there are similarities between God's engagement with Christ Jesus in Rom 8:3–4 and the high priest's engagement with the living goat in Lev 16:20–22. In both cases, one who in himself (or itself) is clean is loaded with sins that are not properly his, and this action is effective περὶ ἁμαρτίας (Rom 8:3).[22] Likewise, at 6:6, Paul speaks of the destruction of τὸ σῶμα τῆς ἁμαρτίας when believers are "crucified" together with Christ. Perhaps, at the least, one could call these "partial frequencies" of Yom Kippur, the sounding of overtones of the scapegoat and Yom Kippur sacrifices, however indistinctly.

THE SHELAMIM AND ROMANS 12:1–2; 15:16

The second strong sacrificial metaphor is that of Rom 12:1–2.[23] Commentators are virtually unanimous in agreeing that when Paul writes, παρακαλῶ οὖν ὑμᾶς (12:1a), he is signaling a turning point from the ground he has laid in chapters 1–11 and the counsels to follow. Jewett is correct in linking the metaphor here with those of 15:16,[24] in a complex of images not unlike what has been observed in the combination of the moral pattern displayed in the Christ Hymn, taken together with Phil 2:17. Like the Christ Hymn,

---

Romans, 139–40), but see also Jewett's discussion of Paul's possible quotation of an imaginary Roman interlocutor (Jewett, *Romans,* 358–39).

22. This particular phrase is not used in reference to the scapegoat, but it is a refrain of the entire Yom Kippur complex: Lev 16:6, 11 (twice), 15–16, 25, 27 (twice), 34.

23. In Jewett's schema, 12:1 introduces the fourth proof, which is concerned with "living together according to the Gospel so as to sustain the hope of global transformation" (*Romans,* ix).

24. Ibid., 724.

it appears that the sacrificial metaphor in 12:1 has as its reference the *shela-mim* sacrifices, the most basic sacrificial pattern of a thank-offering and celebratory meal. It is in the light of the community's willingness to offer itself "as a living sacrifice" that Paul takes his place as λειτουργός of Christ Jesus and ἱερουργός of the gospel of God, for the acceptable offering of the gentiles.

The offering the community is being asked to make in 12:1–2 *might* be lived out in patterns similar to those suggested by the Christ Hymn and the examples of Timothy and Epaphroditus in Philippians, but the pattern of putting the concerns of others first is not explicitly mentioned here. Perhaps one way to understand what behaviors are being commended here would be to place this passage in relationship to the long arc of 3:21–26 to 15:7. The acceptable offering would be that which would lead a people who have been freely reconciled with God and one another to extend the deepest possible welcome to one another. Their act of welcome would be evidence of the transformation of their minds from the divisive patterns of the world around them, patterns of socialization that would separate Jews from gentiles, rich from poor, strong from weak. A more thorough study of these metaphors in relation to Romans as a whole would need to explore how the process of discernment outlined here by Paul relates to the λογικὴ λατρεία he commends to them; to assess whether or not other entailments of the *shelamim*[25] are heard in the letter, and for what purposes; and to study more thoroughly the relationship between Yom Kippur and the more common offerings in the Jewish Temple.

SOME CONCLUDING REMARKS ABOUT ROMANS

This glance in the direction of Romans from the point of view of Paul's use of sacrificial metaphors in Philippians and 1 Corinthians has revealed both their placement at key junctures in the letter (3:21–26 and 12:1–2) and the strong roles they play in establishing an imaginative context for both theological and ethical counsels. In fact, it is in the sacrificial metaphors

---

25. Prominent in this regard would be the frequent references to gift-giving, as both δωρεά and χάρις. Most translations do not reflect the difference between these two terms. Gift-giving, as an entailment of the *shelamim*, is clearly an important theme of Romans, as almost all of Rom 5 is grounded in notions of gift-giving, while it is at 12:1 that the complex reciprocity of God's giving and human giving comes to the surface.

that one can see just how tightly bound are theology and ethics, as a single image, such as the Yom Kippur sacrifice of 3:25, can speak simultaneously of what God has done and is doing, while implying a set of congruent human responses. Sacrifice and metaphor have in common their constant traffic back and forth between the invisible and the visible, the spiritual and the embodied.

From his study of Rom 3:22b–26, Stephen Finlan came to the conclusion that Paul held a supersessionist view toward the Jewish Temple. But when Rom 3 is put in the context of all of the other uses of sacrificial imagery, the issue does not appear as clear. In Rom 3:21–26, Paul announces a new thing that God has done. Whereas the actual Yom Kippur sacrifices accomplished atonement only for the Jewish Temple and the Jewish community, God has chosen to point to the death of Jesus as a place of atonement for the nations. But does that mean that all honor shown to God through the other sacrifices of the Temple is also invalidated? It does not appear that way. The liveliness of the other sacrificial metaphors Paul uses suggest that, while Paul may not have viewed the practice of Temple sacrifice as obligatory for gentiles, he did not anticipate its complete cessation for Jews.

KEEPING THE FEAST

The irony uncovered by this study is that, while sacrifice was so much a part of the warp and woof of daily life in the ancient world that it could be used as an explanatory tool for otherwise difficult-to-grasp spiritual realities, in our own time one can be familiar with talk about religious abstractions such as justification, atonement, Christian fellowship, and such, while failing to pick up on the fuller comprehension of those realities that is conveyed precisely through Paul's use of sacrificial and other cultic metaphors.[26] What we have seen here is that, until one understands

---

26. Attention to the original setting of cultic metaphors when they were a lively and unexpected way of talking about the death of Jesus and the Christian moral life, also makes one aware that much Christian theologizing today has accepted the role of nurse, keeping dying metaphors resting comfortably long after they have lost their true vitality. The question is, can there be any shearing of the tenor from the vehicle, the ethical counsel from the sacrificial metaphor that conveys it, without losing the point of the comparison? As we have seen, sacrificial metaphors are not only a way for Paul to convey a thought he has, but a way for him to arrive at new conceptions

the experiential reality to which the metaphors point, one misses the full-ness of how the metaphors work across an entire letter (both explicitly, and implicitly, through the entailments of the metaphors), to shape Paul's ethical counsels. In addition, there is a tendency to fill in the gaps of one's ignorance with his or her own theological tendencies, experiences, and expectations. When the cultic and sacrificial metaphors are heard with all of their complex resonances, one can discern more clearly how Paul used them persuasively to shape the ethical reflection of his communities over time. The cultic metaphors are far from decorative tropes, but rather carry a great deal of the freight of Paul's moral counsel.

When the sacrificial system is not understood in its particulars, the force of this important body of metaphors is lost. By attending to the specific metaphors at issue in a given passage, and from the point of view of a letter as a rhetorical whole, it is clear that it is in the particulars of a metaphorical reference and its entailments that the ethical "bite" is felt. The most powerful metaphors (the pattern of Christian life as a thank offering; the Christian community as a Passover community; the cruci-fixion of Jesus as God's own metaphor of Yom Kippur to set all people in right relationship with God and one another) have had staying power in the Christian imagination, even though they have become less and less fully understood. Restoring these images to their original palette of sight, smell, taste, emotional effects, and moral commitments awakens one's sense for the living communities who received, discussed, and argued over Paul's Gospel. It is this practice of attention to the living reality to which cultic metaphors point that I understand to constitute "keeping the feast."

---

and a more profound grasp of his own thought. Having discovered how central cultic metaphors are to his train of thought itself, one must ask whether what Paul had to say to the churches he worked among could be conveyed through metaphors and entail-ments that could be apprehended more intuitively by a person in the twenty-first cen-tury. Succinctly, is there any way to sustain his insights *without* "keeping the feast"?

BIBLIOGRAPHY

ANCIENT SOURCES

Aland, Kurt, et al., *Novum Testamentum Graece*. 27th ed. Stuttgart: Deutsche Bibelgesellschaft, 1993.

Andersen, F. I., trans. "2 Enoch." Pages 91–221 in vol. 1 of *The Old Testament Pseudepigrapha*. Edited by James H. Charlesworth. New York: Doubleday, 1983–1985.

Aristotle. *The Art of Rhetoric*. Translated by John Henry Freese. LCL. Cambridge: Harvard University Press, 1926.

———. *Poetics*. Edited and translated by Stephen Halliwell. LCL. Cambridge: Harvard University Press, 1995.

Charlesworth, James H., ed. *The Old Testament Pseudepigrapha*. 2 vols. New York: Doubleday, 1983–1985.

Homer. *The Iliad*. Rev. translation by Peter Jones and D. C. H. Rieu. London: Penguin Books, 2003. Originally translated by E.V. Rieu, 1950.

———. *The Odyssey*. Translated by Robert Fagles. Introduction and Notes by Bernard Knox. New York: Viking, 1996.

———. *The Odyssey*. Translated by A. T. Murray. Revised by George Dimock. LCL. Cambridge: Harvard University Press, 1995.

Josephus. Translated by H. St. J. Thackeray, R. Marcus, and L. H. Feldman. 9 vols. LCL. Cambridge: Harvard University Press, 1956–1965.

Lucian. Translated by A. M. Harmon et al. 8 vols. LCL. Cambridge: Harvard University Press, 1968.

Martínez, Florentíno García, and Eibert J. C. Tigchelaar, eds. *The Dead Sea Scrolls Study Edition*. 2 vols. Grand Rapids: Eerdmans, 1997–1998.

The Mishnah. Translated by Jacob Neusner. New Haven: Yale University Press, 1988.

Ovid. *Fasti*. Edited and translated by James George Frazer. Rev. G. P. Gould. LCL. Cambridge: Harvard University Press, 1989.

Philo. *De Specialibus Legibus*. Translated by F. H. Colson. LCL. Cambridge: Harvard University Press, 1937.

Philodemus. *On Piety*. Edited by Dirk Obbink. Oxford: Clarendon, 1996.

Plato. *Phaedrus*. Translated by Harold North Fowler. LCL. Cambridge: Harvard University Press, 1914.

Seneca. *De Beneficiis*. Translated by John W. Basore. LCL. Cambridge: Harvard University Press, 1935.

Shutt, R. J. H., trans. "Letter of Aristeas." Pages 7–34 in vol. 2 of *The Old Testament Pseudepigrapha*. Edited by James H. Charlesworth. New York: Doubleday, 1983–1985.

Septuaginta. Edited by A. Rahlfs. Stuttgart: Deutsche Bibelgesellschaft, 1935.

Secondary Sources

Aasgaard, Reidar. *My Beloved Brothers and Sisters! Christian Siblingship in Paul*. JSNT 265. London: T&T Clark, 2004.

Aitken, Ellen Bradshaw. "τὰ δρώμενα καὶ τὰ λεγόμενα: The Eucharistic Memory of Jesus' Words in First Corinthians." *HTR* 90 (1997): 359–70.

Anderson, R. Dean. *Ancient Rhetorical Theory and Paul*. Kampen: Kok Pharos, 1996.

Ashton, John. *The Religion of Paul the Apostle*. New Haven: Yale University Press, 2000.

Aune, David. "The Apocalypse of John and the Problem of Genre." *Semeia* 36 (1986): 65–96.

———. "Understanding Jewish and Christian Apocalyptic." *WW* 25 (2005): 233–45.

Batuman, Elif. "Onward and Upward with the Arts: The Bells Harvard Helped and a Russian Legacy." *The New Yorker* (April 2009): 22–29.

Beattie, J. H. M. "On Understanding Sacrifice." Pages 29–44 in *Sacrifice*. Edited by M. F. C. Bourdillon and Meyer Fortes. Based on the proceedings of a Conference on Sacrifice, Cumberland Lodge, England, 1979. London: Academic Press for the Royal Anthropological Institute of Great Britain and Ireland, 1980.

Beers, William. *Women and Sacrifice: Male Narcissism and the Psychology of Religion*. Detroit: Wayne State University Press, 1992.

Beker, J. Christiaan. *Paul the Apostle: The Triumph of God in Life and Thought*. Philadelphia: Fortress, 1980.

Bendlin, Andreas. "Purity and Pollution." Pages 178–89 in *A Companion to Greek Religion*. Edited by Daniel Ogden. Oxford: Blackwell, 2007.

Binder, Donald. *Into the Temple Courts: The Place of the Synagogues in the Second Temple Period*. SBLDS 169. Atlanta: Society of Biblical Literature, 1999.

Black, Max. "Metaphor." *Proceedings of the Aristotelian Society* 55 (1954–1955): 273–94.

———. "More about Metaphor." Pages 19–41 in *Metaphor and Thought*. Edited by Andrew Ortony. 2nd ed. Cambridge: Cambridge University Press, 1993.

Bloomquist, L. Gregory. *The Function of Suffering in Philippians*. JSNTSup 78. Sheffield: Sheffield Academic, 1993.

———. "Subverted by Joy: Suffering and Joy in Paul's Letter to the Philippians." *Int* 61 (2007): 270–82.

Böttrich, Christfried. "'Ihr Seid der Tempel Gottes': Tempelmetaphorik und Gemeinde bei Paulus." Pages 411–15 in *Gemeinde Ohne Tempel, Community without Temple: Zur Substituierung und Transformation des Jerusalemer Tempels und seines Kults im Alten Testament, antiken Judentum und frühen Christentum*. Edited by Beate Ego, Armin Lange, and Peter Pilhofer. Tübingen: Mohr Siebeck, 1999.

Bourdillon, M. F. C., and Meyer Fortes, eds. *Sacrifice*. London: Academic Press, 1980.

Bremmer, Jan N. "Greek Normative Animal Sacrifice." Pages 132–44 in *A Companion to Greek Religion*. Edited by Daniel Ogden. Oxford: Blackwell, 2007.

Brown, John Pairman. "The Sacrificial Cult and Its Critique in Greek and Hebrew (I)." *JSS* 24 (1979): 159–73.

———. "The Sacrificial Cult and Its Critique in Greek and Hebrew (II)." *JSS* 25 (1980): 1–21.

Carter, Jeffrey, ed. *Understanding Religious Sacrifice: A Reader*. New York: Continuum, 2003.

Chilton, Bruce. "The Hungry Knife: Towards a Sense of Sacrifice." Pages 122–38 in *The Bible in Human Society: Essays in Honour of John Rogerson*. Edited by M. Daniel Carroll R., David J. A. Clines, and Philip R. Davies. JSOTSup 200. Sheffield: Sheffield Academic, 1995.

———. *The Temple of Jesus: His Sacrificial Program within a Cultural History of Sacrifice*. University Park: Pennsylvania State University Press, 1992.

Colautti, Federico. "The Celebration of Passover in Josephus: A Means of Strengthening Jewish Identity?" Pages 285–305 in *Society of Biblical Literature 2002 Seminar Papers*. SBLSPS 41. Atlanta: Society of Biblical Literature, 2002.

Collins, John J. "Apocalypse: The Morphology of a Genre." *Semeia* 14 (1979): 1–20.

———. "Early Jewish Apocalypticism." *ABD* 1:282–88.

Collins, Raymond F. *First Corinthians*. Sacra Pagina 7. Collegeville, MN: Liturgical Press, 1999.

Conzelmann, Hans. *1 Corinthians: A Commentary on the First Epistle to the Corinthians*. Hermeneia. Philadelphia: Fortress, 1975.

Cox, Kathryn Lilla. "A Clouded View: How Language Shapes Moral Perception." *USQR* 63 (2010): 84–96.

De Boer, Martinus C. "Paul, Theologian of God's Apocalypse." *Int* 56 (2002): 21–33.

Detienne, Marcel, and Jean-Pierre Vernant. *The Cuisine of Sacrifice among the Greeks*. Translated by Paula Wissing. Chicago: University of Chicago Press, 1986. Originally published as *La cuisine du sacrifice en pays grec*. Paris: Gallimard, 1979.

Donfried, Karl P., and I. Howard Marshall. *The Theology of the Shorter Pauline Letters*. New Testament Theology. Cambridge: Cambridge University Press, 1993.

Douglas, Mary. *Purity and Danger: An Analysis of Concepts of Pollution and Taboo*. Washington, DC: Praeger, 1966.

Dunn, James D. G. "Paul's Understanding of the Death of Jesus as Sacrifice." Pages 35–56 in *Sacrifice and Redemption: Durham Essays in Theology*. Edited by S. W. Sykes. Cambridge: Cambridge University Press, 1991.

———. *The Theology of Paul the Apostle*. Grand Rapids: Eerdmans, 1998.

Dunnill, John. *Covenant and Sacrifice in the Letter to the Hebrews*. SNTSMS 75. Cambridge: Cambridge University Press, 1992.

Eberhart, Christian. "Sacrifice? Holy Smokes! Reflections on Cult Terminology for Understanding Sacrifice in the Hebrew Bible." Pages 17–32 in *Ritual and Metaphor: Sacrifice in the Bible*. Edited by Christian A. Eberhart. RBS 68. Atlanta: Society of Biblical Literature, 2011.

Elliott, Neil. "The Anti-Imperial Message of the Cross." Pages 167–83 in *Paul and Empire: Religion and Power in Roman Imperial Society*. Edited by Richard A. Horsley. Harrisburg: Trinity Press International, 1997.

Engberg-Pedersen, Troels. "Gift-Giving and Friendship: Seneca and Paul in Romans 1–8 on the Logic of God's Χάρις and Its Human Response." *HTR* 101 (2008): 15–44.

Evans-Pritchard, E. E. *Theories of Primitive Religion.* Oxford: Clarendon, 1965.

Fee, Gordon D. *The First Epistle to the Corinthians.* NICNT 7. Grand Rapids: Eerdmans, 1987.

———. *Paul's Letter to the Philippians.* Rev ed. NICNT 11. Grand Rapids: Eerdmans, 1995.

Finlan, Stephen. *The Background and Content of Paul's Cultic Atonement Metaphors.* AcBib 19. Atlanta: Society of Biblical Literature, 2004.

———. "Spiritualization of Sacrifice in Paul and Hebrews." Pages 83–97 in *Ritual and Metaphor: Sacrifice in the Bible.* Edited by Christian A. Eberhart. RBS 68. Atlanta: Society of Biblical Literature, 2011.

Fowl, Stephen E. *Philippians.* Two Horizons New Testament Commentary. Grand Rapids: Eerdmans, 2005.

———. *The Story of Christ in the Ethics of Paul: An Analysis of the Function of the Hymnic Material in the Pauline Corpus.* JSTNTSup 36. Sheffield: Sheffield Academic: 1990.

Fredriksen, Paula. "Did Jesus Oppose the Purity Laws?" *BRev* 11.3 (1995): 19–25, 42–46.

Furnish, Victor Paul. "Belonging to Christ." *Int* 44 (1990): 145–57.

———. *The Theology of the First Letter to the Corinthians.* New Testament Theology. Cambridge: Cambridge University Press, 1999.

Gane, Roy E. *Ritual Dynamic Structure.* Piscataway, NJ: Gorgias, 2004.

Garland, David E. *1 Corinthians.* Baker Exegetical Commentary on the New Testament. Grand Rapids: Baker Academic, 2003.

Garrett, Susan R. "Sociology of Early Christianity." *ABD* 1:89–99.

Geertz, Clifford. *The Interpretation of Cultures: Selected Essays by Clifford Geertz.* New York: Basic Books, 1973.

Gilders, William K. *Blood Ritual in the Hebrew Bible: Meaning and Power.* Baltimore: Johns Hopkins University Press, 2004.

Girard, René. *Things Hidden Since the Foundation of the World.* Translated by Stephen Bann and Michael Metteer. London: Athlone Press, 1987.

———. *La Violence et le Sacré.* Paris: Bernard Grasset, 1972.

———. *Violence and the Sacred.* Translated by Patrick Gregory. Baltimore: Johns Hopkins University Press, 1977.

Gorman, Michael J. *Apostle of the Crucified Lord: A Theological Introduction to Paul and His Letters.* Grand Rapids: Eerdmans, 2004.

————. "Philippians and the Politics of God." *Int* 61 (2007): 256–69.

Hamerton-Kelly, Robert G. *Sacred Violence: Paul's Hermeneutic of the Cross.* Minneapolis: Fortress, 1992.

Haran, Menahem. "The Passover Sacrifice." Pages 86–116 in *Studies in the Religion of Ancient Israel.* VTSup 25. Leiden: Brill, 1972.

Heusch, Luc de. *Sacrifice in Africa: A Structuralist Approach.* Bloomington: Indiana University Press, 1985.

Hogeterp, Albert L. A. *Paul and God's Temple: A Historical Interpretation of Cultic Imagery in the Corinthian Correspondence.* BTS 2. Leuven: Peeters, 2006.

Horn, Friedrich Wilhelm. "Paulus und der Herodianische Tempel." *NTS* 53 (2007): 184–203.

Horsley, Richard A. *1 Corinthians.* ANTC 7. Nashville: Abingdon, 1998.

Howe, Bonnie. *Because You Bear This Name: Conceptual Metaphor and the Moral Meaning of 1 Peter.* BibInt 81. Leiden: Brill, 2006.

Hubert, Henri, and Marcel Mauss. *Sacrifice: Its Nature and Function.* Translated by W. D. Halls. Chicago: University of Chicago Press, 1964. Originally published as "Essai sur la Nature et la Fonction du Sacrifice." *L'Année sociologique* 2 (1899): 29–138.

Hurtado, Larry W. "A 'Case Study' in Early Devotion to Jesus: Philippians 2:6–11." Pages 83–110 in *How on Earth Did Jesus Become a God? Historical Questions about Earliest Devotion to Jesus.* Grand Rapids: Eerdmans, 2005.

Jay, Nancy. *Throughout Your Generations Forever: A Sociology of Blood Sacrifice.* Brandeis University, 1981.

Jeremias, Joachim. *The Eucharistic Words of Jesus.* Translated by Norman Perrin. New York: Scribner's Sons, 1966.

Jewett, Robert. *Romans: A Commentary.* Hermeneia. Minneapolis: Fortress, 2007.

Käsemann, Ernst. *Commentary on Romans.* Translated and edited by Geoffrey W. Bromiley. Grand Rapids: Eerdmans, 1980.

————. "Kritische Analyse von Phil 2:5–11." *ZTK* 47 (1950): 313–60. Translated by Alice F. Carse in *Journal for Theology and the Church* 5 (1968): 45–88.

Keck, Leander. "The Quest for Paul's Pharisaism: Some Reflections." Pages 163–75 in *Justice and the Holy: Essays in Honor of Walter Harrelson.* Edited by Douglas A. Knight and Peter J. Paris. Atlanta: Scholars Press, 1989.

————. *Romans.* ANTC 6. Nashville: Abingdon, 2005.

Kennedy, George A. *New Testament Interpretation through Rhetorical Criticism*. Chapel Hill: University of North Carolina Press, 1984.

Kitts, Margo. "Sacrificial Violence in the *Iliad*." *JRitSt* 16 (2002): 19–39.

Kittay, Eva Feder. *Metaphor: Its Cognitive Force and Linguistic Structure*. Oxford: Clarendon, 1987.

Kittredge, Cynthia Briggs. *Community and Authority: The Rhetoric of Obedience in the Pauline Tradition*. HTS 45. Harrisburg, PA: Trinity Press International, 1998.

———. "Rethinking Authorship in the Letters of Paul: Elisabeth Schüssler-Fiorenza's Model of Pauline Theology." Pages 318–33 in *Walk in the Ways of Wisdom: Essays in Honor of Elisabeth Schüssler-Fiorenza*. Edited by Shelley Matthews, Cynthia Briggs Kittredge, and Melanie Johnson-DeBaufre. Harrisburg, PA: Trinity Press International, 2003.

Klauck, Hans-Josef. *The Religious Context of Early Christianity: A Guide to Greco-Roman Religions*. Translated by Brian McNeil. Minneapolis: Fortress, 2003.

Klawans, Jonathan. "Pure Violence: Sacrifice and Defilement in Ancient Israel." *HTR* 94 (2001): 133–55.

———. "Ritual Purity, Moral Purity, and Sacrifice in Jacob Milgrom's *Leviticus*." *RelSRev* 29 (2003): 19–28.

Knust, Jennifer Wright and Zsuzsanna Várhelyi. "Introduction: Images, Acts, Meanings and Ancient Mediterranean Sacrifice." Pages 3–31 in *Ancient Mediterranean Sacrifice*. Edited by J. Knust and Z. Várhelyi. Oxford: Oxford University Press, 2011.

Lakoff, George. "The Contemporary Theory of Metaphor." Pages 202–50 in *Metaphor and Thought*. Edited by Andrew Ortony. 2nd ed. Cambridge: Cambridge University Press, 1993.

———. "Metaphorical Issues: The Death of Dead Metaphor." *Metaphor and Symbolic Activity* 2 (1987): 143–47.

Lakoff, George, and Mark Johnson. *Metaphors We Live By*. Chicago: University of Chicago Press, 1980.

Lampe, Peter. "The Corinthian Eucharistic Dinner Party: Exegesis of a Cultural Context (1 Cor 11:17–34). *Affirmation* 4:3 (1991): 1–15.

Lanci, John R. *A New Temple for Corinth: Rhetorical and Archeological Approaches to Pauline Imagery*. New York: Lang, 1997.

Langer, Susanne. *Philosophy in a New Key: A Study in the Symbolism of Reason, Rite and Art*. 4th ed. Cambridge: Harvard University Press, 1960.

Lindemann, Andreas. *Der Erste Korintherbrief.* Tübingen: Mohr Siebeck, 2000.

Malina, Bruce J. "The Social Sciences and Biblical Interpretation." *Int* 36 (1982): 229–42.

Marchal, Joseph A. "With Friends Like These...: A Feminist Rhetorical Reconsideration of Scholarship and the Letter to the Philippians." *JSNT* 29 (2006): 77–106.

Martin, Dale B. *Slavery as Salvation: The Metaphor of Slavery in Pauline Christianity.* New Haven: Yale University Press, 1990.

Martin, Ralph P. *Carmen Christi: Philippians 2:5–11 in Recent Interpretation and in the Setting of Early Christian Worship.* Cambridge: Cambridge University Press, 1967.

———. *Philippians.* New Century Bible Commentary. Grand Rapids: Eerdmans, 1976.

McClymond, Kathryn. "Don't Cry Over Spilled Blood." Pages 235–49 in *Ancient Mediterranean Sacrifice.* Edited by Jennifer Knust and Zsuzsanna Várhelyi. Oxford: Oxford University Press, 2011.

McFague, Sallie. *Metaphorical Theology: Models of God in Religious Language.* Philadelphia: Fortress, 1982.

Meeks, Wayne A. "'And Rose Up to Play': Midrash and Paraenesis in 1 Corinthians 10:1–22." *JSNT* 16 (1982): 64–78.

Milbank, John. "Can a Gift Be Given? Prolegomena to a Future Trinitarian Metaphysic." *Modern Theology* 11 (1995): 119–61.

Milgrom, Jacob. "Leviticus." Pages 151–97 in *The Harper Collins Study Bible NRSV.* Edited by Wayne A. Meeks et al., with the Society of Biblical Literature. New York: HarperCollins, 1993.

———. *Leviticus 1–16: A New Translation with Introduction and Commentary.* AB 3. New York: Doubleday, 1991.

Mitchell, Margaret M. *Paul and the Rhetoric of Reconciliation.* Tübingen: Mohr Siebeck, 1991.

Newton, Michael. *The Concept of Purity at Qumran and in the Letters of Paul.* Cambridge: Cambridge University Press, 1985.

Nussbaum, Martha C. *The Therapy of Desire: Theory and Practice in Hellenistic Ethics.* Princeton: Princeton University Press, 1994.

Ortony, Andrew, ed. *Metaphor and Thought.* 2nd ed. Cambridge: Cambridge University Press, 1993.

Osiek, Carolyn. *Philippians, Philemon.* ANTC 11. Nashville: Abingdon, 2000.

Perkins, Pheme. "Philippians: Theology for the Heavenly Politeuma." Pages 89–104 in *Pauline Theology 1: Thessalonians, Philippians, Galatians, Philemon*. Edited by Jouette M. Bassler. Minneapolis: Fortress, 1991.

Price, Simon. *Religions of the Ancient Greeks*. Vol. 9 of *Key Themes in Ancient History*. Edited by P. A Cartledge and P. D. A. Garnsey. Cambridge: Cambridge University Press, 1999.

Prosic, Tamara. *The Development and Symbolism of Passover until 70 CE*. JSOTSup 414. London: T&T Clark, 2004.

Richards, I. A. *The Philosophy of Rhetoric*. 2nd ed. Oxford: Oxford University Press, 1976.

Ricoeur, Paul. *The Rule of Metaphor: Multi-Disciplinary Studies of the Creation of Meaning in Language*. Translated By Robert Czerny with Kathleen McLaughlin and John Costello, SJ. Toronto: University of Toronto Press, 1977.

Routledge, Robin. "Passover and Last Supper." *TynBul* 53 (2002): 203–21.

Rowland, Christopher. *The Open Heaven: A Study of Apocalyptic in Judaism and Early Christianity*. New York: Crossroad, 1982.

Sanders, E. P. *Judaism: Practice and Belief 63 BCE–66 CE*. Philadelphia: Trinity Press International, 1992.

———. *Paul and Palestinian Judaism*. Philadelphia: Fortress, 1977.

Schön, Donald A. "Generative Metaphor: A Perspective on Problem-Setting in Social Policy." Pages 137–63 in *Metaphor and Thought*. Edited by Andrew Ortony. 2nd ed. Cambridge: Cambridge University Press, 1993.

Schottroff, Luise. "Holiness and Justice: Exegetical Comments on 1 Corinthians 11:17–34." *JSNT* 79 (2000): 51–60.

Siker, Jeffrey S. "Yom Kippuring Passover: Recombinant Sacrifice in Early Christianity." Pages 65–82 in *Ritual and Metaphor: Sacrifice in the Bible*. RBS Edited by Christian A. Eberhart. 68. Atlanta: Society of Biblical Literature, 2011.

Smith, W. Robertson. *The Religion of the Semites: The Fundamental Institutions*. 2nd ed. New York: Meridian, 1956.

Soskice, Janet Martin. *Metaphor and Religious Language*. Oxford: Clarendon, 1985.

Still, Todd D. "More Than Friends? The Literary Classification of Philippians Revisited." *PRSt* 39 (2012): 53–66.

Stökl Ben Ezra, Daniel. *The Impact of Yom Kippur on Early Christianity: The Day of Atonement from Second Temple Judaism to the Fifth Century*. Tübingen: Mohr Siebeck, 2003.

Stowers, Stanley. "Friends and Enemies in the Politics of Heaven: Reading Theology on Philippians" Pages 105–21 in *Pauline Theology 1: Thessalonians, Philippians, Galatians, Philemon*. Edited by Jouette M. Bassler. Minneapolis: Fortress, 1991.

———. "Greeks Who Sacrifice and Those Who Do Not: Toward an Anthropology of Greek Religion." Pages 293–333 in *The Social World of the First Christians: Essays in Honor of Wayne A. Meeks*. Edited by L. Michael White and O. Larry Yarborough. Minneapolis: Fortress, 1995.

———. *Letter Writing in Greco-Roman Antiquity*. LEC 5. Philadelphia: Westminster, 1986.

———. "The Religion of Plant and Animal Offerings versus the Religions of Meanings, Essences, and Textual Mysteries." Pages 35–56 in *Ancient Mediterranean Sacrifice*. Edited by J. Knust and Z. Várhelyi. Oxford: Oxford University Press, 2011.

———. *A Rereading of Romans: Justice, Jews, and Gentiles*. New Haven: Yale University Press, 1994.

Thiselton, Anthony C. *The First Epistle to the Corinthians: A Commentary on the Greek Text*. Grand Rapids: Eerdmans, 2000.

Thurston, Bonnie B., and Judith M. Ryan. *Philippians and Philemon*. Sacra Pagina 10. Collegeville, MN: Liturgical Press, 2005.

Tolbert, Mary Ann. *Sowing the Gospel: Mark's World in Literary-Historical Perspective*. Minneapolis: Fortress, 1989.

Tylor, Edward Burnett. *Primitive Culture: Researches into the Development of Mythology, Philosophy, Religion, Language, Art, and Custom*. 3rd ed. 2 vols. New York: Gordon, 1977.

———. *Religion in Primitive Culture*. New York: Harper and Row, 1958.

Ullucci, Daniel. "Contesting the Meaning of Animal Sacrifice." Pages 57–74 in *Ancient Mediterranean Sacrifice*. Edited by Jennifer Knust and Zsuzsanna Várhelyi. Oxford: Oxford University Press, 2011.

Watson, Duane F. "A Rhetorical Analysis of Philippians and its Implications for the Unity Question." *NovT* 30 (1988): 57–88.

Watts, James W. *Ritual and Rhetoric in Leviticus: From Sacrifice to Scripture*. Cambridge: Cambridge University Press, 2007.

White, L. Michael. "Morality between Two Worlds: A Paradigm of Friendship in Philippians." Pages 201–15 in *Greeks, Romans, and Christians: Essays in Honor of Abraham J. Malherbe*. Edited by David L. Balch, Everett Ferguson, and Wayne A. Meeks. Minneapolis: Fortress, 1990.

Williams, David J. *Paul's Metaphors: Their Content and Character*. Peabody, MA: Hendrickson, 1999.

Williams, Jarvis J. *Maccabean Martyr Traditions in Paul's Theology of Atonement: Did Martyr Theology Shape Paul's Conception of Jesus's Death?* Eugene, OR: Wipf & Stock, 2010.

Willis, Wendell. "First Corinthians 8–10: A Retrospective after Twenty-Five Years." *ResQ* 49 (2007): 103–12.

Wire, Antoinette Clark. *The Corinthian Women Prophets: A Reconstruction through Paul's Rhetoric.* Minneapolis: Fortress, 1990.

———. "Response: The Politics of the Assembly in Corinth." Pages 124–29 in *Paul and Politics: Ekklesia, Israel, Imperium, Interpretation: Essays in Honor of Krister Stendahl.* Edited by Richard A. Horsley. Harrisburg, PA: Trinity Press International, 2000.

Witherington, Ben, III. *Conflict and Community in Corinth: A Socio-rhetorical Commentary on 1 and 2 Corinthians.* Grand Rapids: Eerdmans, 1995.

Wuellner, Wilhelm. "Where Is Rhetorical Criticism Taking Us?" *CBQ* 49 (1987): 448–63.

Ancient Sources Index

Modern Authors Index

Subject Index

agency, 3, 14, 23, 113–14, 165–66
Akedah, 109, 162
alms, 4
altar, 40, 44, 130, 142
   and blood, 2, 37, 58, 73
   and burnt offerings, 46, 54 n. 53, 101
   metaphorical, 93
   removal of, 61
animals, 1, 2, 46, 73. See also bulls, lamb,
   ram, sheep
apocalyptic,
   as a literary genre, 52, 104, 105
   as a worldview, 22, 102–7, 111, 129,
     161
apocryphal texts, 4
apotropaism, 55–56, 62
Aristeas, 4, 5
Aristotle, on metaphors, 8–9, 16–17, 19,
   20, 26
   on rhetoric, 30
Azariah, 4, 5
atonement, 77, 89, 91, 121, 148–49, 152–
   54, 163–69, 171. See also Yom Kippur;
   sacrifice, atoning
   and martyrdom, 78
   as an interpretation of sacrifice, 75
   Jewish practice of, 23, 67
   metaphors drawn from, 3, 7, 24–25,
     91, 113, 133–34, 154, 161
   within the Jewish sacrificial system, 2,
     28, 45
Babylonian exile, 5, 61–62, 146
belief, 8, 102, 112. See also faith, *pistis*
   in sacrificial practice, 39 n. 6, 63, 75

   in Jesus Christ, 83–84, 92, 100, 110–
     11, 113, 132, 155
belonging, 119, 140
   to a community, 120, 124, 137, 140–
     41, 157, 161
   to Christ, 120, 140–41, 161
   to Israel, 57 n. 59
   to God, 120, 124, 137, 157
blamelessness, 83, 122. See also
   spotlessness
blood, 72–73, 149, 157, 165–66, 168
   and life, 2, 45, 71, 111–12, 165–66
   as apotropaic rite, 56
   as atoning, 2
   as cleansing, 45,
   consuming, 65
   manipulation, 23, 37, 58
   origins of use in sacrifice, 71–72
   of Jesus Christ, 23, 133, 146, 149, 151–
     54, 165–66, 168
   covenantal, 146, 149, 151–54, 79
   of the Passover lamb, 56, 133, 146
   poured out, 37, 111
body, 1, 26, 44, 86, 95, 122–23, 125, 132,
   136 n. 13, 137
   and healing, 125 n. 15
   and holiness, 26
   as sacrifice, 5
   as temple, 9, 30, 118, 122, 136
   community as, 118, 120, 122, 132,
     137, 140, 148
   discerning the, 10, 42, 148, 153, 157
   for others, 149, 153
   Israel as a, 123
   male, 40, 72

cultic meals, 144, 150
cultic specialists, 74
Greco-Roman, 28, 35, 41, 53, 132, 150, 165
Jewish, 4, 35–36, 43, 48, 53, 68–69, 79, 83, 129, 132
Temple, 4, 48–49, 50
practices, 6, 13, 28, 49, 143
daily life, 68, 93–94, 107, 113, 136–37, 147, 171
as offering, 5
death, 22, 56, 81–84, 88, 90, 92, 100, 107–9, 113, 114–15, 133, 152 n. 86, 165–67
and life, 1, 2, 23, 24, 56, 71, 90–92, 165
of Christ Jesus, 7, 10, 13–15, 17, 19, 25–26, 28, 43, 55, 70, 86, 89, 91, 108–9, 111–14, 118, 125, 132–33, 137, 142, 147–48, 151, 154, 156, 165, 166–68, 171
of a martyr, 3, 78,
of sacrificial victims, 2, 41, 42, 56, 66, 73, 133, 165
defilement, 124, 130. See also uncleanness
deliverance, 62, 123, 133, 135, 139, 145, 150 n. 77, 155–56. See also freedom; liberation
Diaspora, 4, 50
doctrine, Christian, 2, 10
ekklesia, 30, 40, 61, 68, 102, 122, 126, 129, 135, 140, 143, 155
encouragement, 3, 89, 104–5, 113, 125, 141, 143, 147
entailments. See metaphors, entailments of
Epaphroditus, 17, 31, 51, 53, 84, 87, 90, 94, 100–101, 106, 109–10, 114, 123, 170
Ephesus, 117
ethics, 4, 6, 47–48, 68, 69, 81, 86–87, 92, 125, 131, 147, 161, 170–72
ethical living, 43
ethical reflection, 11, 117, 172
ethical interpretation, 64

execution of Jesus, 3, 14, 23, 25, 27–28, 83
exegesis, 6, 10, 30, 39, 48, 144
exodus, 55, 60, 143, 146
expiation, 2, 64, 72
factionalism, 3, 8, 31, 120, 124, 128, 145, 152, 157
faith, 36, 49, 78, 84, 92, 107, 161, 164 n. 12, 166, 167 n. 16. See also belief, pistis
community of, 22
in Jesus Christ, 43, 49, 167 n. 16
faithfulness, 5, 7, 10, 17, 52, 56, 60, 62, 76, 86–87, 92–94, 101–2, 104–7, 110–11, 123, 124, 127, 140, 147, 156, 164–67. See also pistis.
feast, 2, 37–39, 42, 52, 56, 65, 74, 81, 109, 117, 123, 131, 134–38, 142, 146–47, 149, 150–51, 155, 157, 163, 172. See also Passover
of unleavened bread, 57–58, 124, 131, 135, 154, 161
firstfruits, 56, 121, 154, 162
flour, 4
fragrance, 5, 53, 84, 94, 106, 166
freedom, 60, 81, 100, 119–20, 133–35, 138–39, 143, 151. See also deliverance; liberation
friendship, 55, 81, 113, 115
and gift-giving, 95–102
letter of, 82
Gentiles, 36, 49, 50, 59, 62, 83, 86, 91, 100, 123–24, 126, 132, 135, 143, 155, 162–66, 168, 170–71
gifts and gift-giving, 17, 24, 53, 85, 92, 95–102, 106, 113–15, 160, 167 n. 16
sacrifice as, 5, 44–45, 64–65, 74, 77, 80, 84–85, 92, 95–102, 106, 113, 115, 170
glory, 1, 5, 51, 57, 92, 96, 100, 109, 111–12, 164
gods, 37–44, 65, 74–77, 111, 127, 140
grain, 77, 130, 132
Greco-Roman, context, 6, 22, 31. See also cult, Greco-Roman
religion, 23, 30

sacrifice (cont.)

atoning, 3, 7, 23–25, 28, 45, 67, 75, 78, 89, 91, 113, 121, 133–34, 149, 152–54, 161, 163, 171

blood, 2

burnt. *See* offering, burnt

civic, 40, 44

commensal, 36–41, 42, 52, 62, 65, 80–81, 87–88, 109, 111, 114, 140, 149–50, 155

covenantal, 41–43, 56, 109, 149, 151–52

critique of, 43–44

daily life as, 5, 94, 107,

death of Jesus as a, 14, 23, 58

dedicatory, 36, 45, 51, 114

evolutionary view of, 47–48, 63–64, 67, 71, 78

expiatory, 64–65, 68

Greco-Roman, 35, 36–43, 44, 53

interpretations of, 3–5, 63–64, 75, 88, 95, 109

Jewish, 35, 45–49, 52, 59, 128, 134, 165

Levitical, 3, 45, 53–54, 109,

martyrdom as, 3

metaphors of, 1–4, 7–10, 13–34, 43, 48, 50–53, 80, 83–85, 87, 91–92, 102, 104, 106–8, 111–15, 117, 119, 121–22, 149, 157, 159–63, 165–67, 169, 171–72

moods of, 2, 36, 47, 52, 64, 99, 107, 109, 167, 172

narratives of, 109

patterns of, 8, 17, 29, 30, 35–36, 38, 46, 67–68, 84, 86, 88–92, 94–95, 97–98, 100–102, 109–14, 123, 154, 156, 161, 167, 170

practice of, 2, 5, 6, 8–9, 13, 28, 48, 63–64, 70, 74–80, 86, 106, 128, 136, 166–67, 171

prophetic critique of, 3, 76–79

propitiatory, 59, 62

rhetoric and, 9, 13–34, 40, 74–80

risk and, 99, 109

of thanksgiving, 2, 4, 10, 17, 24–25, 32, 35, 40–41, 45, 47, 51– 53, 55, 57, 81–82, 84, 86–88, 91, 93–94, 101, 109–10, 112–13, 117, 156, 170, 172

of well-being, 4, 38, 41, 45, 51, 52 n. 50, 64 n. 4, 81, 83, 112

sacrificial meat, 140–42

sacrificial system, 1, 2, 7, 11, 45, 50, 52, 59, 155, 165, 172

self-, 94, 101, 170

slaughter-, 36

theology of, 8, 15–16, 160

sacrificer, 66, 73, 80

sacrifier, 66–67, 88, 94, 111

salvation, 9, 56, 68, 78–79, 86–87, 92, 123, 125, 139, 151, 167

sanctuary, 45, 48, 54 n. 53, 61, 68, 168

scapegoat, 7, 70, 71, 128–29, 162, 167, 169

scum, 128–29, 130

servant, 25, 60, 90–91, 94, 129

shame, 1, 5, 22, 42, 61, 83

sheep, 5, 36, 41

shelamim, 10, 46, 81, 108, 112

entailments of, 50–53, 114–15, 170

importance of, 46, 81

metaphors of, 19, 87, 111, 117, 155, 161–62, 169–70

meaning of, 46

ritual pattern of, 35, 86, 109, 112

sin, 2, 45, 64, 68, 71, 91, 112, 133, 139, 148, 164–65, 169

Sinai, 143–44, 146, 151

slave, slavery, 6, 9, 22, 26, 60, 62 , 82, 86, 90, 92, 100, 109, 111, 119, 120, 122, 128, 134, 138–39, 150–51, 155, 168

smoke, 1, 37, 46, 82, 106

spiritualization, 4, 77–79, 91

in Philo, 93

spotlessness, 123. *See also* blamelessness

status, 79, 100, 156

of Jesus Christ, 81–82

of learned specialists, 79

reflected in sacrificial practice, 40–41

reversal in Christian community, 23,
    115, 139, 156
values reflected in metaphors, 22
steward, 37, 127
suffering, 52, 105–12, 125–26, 161
    and joy, 10, 52, 81–82, 88, 107–12,
        115, 161
    and obedience, 51–52
    as sacrificial, 93
    endurance of, 51, 84
    of Christ, 91
    personal, 51
supersessionism, 7–8, 77, 171
temple, 1, 4, 9, 30, 35, 43, 47–49, 117–20,
    122, 126–29, 136–37, 141. *See also*
    Temple
Temple (Jerusalem) 4, 6–9, 26, 45, 48–49,
    50, 53, 55–62, 68–69, 76, 79, 83, 96,
    119, 122, 126–29, 136, 142–43, 166–
    67, 170–71
theology, 6, 9
    of sacrifice, 8
Timothy, 17, 31, 84–87, 90, 94, 100–101,
    109–110, 114, 123, 170
Torah, 4, 33, 47, 61–62, 64, 68, 79, 127
trust, 5, 52, 110, 166
uncleanness, 136, 138
unity, 19, 31, 32, 57, 61–62, 65–67, 98,
    113–14, 123–24, 134, 137, 140, 154,
    157
    of Philippians, 82
    thematic, 143
victim, 36, 37, 42, 44–45, 65–67, 73–74,
    106, 109, 165
vindication, 3, 15, 22, 52, 82, 166, 168
violence, 41, 42, 48, 51, 69, 70–72, 80,
    152, 165–66
vow, 2, 51
wilderness, 71, 93, 129, 143–46, 155–57
worship, 5, 13, 43, 46, 52–53, 57 n. 59, 65,
    94, 148
yeast, 17, 25, 130–32, 134, 141, 149. *See
    also* leaven
Yom Kippur, 2, 7, 35 n. 2, 59, 71, 129, 133,
    162, 163–69, 170–72

CPSIA information can be obtained at www.ICGtesting.com
Printed in the USA
BVOW05s1909200915

418719BV00001B/1/P